British Bangladeshi Muslims in the East End

Manchester University Press

British Bangladeshi Muslims in the East End

The changing landscape of dress and language

Fatima Rajina

MANCHESTER UNIVERSITY PRESS

Copyright © Fatima Rajina 2024

The right of Fatima Rajina to be identified as the author of this work has been asserted in accordance with the Copyright, Designs and Patents Act 1988.

Published by Manchester University Press
Oxford Road, Manchester, M13 9PL

www.manchesteruniversitypress.co.uk

British Library Cataloguing-in-Publication Data
A catalogue record for this book is available from the British Library

ISBN 978 1 5261 7294 5 hardback
ISBN 978 1 5261 9494 7 paperback

First published 2024
Paperback published 2026

The publisher has no responsibility for the persistence or accuracy of URLs for any external or third-party internet websites referred to in this book, and does not guarantee that any content on such websites is, or will remain, accurate or appropriate.

EU authorised representative for GPSR:
Easy Access System Europe – Mustamäe tee 50,
10621 Tallinn, Estonia
gpsr.requests@easproject.com

Typeset by Newgen Publishing UK

Contents

List of figures   *page* vi
Acknowledgements   vii

Introduction   1
1 From Shurma to Thames, from Desh to Bidesh:
   History of migration   19
2 Shaping of identity: The relationship with South Asian clothes   54
3 Visibly Muslim: The aesthetic choices   85
4 Being Bengali: More than just the language   115
5 Audibly Muslim: Arabic as the lingua franca?   147
Conclusion   178

Index   186

Figures

0.1	Outside Modern Saree Centre on Brick Lane.	*page* 1
2.1	Shantanu and Matsyagandha. *The Boat-Woman and the Noble*.	63
4.1	The front of the East End Community School.	116
4.2	Anwara Begum reading from a Bengali book to a group of children sitting across the floor.	117
4.3	Nurul Hoque teaching children Bengali.	117

Acknowledgements

بِسْمِ ٱللَّهِ ٱلرَّحْمَٰنِ ٱلرَّحِيمِ
In the name of God, the Most Gracious, the Most Merciful

This project began more than ten years ago when I was accepted to do a PhD at the School of Oriental and African Studies (SOAS). Studying for a PhD was never the plan, but it has introduced me to people and communities that have defined this project, reshaped my approach to the world, and changed my life in many ways.

But this journey began before I was accepted at SOAS. It began with my late naniji picking me up at school wearing a *sari* and her cardigan; with private conversations with my friends. My elders shared random anecdotes, past and present, when they told their migration stories and talked of how dress and language had played a crucial role in defining who they are today.

Language and dress ultimately form a crucial part of our identities that has always fascinated me: one that I knew I wanted to question further when embarking on this journey. One that would never have happened without the community of people who helped steer me in the right direction.

From that community, I want to thank a generous number of people who gave me so much of their time and thoughts that contributed to my intellectual growth. People who were honest, invested in my project, very gently offered me their guidance and sharp observations, and believed in what I was trying to achieve.

I would like to thank Dr Fahad, who set up the Nohoudh scholarship, which funded my PhD at SOAS and allowed this project to come into fruition; Dr Katherine Zebiri, for the unfettered support you gave me over the years as my PhD supervisor; and Professor Muhammed Abdel-Haleem at the Centre of Islamic Studies at SOAS.

While writing this book, I have had numerous people who lent me their unconditional support and care. In particular, I want to thank everyone at the Stephen Lawrence Research Centre at De Montfort University in

Leicester, for giving me the space and time to develop and turn my thesis into a book. To Dr Lisa Palmer, you have taught me to think gracefully about the world, race and minoritised communities. Our conversations during meetings informed me so much on how to approach this book and other projects I have planned.

I am also truly indebted to the amazing friends who read the chapters for me and gave me thorough feedback. I admire their work, scholarship and research, and it was therefore a huge honour for me that they gave up their time. So a big thank you to Luisa Barbosa, Sharaiz Chaudhry, Azfar Shafi, Kamran Khan, Asma Hussain, Hafsa Kanjwal, Khadijah El Shayyal, Amandla Thomas-Johnson and Mohammed Mumith. You all provided valuable comments and suggestions that helped me think through the chapters carefully.

A heartfelt thank you to Thomas Dark for believing in my project and commissioning the book. To the editors at Manchester University Press, including Shannon Kneis and Laura Swift, thank you for your patience and guidance. And a big shout out to the incredibly talented Waheeda Rahman-Mair, who produced the gorgeous cover.

This book could not have been completed without the love, support and encouragement of so many people in my life. Without them, this journey would have been non-existent. My family and friends have patiently stood by me during the very difficult moments and have always pushed me to produce the best work. Their insights, readings and criticisms helped me nourish my own understanding of this project. My family prayed for me in silence while I remained absent for long periods; I will forever love you for your patience, and for always filling my life with such positivity.

I want to thank my mum and dad. My parents have been a source of many life lessons, and their perseverance while facing hardships is something I hope I will be able to mirror in my own life. Nadiya Hussein aptly shared in her documentary, *Chronicles of Nadiya*, 'Sometimes you feel like you are the one who made you. You forget these are the people, who quietly sit and pray for you, and think about you.' Along with my parents, my dear mother-in-law has been a huge influence on me. Her generosity and kindness ground me in my thinking. The three relatives who ensured I was always eating, because at times I would forget, were my mum; mother-in-law; and sister-in-law, Shuva. They nourished me throughout this journey, and I will forever remain indebted to them.

So many of the moments of love and joy I experienced on the journey of life have come from my ever-thoughtful friends. I have nothing but love and admiration for Wedeb Kiros, Michela Di Bellonia, Saima Zia, Saima Khan, Asbath Chowdhury and Omayma El Ella. I adore everyone at Nijjor

Manush – friends and comrades I have been organising with for over half a decade.

Above all, so much of my intellectual growth during the writing process for this book stems from the many conversations I had with my partner-in-crime, bhondu and dear husband, Areeb Ullah. I met you when I was writing my PhD in SOAS library, and there are days I wonder if we would ever have met if it hadn't been for this project. You have brought so much joy and thought to it that a simple thank you will never be enough. Know that I love you deeply, and may all those conversations still continue where I learn from your sharp and thoughtful insights. I love you.

Last but not least, I am grateful to the Bangladeshis from East London who took time out of their lives to allow me to gain even a small insight into their lives. I have made many friends on this beautiful road, and attended the wedding of two of the research participants. I learnt a great deal from every single participant. Thank you to you all. Your stories, narratives and memories are what make this book what it is; without you, it would not exist.

Introduction

It was a cold April afternoon in 2014, and I was walking down Brick Lane to meet my next interviewee. I was in the midst of my PhD research and hoped to secure another interview. But as I walked through the green arches of Bangla Town on Brick Lane, I noticed something had changed. There was only one *sari* shop left on Brick Lane. Perched on the southern end of Brick Lane, four tall mannequins, armed with hairdos reminiscent of the 1980s, stood tall under the fading yellow-and-red sign of the Modern Saree Centre. In its heyday, Bangladeshis would come from Portsmouth to Poplar to visit the Modern Saree Centre and other *sari* shops scattered across Brick Lane before the arches of the Truman Brewery.

Figure 0.1 Outside Modern Saree Centre on Brick Lane. Image by the author.

But shopping habits for Bengalis in Tower Hamlets and beyond have changed over the years, with many *sari* shops on Brick Lane either closing down or migrating to other places, such as Bethnal Green Road or Whitechapel. While thinking about the changing face of Brick Lane, I began to wonder what drove this, and whether the Bangladeshi community's relationship with garments such as the *sari* had changed, too, over time. This question drove me down the rabbit hole of trying to figure out why Bangladeshi dress habits had changed. Was it politics? Economics? Religion? The War on Terror?

These questions constantly came back to me and made me think about my own family's migration pattern and our conversations about our relationship with our ancestral homeland of Bangladesh. I had already taken a keen interest in the political development of the wider British Muslim community and personally observed these changes myself within it. For example, the fixation on Muslim women's bodies; their sartorial choices; and how they evoked much speculation, interrogation and commentary became a routine feature for Muslims. I witnessed many of my female relatives going through tumultuous journeys to figure out what it meant to be a Muslim woman in Britain. Growing up in Luton, as in many Muslim-majority areas, I noticed a shift in sartorial choices with the wearing of the *hijab*, *jilbab* and *niqab* becoming more prevalent.

In particular, what struck me most was how these garments provoked such visceral reactions worldwide, especially in the West, exposing how such attitudes rest on the way dominant societies understand and interpret these garments. As a result, multiple European countries have legislated banning the *hijab*, further extending the ban to the *niqab*. Although there have been no such bans in the UK, policymakers have hinted at the idea of banning the *niqab*, or have made derogatory comments about the garment. Former Home Secretary Jack Straw, in 2006, represented Blackburn, where there is a sizeable Muslim community. In his local paper, the *Lancashire Telegraph*, he famously wrote that he felt uneasy with the *niqab* and would ask his female constituents to remove it when visiting his weekly surgery. His positioning caused a nationwide discussion about freedom of expression and Muslim women's clothing choices. He insisted that he had no problem with the *hijab* (the headscarf) and would defend 'the right of any women to wear a headscarf',[1] but it was the *niqab* (the additional piece of fabric tied behind the head that covers the entire face apart from the eyes) that sat uncomfortably with him, causing him to question whether Muslim women *really* choose to wear it or not. Several years later, in a similar vein, former British Prime Minister Boris Johnson wrote a column for the *Daily Telegraph* referring to Muslim women who wear the *niqab* as 'looking like letter boxes', and compared them to bank robbers.[2]

While the fixation on female Muslims was widespread, I wondered why little attention was given to the clothing choices made by Muslim men. I wanted to know more about what men choose to wear, why they decide to wear what they do and how such choices are informed. What shapes those decisions? I was curious to learn more about this, but I also wanted to investigate how a racialised community, such as that of the British Bangladeshi Muslims, related to their linguistic identities. Where did they articulate their Bengali? What about Arabic? What is the locus here that determines which language is given more importance? Did they express their religious reference in Bengali terms or Arabic? Which language did they fall back on? Muslim communities do not exist outside the grip and structures of the societies they find themselves in, where there is a ceaseless interplay of interests with racism and (gendered) Islamophobia within the cultural and political terrain. And these then inform the everyday choices of which clothing items are considered religious while determining that others do not meet religious requirements. While the UK's political landscape shapes people's choices, it is also further amalgamated by global political moments.

My first interview for my PhD was held in a small café on New Road – a few minutes walk from Whitechapel Station, East London. The café was bustling with young people walking in wearing their school uniforms, grabbing their after-school snacks, and with workers in the area catching up with friends and family. This interview set the tone for my research. I met Shamim (not his real name) in the afternoon. He wore trousers with a jumper and the shirt collar sticking out. We spoke for a few hours, and during the discussion about men's clothing choices he captured my attention and neatly situated how dress for Muslim men is as intricate as it is for Muslim women. Shamim explored this notion by sharing an anecdote about his father:

> My dad used to do something really funny. He used to be very well dressed at home, he would still wear a shirt and a jumper at home, and then he'd wear a *lungi*. I found it really interesting. My dad, on purpose, he's a very educated man, very well known, and when he saw people wearing *lungi*s much in Brick Lane, he used to walk out in a *lungi*, he didn't care 'cause he never didn't care [*sic*]. He used to have this political leader that he was following in Bangladesh – his name was Abdul Hamid Bashani; my dad was like quite high up in his political party and that guy came to the UK in a *lungi*, boarded the plane, came to the UK in a *lungi* – very similar to what Gandhi did in his dhoti, so there was a demonstration, which is 'I am here but I am me and if I am from somewhere else this is a part of it.'

Shamim's relationship with clothes is shaped by his father and the political representation that South Asian politicians adhered to while visiting the UK. Their unwavering pride in their cultural heritage and spatial boundaries did not alter their decision on what to wear. When I enquired about his relationship with language and the role it played in his life, he shared:

> my mum said something to when I was really small in the kitchen, I remember. She told me: 'I never want to hear a word of English at home.' I didn't ask why, but she explained, 'Look, I can speak English, and your dad can speak English. And you will be speaking English all the time outside, in school, at work … but Bengali is what you need to practise, so I want you to ask for everything in Bengali, and only if you don't know how to ask or what it is, then I'll explain in Bengali words to you, and you will use that from now on. How is that?'.

Shamim's exposure to the language was predicated on his parents' political choices of demarcating spaces and allocating a specific language to each space. Choosing which language to speak was a manifestation of the dominant language they needed access to at that moment. I will gauge these thoughts in further detail in the forthcoming chapters looking at dress and language as separate categories and how they have evolved for the British Bangladeshi Muslim community in the East End of London. One thing to note here is how negotiating dress and language is predicated by the political, and demarcations oscillate between the public and the private. At times, these boundaries become blurred between what is public and/or private in a borough such as Tower Hamlets, where much of the public space is seen as being inclusive of the private because of the large demographic of Bangladeshis in the area. Shabna Begum argues that the local East End Bengali community reinscribed a particular Sylheti model of homemaking in this new space where the 'home reaches out into wider uthaan (courtyard) and para (neighbourhood)'.[3] The recreation of this model in the East End provided the possibility of asserting a distinct identity while continuously contesting the process of '"claiming" and "making" space in East London', marking the area as the heartland of the Bangladeshi community in the British Bangladeshi imagination.[4]

In this sense, I want to examine the role of ethnicity and religion in the process of identity negotiation, formation and identification amongst the British Bangladeshi Muslim community in the East End. The research deals with two interrelated factors: dress and language, and their perceptions and developments, through a case study of the community that populates the areas of the London Borough of Tower Hamlets and Newham. Most participants were from Tower Hamlets, more so than from Newham. The book explores the relationship between dress and language and the meaning attributed to them by the research participants. It also argues that the participants who spent their formative years in Britain were likely to draw from their religious traditions to inform their relationship with dress and language. In contrast, others drew their identifications more from their Bengali identity via their parents. Further to this, the book addresses the relationships between the constructions of an ethnic identity vis-à-vis a religious identity, and the fact that it is messy and not always very clear-cut. There are convergences and divergences explored in the language and dress chapters, respectively.

The decision to opt for language as a variable stems from the Bengali people's historical struggles to preserve their linguistic identity. I was curious to understand the role of language amongst British Bangladeshi Muslims and how it shapes their identities while suggesting that, because of the commitment of some of the research participants to their faith, their heritage language and clothing are prioritised differently. The prioritising of their faith has relegated their heritage language and dress to the site of contestation over the political accommodation of cultural difference. This is a striking observation, considering the Bengali language's prominent role in Bangladesh's independence movement. Observing the shift towards a more faith-based identity also added to the decision to enquire about the role of Arabic in the participants' lives and how particular Persian-origin terms within Bengali were kept alive. In a post-9/11 world, Arabic has become more pronounced for non-Arab Muslims, – although this interest in the language is beyond simple memorisation and recitation, as there is a concerted investment in learning to speak the language to acquire a deeper understanding of the faith through Arabic – the language of the Qur'an.

The focus on dress arose from the British Bangladeshi Muslim communities' aesthetic transformation over the years. When accessing archival footage and photographs of the East End following the Bengali community's migration to the UK, it is evident that most women and some men dressed in ethnic clothing. During the 1970s and 1980s, women were visible in their brightly-coloured *sari*s with long coats resembling a trench coat, and the younger women, probably unmarried, could be seen in their *shalwar kameez*es. On the other hand, men dressed in the latest trends, with some in their *lungi*s and *funjabi*s. More recently, there has been a shift in this aesthetic, and more British Bangladeshi Muslims are now seen in *hijab*s, *jilbab*s, *niqab*s, *thobe*s and beards. I want to explore further when and where this shift occurred, and what role, if any at all, ethnic clothing had in their lives. Furthermore, what did the ethnic clothing symbolise for the research participants contemporarily in forming their identities as racialised and religious minorities in the UK?[5]

Interventions

Following the terrorist attacks of 7 July 2005, British Muslims, particularly young people, have come under unprecedented public scrutiny, as it was not hardened al-Qaeda operatives who perpetrated the attack, but British

Muslims who were born and raised in the UK.[6] This attack created a sense of panic amongst Muslims living in Britain, resulting in a societal dynamic of 'integration' vs. 'seclusion', forcing Muslims to redefine their identities as either 'moderates' or 'extremists'. Words such as 'Muslim' and 'young Muslims' together often triggered associations with violent extremism. Young Muslims, just like their non-Muslim peers, face similar everyday challenges of adolescence, while also contending with issues unique to their 'Muslimness'. A young generation of Muslims, without choice, have had much of their identity shaped by external events. These events have come to proliferate and amplify their religious identity, which is then managed through and under the panopticon of the surveillance- and securitisation-led state through the Prevent Strategy.

Building upon the legacies of the terrorist attacks in the United States on 11 September 2001 and the subsequent rise of anti-Muslim racism in western societies in particular, many non-Muslims in Britain were asking questions about the compatibility between British Muslims and the Islamic world more generally. The discussions that ensued centred around the tensions between what is perceived to be the Islamic world and its occidental counterpart, as terms such as 'Islam' and 'terrorism' are seen as almost synonymous.[7] The bombings and acts carried out by a few Muslims and the justification of such acts using the Qur'an led to questions such as: is Islam the problem? Or is it the Muslims who are practising it? Is Islam compatible with the 'modern' world or the West? How can Muslims be integrated into western societies, especially if these Muslims' allegiance lies with their religion rather than with the state within which they reside? Or are Muslims more loyal to their parents' country of origin?

Whether academics, journalists or policymakers, all parties have contributed to this field of enquiry of British Muslims. Whatever the accomplishments of these various organisations and individuals, be it research, publicity stunts or policies, one thing is clear: discussion of Muslims' integration has become a contentious topic leading into the twenty-first century. It is of interest and relevance to a broad spectrum of people ranging from policymakers to community leaders. In this regard, my research has implications for scholarly and public debates on the cultural integration of religious minorities, British Muslim identity construction and intergenerational differences amongst immigrant communities. I consciously attempt to move away from simplistic framings of Muslims by shifting the locus away from the West-vs.-Islam dichotomy. However, I am also cognisant of how 'integration' has been used to frame racially minoritised communities, thereby placing the burden of conviviality on them.[8] As a result, conversations concerning British Muslims tend to be framed around integrationism when it operates as a guise for demanding an assimilationist project for Muslims – the vast majority of whom are racialised as non-white.

The main purpose of using the intergenerational analysis is to demonstrate, through semi-structured interviews and general observations of the Bangladeshi community in East London, the various ways the community in the East End has developed and continues to develop its identifications through their contestations. I suggest that British Bangladeshi Muslims are forging a multifarious understanding of dress and language influenced by various factors, including, but not limited to, the pressures within and outside the community. I explore the articulation of multiple generations' experience with dress and language, what they represent for them, and how they place them in relation to their ethnic and religious identities. I wish to interrogate their perceptions of these variables and gain insights into some concrete thoughts on the changing trends in language usage and the adoption of specific clothes for both men and women. Gauging the continuously shifting social categories and markers, and where, when and how they are merged or dismantled, is of importance. For example, why is there more of a focus on Arabic than Bengali terms, where the latter, historically, functioned as a marker of South Asian Muslims' religious expression? How do the different generations feel about their heritage-origin clothes, such as the *sari*, *shalwar kameez*, *lungi*, *funjabi* and so on?

This book on British Bangladeshi Muslims is historically situated, as I draw upon the historical interaction between the British and Bengalis across the Bengal (consists of today's Bangladesh and West Bengal in India). British presence in the Bengal modified the meaning of dress, particularly the *sari*, and notions around modesty and respectability politics. I also focus on the history of the Bengali language, fomenting a pivotal moment in history for Bangladesh's independence. Additionally, the research participants incorporated other discursive fields, intersecting with British colonial history in India: the global Islamic revival (this is a prevalent topic in the dress and language chapters), merging with recent shifts in policies and practices around integration and multiculturalism in the UK and the impact of Bangladesh's independence to the present day in East London. These variegated and broad historical situations provide the socio-historical backdrop for the book, which I explore in detail in Chapter 1. Saba Mahmood has argued that 'representation of facts, objects and events are profoundly mediated by the fields of power in which they circulate'.[9] Although Mahmood is making this intervention concerning imageries of Muslims, I contend that such an analysis applies to how Muslims make their everyday 'choices' and locate themselves within the political landscape. The fields of power craft the paradigms available to the Muslim subject and how to position themselves, because they are continuously made and remade through local, national and global politics.

This book aims not to gauge and analyse Muslims as the terrorists versus the oppressed paradigm. Nor am I interested in humanising Muslims via the 'just like us' discourse. Concepts such as diversity and integration are concerns brought up by some of the research participants. However, my preoccupation in this book is not to interrogate these categories. Instead, I am keen to identify how Muslims inhabit, embody and acquaint themselves with the contested meanings around dress and language. I am interested in how that process takes place. In particular, I want to situate how the research participants have consumed the debates surrounding these issues and how those debates may have influenced them to unravel aspects of their identities. These particular points were raised following the political upheaval in Tower Hamlets when the borough's former Mayor Lutfur Rahman made a comeback in 2022 after he had been banned from political office following a guilty verdict in a court case.[10] Some research participants used the media discussions of Tower Hamlets to pose questions internally about what constitutes Bengali culture and what it means to be British and Muslim. How can one negotiate the Bengali, British and Muslim identities when faced with scrutiny? I heard some of these commentaries while spending hours in different cafés across East London. This book also aims to contribute to the current sociological and anthropological literature on British Muslims. I will be doing this by providing an in-depth study of a specific ethnic minority community, hopefully adding to the complexity of British Muslims overall, away from the homogenised impositions of dominant narratives.

Why this community?

My interest in the Bangladeshi community stems from personal experiences of seeing the changes and perceptions of dress and language amongst my close and extended family. Seeing photos of my grandmother, who came to the UK in the 1970s during the reunification decade, when many Bangladeshi women and their children joined their fathers and husbands in the UK, makes me think about the drastic changes and shifts in identity since. My grandmother is wearing a *sari* with a long overcoat in many of her photos. She used the *asol* (end of the *sari*) in the pictures to cover her hair. Culturally, a married woman was expected to have her hair covered in photos, especially outside the domestic space, as this functioned as a marker of respectability. My aunts and my mother, the younger women of my family, wore the *shalwar kameez* to denote their single status. Although unmarried, they were still required to adhere to respectability politics around guests in the domestic space and to cover their heads with the scarf. While the *sari* operated as a sign, publicly, that the woman was married, the *shalwar kameez* signified the opposite. Although these boundaries no longer apply in the same way, participants made these references to how these garments were employed to situate a Bangladeshi woman.

Much has changed since then, and many, though not all, of the older women, particularly those who belong to my late grandmother's generation, are likely to wear the *jilbab* with a *hijab*. From my grandmother's time, there was a cultural shift whereby my mother's generation continued to wear the *shalwar kameez* even after getting married. In many cases this was frowned upon, as a woman was expected to switch to wearing a *sari* after marriage. This switch signifies her married status and is viewed as a rite of passage into womanhood; she has left her *meye bela* (girlhood) behind, and is no longer a *furi* (girl) but is a *beti* (lady/woman). My granddad wore suits, and I do not have any concrete memories of seeing him in a *funjabi*, but I do recall seeing him in a *lungi* around the house. My uncles came to the UK as young boys and grew up in the UK as second-generation Bangladeshis. They wore what other teenagers were wearing in the 1970s and 1980s. But after 9/11 and the London attacks of 7 July 2005, known as 7/7, some of the women in my family started wearing the *hijab* with their South Asian clothes. Meanwhile, others wore the *hijab* with *jilbab*s, and completely discarded their South Asian dress. In contrast, the men started growing their beards at a time when many Muslim men began wearing *thobe*s to the mosque and were choosing to get married in them.

Noticing these trends changing over the years, I have found the way identity transforms and changes with time fascinating. Geopolitics, racism, exclusion and many other factors make people question their sense of home, and the constant cultural navigations that they are contesting yet recontesting. But despite using terms such as identity and belonging, this book does not attempt to make the Muslim more legible. Muslims do not require an enquiry to understand or situate them as safe or a non-danger. Instead, the book aims to establish that Muslims come forth with textured voices of lived experiences, and that such experiences warrant much more rigorous theorising. The research participants for the book use a dialectical engagement in their local areas as a way to mark their place. The participants' honesty and portrayal of the banality of the everyday was refreshing. They expressed how their locality shaped more of their choices than how they were discussed as the 'other' in the wider political context. In fact, many spoke of the ever-present nature of coloniality. Nevertheless, as uttered by the former director of the Institute of Race Relations, Ambalavaner Sivanandan, they understood that we are here because they were there.[11]

British Bangladeshis, Muslim community and the literature

British Muslims have the youngest age profile of all the faith communities in Britain. Census data from the 2011 Census showed that around 33 per cent of the Muslim population was aged fifteen years old or younger, compared to 19 per cent of the population as a whole.[12] At the time of the 2001 Census, 34 per cent of Muslims in Britain were under the age of sixteen, and over 50 per cent were younger than twenty-five years old. Muslims in 2011 formed 4.8 per cent of the population in England and Wales. The population of Muslims in 2001 amounted to 1.55 million, which increased to 2.71 million in 2011. There are 77,000 Muslims in Scotland and 3,800 in Northern Ireland, with 47 per cent of Muslims born in the UK.[13] The vast majority of these young British Muslims are second- or third-generation from migrant communities, some being first-generation unaccompanied refugees and asylum seekers. Two-thirds of the Muslims originate from South Asian heritages (Pakistan, Bangladesh and India), along with significant numbers from the Middle East, North Africa and Sub-Saharan Africa.[14] As of 2021, the Muslim population has increased to 3.9 million from 2.7 million, making up 6.5 per cent of the population of England and Wales.

According to the 2001 Census, the overwhelming majority of Bangladeshis in Britain were Muslim, with 92 per cent identifying themselves as such (283,063 Bangladeshis).[15] A decade later, this figure increased to 451,529 in the 2011 Census and 90 per cent of these identified themselves as Muslim.[16] Bangladeshi Muslims account for almost 17 per cent of Britain's Muslim population, the second largest group after Pakistanis. Bangladeshi Muslims are typically Sunnis, allied to the syncretic Barelvi tradition emphasising the role of customs, shrines and *pirs*.[17] From 2001 to 2011, the Muslim population of the London Borough of Tower Hamlets increased by 19 per cent, from 71,000 to 88,000. Census data from 2021 records that nearly 644,841 people identified as British Bangladeshi, making up 1.1 per cent of the population in England and Wales, and that 34.6 per cent of that population live in Tower Hamlets.[18]

In the UK, religious organisations have grown within Bangladeshi communities, many of which have roots and funding from Muslim-majority countries in the Middle East, Pakistan and Bangladesh (the Dawat'ul Islam being the most influential).[19] Little work has been done on the Bangladeshi community and the role of religion, although preliminary work suggests that the impact of religion has been shaped in local spaces, and by local issues, concerns and struggles.[20] By contrast, relatively more studies were produced by 'insiders' who looked at notions such as identity, diaspora, multiculturalism, integration and postcolonial migration.[21] In his book *Islam and Identity Politics among British-Bangladeshis*, Ali Riaz provides a more contemporary analysis of identity:

first to underscore the fact that identity politics among the British-Bangladeshi community has undergone a dramatic shift in the past decade and to explore the challenges, opportunities and dilemmas for members of the community and the British state; second, to address a lacuna in the extant literature on the interplay of Islam and Europe in the era of globalization and the future of multiculturalism in Britain.[22]

Similar to Riaz, Aminul Hoque also explores the role of Islam; however, he focuses on this topic by centring the lives of third-generation young Bangladeshis in Tower Hamlets and the development of what he coins a 'Br-Islamic identity'.[23] In his thesis, *British-Islamic Identity: Third-Generation Bangladeshis from East London*, published as a monograph in 2015, Hoque explains how he spent most of his fieldwork with six young research participants in Tower Hamlets, and investigated how they negotiate their Bengali identity with their Islamic, as well as their British, identity. He investigates this by examining the various strategies young Bangladeshis employ to engage and activate their multifaceted identities, which is done through the gaze of an 'other'.

With regard to the Bangladeshi community, one of the most seminal works produced on the community is the book *Across Seven Seas and Thirteen Rivers* by Caroline Adams, who worked in the schools and youth service of Tower Hamlets.[24] Her book is divided into two sections: the first deals with the journeys and stories of lascars (Indian seamen working on British ships), the history of Sylhet, the recruitment of the lascars in the Bengal and their arrival in Britain; the second consists of ten interviews with the lascars who stayed in Britain, and provides an expressive and accessible insight into the men's lives as they adjust to a new environment and country while continuing a relationship with 'back home', which was changing after the end of the British Raj and creating a new community. Shabna Begum's work is a part of the renewed interest in the Bangladeshi community in the East End, which looks at the Bengali squatters' movement in the 1970s.[25] Begum's is a critical intervention where she shows how the Bengali community, whilst also fighting racism, was able to build and find community through squatting. However, this is foregrounded by challenging the hegemonic forming of who did the squatting (read: white people) and was at the core of the literature. She incisively shows how Bengalis were treated as passive and, within this terrain, regulated simply as existing there and photographed, but never engaged with directly with regard to how they were making history by demanding better housing for themselves and the wider community. Moving away from the hegemonic framing of squatting and squatters, Begum interjects by considering the political and epistemic implications when a group is excluded from our understanding of East End history.

Similar to Adams, Katy Gardner provides us with an insight into the migratory pattern and how it can be understood as a gendered as well as an embodied experience. Gardner also traces the lives of former lascars from Sylhet and their monopolisation of the sector 'as a number of serangs (foremen) had begun to control employment and generally favour their kinsmen and fellow countrymen as employees'.[26] Gardner refers to this as 'chain migration', through which more and more Sylhetis started arriving in Britain and making it their home. Gardner carefully considers the relationship between *desh* (home) and *bidesh* (abroad) through a transnational lens,[27] and the ways remittances permeate the lives of Bengalis.[28] While Gardner's work questions the boundaries around life in the UK and Sylhet, factoring in how migration impacts those who stay behind in Bangladesh and not just those who do the migrating, Nilufar Ahmed provides insights into the way gender and religion transpire for first-generation Bangladeshi women who leave the village to build a new life in the UK.[29] Like Gardner, Ahmed locates transnationalism at the heart of her analysis for this longitudinal study, and examines how Bangladeshi women in the diaspora become the bearers of culture and tradition. Using Sivanandan's aphorism of 'we are here because you were there', referencing the former colonised people's presence in the metropole of empire, is an important connector to understand how placings and multiple sites operate to make sense of Bangladeshis in the UK, particularly in East London.

In contrast, David Garbin and John Eade[30] focus on contemporary issues related to identity politics, urban space, and the negotiation of space in London between Bangladeshis and non-Bangladeshis. In their other work, Eade and Garbin suggest that, through the 1960s and into the early 1970s, the first generation of migrants were actively involved in the politics of the subcontinent; however, this changed with events affecting the local community in the 1970s, which I highlight with the killing of Altab Ali.[31] Additionally, Eade and Sarah Glynn provide an insight into the local as well as transnational politics of the community.[32] Glynn, in her article 'Bengali Muslims: The New East End Radicals?', analyses the Bangladeshi community in East London and compares its struggles with those of the Jewish community of the East End. In this article, Glynn tries to move away from identity politics and focuses on the influence of socio-economic background and ideology in formulating one's politics.[33] She also traces the role of the independence of Bangladesh and its impact on the community in London, and how it shaped the community's involvement in local politics, which coincided with the anti-racist movement at the time.[34] Another significant contribution by Glynn considers how the Bengali community was politically organised in the past, using a primarily Marxist lens.[35] While this is an important lens to locate the Bengali community's positioning in the East End, it nonetheless remains limited and engages little with colonial history, diluting the presence of race and how much it has informed the ways in which the community was treated socially, culturally and politically.

In Benjamin Zeitlyn's 'Growing up glocal in London and Sylhet', the author explores the Bangladeshi community through the lens of Bangladeshi children, transnationalism and their relationship with their Bengali identity.³⁶ Zeitlyn interrogates the complexities faced by young Bangladeshi children, and the multiple ways in which the young children negotiate their identities in different settings. He intricately examines and observes the children within a school context and explains the varying contradictions by highlighting the differences among practices, ways of being, beliefs, identities or ways of belonging. His fieldwork took place in Islington, providing an alternative insight, as Tower Hamlets commonly becomes the primary research site for studying the British Bangladeshi community. Zeitlyn's thesis will be highly relevant for my discussion on language (see Chapter 5), as it will complement the data I collected on Bangladeshis and their linguistic identities from across Tower Hamlets and Newham with his findings from Islington. This could provide insightful comparisons and the observed distinctions could illustrate that the existence of isolated ethnic enclaves (Tower Hamlets, in particular, is treated in this way) are not the only way in which ethnic and linguistic identity could be preserved. Similarly, Justin Gest's *Apart: Alienated and Engaged Muslims in the West* reveals how identity constructions for the young British Bangladeshi Muslim communities in East London are based upon the conditions of reproduction and transformation of a religious identity, which is critically linked to a range of interconnected political divisions and distinctions.³⁷ Gest conducted his research in London's East End and Madrid, drawing on over 100 interviews with various figures and leaders within the two Muslim communities. From these interviews, he examines the daily lived experiences of young Muslims of Moroccan and Bangladeshi origin and their daily negotiations with discrimination, racism, religion and inequality.

Methodology

Forty-three British Bangladeshi Muslims were interviewed in the form of semi-structured interviews, their ages ranging from nineteen to sixty. The interviews sought to examine the socio-political experience of dress and language in the participants' lives while considering how much their local experiences shaped their identifications with the two variables. Although the focus was primarily to seek people's insights into how they choose to wear the clothes they wear and the language/s they speak, most of the conversations also focused on more biographical themes of migration, settlement, housing and historical experiences of racism.

In Tower Hamlets, initial access to interviewees was gained with the help of my personal networks and contacts. After the initial interviews were conducted, snowball sampling began. Alongside the snowball sample, I contacted a broader range of relevant organisations. Drawing on my personal networks helped to ensure sample selectivity was minimised, but it was not completely eradicated. All the interviews were conducted by the author in English, with many having references in Sylheti. Most of them took place in interviewees' homes and local community centres to ensure that participants were as relaxed and comfortable as possible and to minimise any power asymmetry between the researcher and participants. It was clear from the data generated that the my 'insider' status helped to build rapport, and the interviews were rich. The majority lasted approximately 100 minutes. All were audio-recorded and transcribed, with the names of participants replaced by pseudonyms.

Organisation of the book

This book consists of seven chapters, including an introduction and conclusion, with the introduction providing an overview of the book's objective and the core questions that will be tackled.

Chapter 1 will provide the necessary context for later discussions on the British Bangladeshi community. I explore the history of British Bangladeshi migration and how the community has established itself in the East End. I investigate why, historically, East London became the Bangladeshi community's location of choice for migration and eventual settlement. This is achieved by tracing the relationship created between Bengal and the East End via the East India Company, which had its headquarters in the East End, and the Partition of India and West/East Pakistan, where East Pakistan later became the independent state of Bangladesh. I critically engage the history of the British presence in the Bengal and the exchanges and impositions during that time. It is crucial to incorporate this history, as the arrival of lascars, which I discuss in thorough detail in this chapter, became a crucial component in understanding the early migration patterns from the empire to the metropole of empire.

I also problematise the terms Bengali and Bangladeshi, particularly given that all my research participants identified with both terms and used them interchangeably during the recorded interview, as well as in conversations after the recording. The former term has been around for centuries and marks ethnicity, whereas the latter came into existence with East Pakistan's independence when it was renamed Bangladesh. The renaming of the state led to the incorporation of 'Bangladeshi' into popular discourse and public policy documents. The adoption by each research participant of 'Bengali' or 'Bangladeshi' varied, depending on which dimension of their ethnicity and/or spatial origins they wanted to emphasise.

The second chapter discusses how opinions regarding clothing and attire have evolved. I critically analyse the research participants as they relate sentimentality and significance to clothing, as well as how their relationship has evolved over time and what factors have influenced those changes. Why do people dress in the ways that they do? Why do they now think differently about clothing that is seen as religious or cultural? My area of focus in the chapter is mainly on how and why research participants conceptualise clothing in various circumstances. I focus on particular South Asian clothing, including the *sari*, *shalwar kameez*, *lungi* and *funjabi* (garments also worn in other South Asian nations; this is why I do not wish to call them Bangladeshi).

In the third chapter, I focus on the shifting relationship with clothes and dress associated with Islam. I want to consider the impact of the broader political terrain and how this has informed people's consciousness around their Muslimness vis-à-vis dress. I factor in the challenges the research participants may have encountered within the community and outside it. How did the participants convey their embodied reflections? How did they negotiate their decisions with the looming effects of the West's obsession with Muslims' dress (this is, of course, highly gendered)? To analyse this phenomenon and the way clothes are being reconfigured, I look at specific clothes chosen by British Bangladeshi Muslims to assert their Muslim identity, including growing a beard, the *jubba* (*thobe*), *hijab*, *jilbab* and *niqab*.

Chapter 4 will observe how participants relate to their heritage language: Bengali. I consider how specific spaces determine the use of the language. I interrogate how some are concerned about the language 'dying' because fewer Bengalis speak it, and even then it is at a conversational level. I gauge how the participants describe its role in their lives and how it informs their understanding of their heritage identity. The conversations around the Bengali language rested on its losing importance and that it will only retain any value as a mother tongue within the community. I also point to how these experiences of cultural expressions are described, processed and interpreted through the idiom of identity, particularly an ethnic identity.

The fifth chapter examines the research participants' use of language, the way they discuss the Bengali religious terms and their link to Arabic. I observe the manner in which research participants characterise the languages they use and how that aids the formation of their ethnic and/or religious identities. I take into account their experiences redefining their relationships with various languages, both in their interactions with the British culture as a whole and in their more intimate experiences as children growing up with other Bangladeshis. I point to the ways in which these experiences of religious and ethnic expressions are described, processed and interpreted through the idiom of identity, particularly a religious identity. The majority of the research participants employ religion in their everyday engagement with the world to create their distinctive imaginings of language/s.

The conclusion will synthesise the book's key conceptual contributions, with a focus on the intervention made into debates on identity in a postcolonial setting and belonging vis-à-vis dress and language. It also considers the ever-changing conversations around identity constructions by ethnic minorities in the United Kingdom and the political imaginaries reflected in this research, using Stuart Hall's constructions of cultural identity and its breakdown.

Notes

1 Press Association, 'Straws asks Muslim women to remove veil', *Guardian*, 5 October 2006.
2 F. Rajina, 'If the Conservatives are to truly tackle Islamophobia, Boris Johnson must be reprimanded', *The Metro*, 7 August 2018. For the original article, see B. Johnson, 'Denmark has got it wrong. Yes, the burka is oppressive and ridiculous – but that's still no reason to ban it, *Daily Telegraph*, 5 August 2018, www.telegraph.co.uk/news/2018/08/05/denmark-has-got-wrong-yes-burka-oppressive-ridiculous-still/ (accessed 4 April 2024).
3 S. Begum, 'From Sylhet to Spitalfields: Exploring Bengali migrant homemaking in the context of a squatters' movement, in 1970s East London' (PhD dissertation, Queen Mary, University of London, 2021), p. 21.
4 C. Alexander, 'Making Bengali Brick Lane: Claiming and contesting space in East London', *British Journal of Sociology* 62:2 (2011), 201–220.
5 The *sari* is a length of material, looking more or less like a very long scarf, worked with a loose bodice, called a blouse, and a petticoat to help secure the pleats of the *sari* at the front. The *shalwar kameez* (also known as 'Punjabi dress') consists of three parts: *kameez* (shirt), *shalwar* (trousers), and *dupatta* or *uruna* (the latter means scarf in Sylheti). The *funjabi*, also known as *punjabi*, is a *kurta*-like top – a loose shirt – over a pair of trousers, or sometimes worn over a *lungi*; a *lungi* is a sarong worn by men around the waist and just above the ankle, usually made of cotton. *Hijab* throughout the book refers to the headscarf worn by Muslim women; the *jilbab* is a long and loose-fitted garment worn by Muslim women, the *niqab* being the separate piece of fabric used to cover the face by tying a knot at the back of the head. The *thobe* is an ankle-length garment similar to a robe, usually white, worn by men in West Asia and North Africa.

6 K. Baxter, *British Muslims and the Call to Global Jihad* (Clayton, VIC: Monash University Press, 2007), p. 1.
7 M. E. T. El-Mesawi and T. Khriji, 'Islam and terrorism: Beyond the wisdom of the secularist paradigm', *Intellectual Discourse* 14:1 (2006), 47–70.
8 V. Redclift, F. Rajina and N. Rashid, 'The burden of conviviality: British Bangladeshi Muslims navigating diversity in London, Luton and Birmingham', *Sociology* 56:6 (2022), 1159–1175.
9 S. Mahmood, 'Feminism, democracy and empire: Islam and the war on terror', in J. W. Scott (ed.), *Women's Studies on the Edge* (Durham, NC: Duke University Press, 2008), pp. 81–114 (p. 97).
10 K. Devlin, 'Lutfur Rahman elected mayor of Tower Hamlets despite five-year ban for "corrupt and illegal practices"', *Independent*, 6 May 2022.
11 G. Younge, 'Ambalavaner Sivanandan obituary: Director of the Institute of Race Relations who helped change the way Britain thought about race', *Guardian*, 7 February 2018.
12 S. Ali, 'British Muslims in numbers: A demographic. Socio-economic and health profile of Muslims in Britain drawing on the 2011 Census' (2015), Muslim Council of Britain, www.mcb.org.uk/wp-content/uploads/2015/02/MCBCensusReport_2015.pdf (accessed 5 June 2023), p. 16.
13 Ibid.
14 S. Hamid, 'British Muslim young people: Facts, features and religious trends', *Religion, State and Society* 39:2–3 (2011), 247–261.
15 Office for National Statistics, *Census National Statistics* (London: Office for National Statistics, 2001).
16 Office for National Statistics, *Census National Statistics* (London: Office for National Statistics, 2011).
17 A Sufi master or guide. See D. Garbin, 'Bangladeshi diaspora in the UK: Some observations on socio-cultural dynamics, religious trends and transnational politics, paper presented in a conference on human rights and Bangladesh' (PhD dissertation, SOAS, University of London, 2005); S. Glynn, 'Bengali Muslims: The new East End radicals?', *Ethnic and Racial Studies* 25:6 (2002), 969–988.
18 Office for National Statistics, *Census National Statistics* (London: Office for National Statistics, 2021).
19 J. Eade and D. Garbin, *The Bangladeshi Diaspora: Community Dynamics, Transnational Politics and Islamist Activities* (London: Foreign and Commonwealth Office, 2005).
20 J. Eade, 'Nationalism, community and the Islamization of space in London', in B. D. Metcalf (ed.), *Making Muslim Space in North America and Europe* (Berkeley: University of California Press, 1997), pp. 217–233.
21 A. Hoque, *Being Young, Male and Muslim in Luton* (London: UCL Press, 2019); S. Mia, 'Navigating histories: An exploration of second generation high-achieving British Bangladeshi Muslim young women living in north-east London' (PhD dissertation, Goldsmiths, University of London, 2015).

22 A. Riaz, *Islam and Identity Politics among British Bangladeshis: A Leap of Faith* (Manchester: Manchester University Press, 2013), p. 5.
23 A. Hoque, *British-Islamic Identity: Third Generation Bangladeshis from East London* (London: Institute of Education Press, 2015).
24 C. Adams, *Across Seven Seas and Thirteen Rivers: Life Stories of Pioneer Sylheti Settlers in Britain* (London: Thap, 1987).
25 S. Begum, *From Sylhet to Spitalfields: Bengali Squatters in 1970s East London* (London: Lawrence and Wishart, 2023).
26 K. Gardner, *Global Migrants, Local Lives: Travels and Transformation in Rural Bangladesh* (Oxford: Oxford University Press, 1995), p. 35.
27 K. Gardner, *Age, Narrative, and Migration: The Life Course and Life Histories of Bengali Elders in London* (Oxford: Berg, 2002).
28 K. Gardner, 'Keeping connected: Security, place, and social capital in a "Londoni" village in Sylhet', *Journal of the Royal Anthropological Institute* 14 (2008), 477–495.
29 N. Ahmed, *Family, Citizenship and Islam: The Changing Experiences of Migrant Women Ageing in London* (Abingdon: Routledge, 2016).
30 J. Eade and D. Garbin, 'Changing narratives of violence, struggle and resistance: Bangladeshis and the competition for resources in the global city', *Oxford Development Studies* 30:2 (2002), 137–149.
31 J. Eade, 'Nationalism and the quest for authenticity: The Bangladeshis in Tower Hamlets', *Journal of Ethnic and Migration Studies* 16:4 (1990), 493–503; J. Eade, *The Politics of Community: The Bangladeshi Community in East London* (London: Gower, 1989). D. Garbin, 'A diasporic sense of place: Dynamics of spatialization and transnational political fields among Bangladeshi Muslims in Britain', in M. P. Smith and J. Eade (eds), *Transnational Ties: Cities, Migrations, and Identities* (New Brunswick, Transaction, 2017), pp. 147–161.
32 J. Eade, 'Representing British Bangladeshis in London's East End: The global city, text, performance and authenticity', in S. McLoughlin, W. Gould, A. J. Kabir and E. Tomalin (eds), *Writing the City in British Asian Diasporas* (Abingdon: Routledge, 2011), pp. 49–69.
33 Glynn, 'Bengali Muslims'.
34 S. Glynn, 'The spirit of '71: How the Bangladeshi War of Independence has haunted Tower Hamlets', *Socialist History Journal* 29 (2006), 56–75.
35 S. Glynn, *Class, Ethnicity and Religion in the Bengali East End: A Political History* (Manchester: Manchester University Press, 2014).
36 B. Zeitlyn, 'Growing up glocal in London and Sylhet' (PhD dissertation, University of Sussex, 2010).
37 J. Gest, *Apart: Alienated and Engaged Muslims in the West* (London: Hurst, 2010).

1

From Shurma to Thames, from Desh to Bidesh: History of migration

The Bangladeshi community in Britain began to take root, on the territory marked out by the first few casual pioneers who had found the way 'across seven seas and thirteen rivers' from Sylhet to Aldgate. Here at last was the memorial to those thousands of nameless sailors who died in cold water and blazing engine rooms. The Empire had finally come home.[1]

Background

The presence of Bengalis in Britain precedes the British empire. The first recorded note of a Bengali in Britain was in 1616 when the 'Mayor of London attended the baptism of "Peter", an East Indian from the Bay of Bengal, who had arrived in 1614 and [been] given a "Christian" name by James I'.[2] The broader relationship between Britain and the Bengal (consisting of today's West Bengal state in India and Bangladesh) is a crucial geographic historical moment we have to factor in to understand the more recent migration waves of Bengalis arriving in Britain and settling in the East End.[3] The East India Company (EIC), which went on to rule over parts of India, began trading there from the city of Kolkata in West Bengal. I also, importantly, situate the historical development of the Language Movement in East Pakistan and document how this movement became one of the essential facets of the independence movement in Bangladesh. By providing a wider historical context of the relationship between the British during the British empire and the Bengal, the post-Partition maladies enable us to be more cognisant of how such interactions created possibilities and offered early migration passages between the Bengal and Britain.

After I explore the Bengalis' arrival in Britain before the Second World War, the following segment considers the varying migration periods of the 1950s, 1960s, and 1970s, before and after the independence of Bangladesh in 1971. These contexts emphasise how the articulation of geography and space, even with the distance between Britain and Bengal, forges a geographic intimacy. Bengalis, who may have never stepped foot in Britain before, would probably have had a level of familiarity because of their proximity to the metropole via empire. While contextualising those specific periods, this chapter also examines the community's anti-racist activism in relation to the growing antagonism they faced on the East End streets. The continuous experience of state-sanctioned racism meant that Bengalis were suddenly confronting questions about home and where home was, and if this was the fight they were putting up with in East London. The 1970s became the decade that ruptured the myth of return and saw the emergence of Bengalis building coalitions and alliances with other racially minoritised communities from former colonies in order to fight back, while the 1980s and 1990s stand out as decades of containment where the radical flavour of the community was indexed through the cooption of many into the political mainstream. A further discussion scoping the current literature in place and looking at this community's history will provide room for a close examination and contestation of the findings in existing research, replacing them where necessary with new considerations and alternative ways of theorising racially minoritised communities.

Once we get to the early 2000s, much of the discourse around the community's ethnic and racial positioning shifts to a more explicitly religious one. However, such new interventions were hasty in conceptualising the *British Muslim*. When it comes to the exploration of the image, discrimination, stereotyping and ethno-religious identity of a minority group in a western migratory setting, British Bangladeshi Muslims received much attention in the post-7/7 hysteria surrounding Muslims and Islam in Britain. This focus has often been viewed through a securitised lens with a spotlight on the role of the East London Mosque. Some studies have suggested that, though Bangladeshis are more secular than their South Asian Muslim counterparts, the second generation are going back to their religious roots, asserting their distinctive character by identifying with the global *ummah* of Islam.[4] Meanwhile, the first generation identify more closely with their ethnic identity and are, allegedly, more willing to integrate. My focus is not so preoccupied with integration or who is more inclined to integrate. Instead, I am more invested in exploring how the pressures of being Muslim shape and determine the community's relations to itself via dress and language. How are the boundaries drawn with regard to what to wear? How do Muslims negotiate their language use while located within the cultural and political terrain as a 'suspect community'?

The British Raj and the lascars

For hundreds of years, the Bengal has been a nexus for migration between the Indian subcontinent and Britain.[5] It was only after the Battle of Plassey in 1757 that the East India Company ruled the Bengal, employing Bengali seamen, known as lascars or lashkars, for their knowledge of trade routes from Kolkata to the docks in East London.[6] These men 'came from Bengal Presidency',[7] and, according to Ansar Ahmed Ullah, the word *lascar* was then used to describe 'any sailor from the Indian subcontinent or any other part of Asia, but came particularly to refer to people from West Bengal and modern-day Bangladesh'.[8] However, Sophie Gilliat-Ray points out their diversity and notes that 'Pathans, Punjabis and Mirpuris were recruited in Bombay, while Bengalis, especially from the Sylhet region, were recruited in Calcutta', and the sailors started to form a community in East London, especially in the dock areas.[9] In his book *Counterflows to Colonialism: Indian Travellers and Settlers in Britain 1600–1857*, Michael H. Fisher argues that far more Muslims than Hindus 'went to Britain, often supported by traditions of travel through the wider Islamic world that already linked Europe and Asia'.[10]

Since at least 1873, Sylhetis have been recorded as working in London restaurants, and contributed to the growing numbers of 'Muslim seamen' who 'formed a substantial section of the "visible" migrant population in Britain'.[11] According to Fisher, the lascars who stayed married local white British women. From the seventeenth century, 'Indian sailors became a visible feature of British society, particularly, but not exclusively, in the dock areas of east London'.[12] Sake Dean Mahomed was one of the most prominent figures from the Bengal who arrived and permanently settled in England in the eighteenth century.[13] An account of marriages between Bengali men and English women reads: 'Many Bengali Lascars and destitute servants found it difficult to gain employment in England and became musicians playing Indian drums, tambourines and sitars in the streets of the East End. Some eventually entered into relationships with local English women and a generation of Bengali-British children was born.'[14]

Ali Riaz argues that, amongst South Asians, Sylhetis, originating from the north-eastern region of Bangladesh, were the first 'to establish a significant presence in Britain'.[15] The connection with Sylhet, then known as Srihatta ('a prosperous centre of trading' in Sanksrit), was established via the EIC, 'officially [coming] under the control of the EIC in 1765, but it took almost two decades for them to establish their dominance'.[16] Ullah and John Eversley speculate that, although there is no clear evidence about the reasons why so many seamen came from Sylhet, one explanation could be that 'the serangs (recruiter and in charge of lascars) who operated in the streets of Calcutta chose to recruit crews from their own birthplace – that is, Sylhet. Crews were also recruited in Calcutta to carry Assamese tea, including tea from Sylhet.'[17]

Katy Gardner and Abdus Shukur contend that by 'the beginning of the twentieth century many Sylhetis had gained enough experience to become brokers themselves', explaining how and why Sylhetis had 'near monopoly', as many favoured 'their own kinsmen and fellow-villagers'.[18] This is further attested by Haji Kona Miah, a seaman interviewed and quoted in Caroline Adams's book, *Across Seven Seas and Thirteen Rivers*, who said 'The Sylhet people were in the ship because these people follow each other, and some went there and others saw them, and they thought they could get jobs too. It all started before we were born.'[19] Notably, John Eade and David Garbin argue that the predominance of Sylhetis was primarily due to geographical location and 'the proximity of the Surma and Kushiara rivers which linked Sylhet to Southern Bengal and to Kolkata (Calcutta)', giving access to local Sylhetis to embark on the ships and find jobs.[20] In conjunction with this, according to Gardner, during the rainy season the river traffic brought cargo ships that would stop at Markhuli, Enatganj, Sherpur, Maulvibazar, Baliganj and Fenchuganj in Sylhet.[21] In this vein, one possible factor causing Sylheti men to join the British merchant navy ships for employment may have been Sylhet's long-established boat-building tradition. This tradition, as argued by Riaz, was due to the favourable geographical location of Sylhet – an area that was surrounded by waterways, particularly during the monsoon season, and was also 'due to its close proximity to the trade route (between Assam and Calcutta, and between the seaports of the Bengal delta) and due to the need to transport the most precious commodity of the region (limestone locally known as *chunam*)'.[22] This is elaborately reflected in the autobiography of Robert Lindsay, an administrator ('resident collector') of Sylhet from 1778 to 1790.[23]

Strikingly, upon the arrival of the lascars in England, issues pertaining to questions of identity, belonging and othering became a point of contention amongst the English in the nineteenth century. The general assumption is that matters of identity, particularly conversations around race, became more contentious and prevalent in a postcolonial context. However, this is untrue, as discussions around race and identity were present. As a result, the lascars were seen as complete outsiders and not considered English, despite living in England for many years. According to Diane Robinson-Dunn (2003), this was the case because the lascars were not born in England. Yet, paradoxically, it was because 'their circumstances and lifestyles resembled those of other English people who seemed to threaten the social order and were, therefore, considered outsiders existing beyond the pale of the true English nation'.[24] The English thus constructed and defined an English identity in relation to the empire where those coming from 'over there' were viewed suspiciously and were not included in that new identity, which, as Robinson-Dunn contends, was due to 'the role of imperial politics within the metropole'.[25]

The 'otherisation' of South Asian men was being forged in the metropole, providing a distance from the 'subjects' in the subcontinent. As the 'subjects' started appearing on the streets of London, and in proximity to the English, this seemed to challenge power dynamics bound by space and location. Furthermore, while the lascars were arriving, there were also South Asian women coming to the UK. They came as *ayahs* (Indian nannies, nurse maids and servants) who 'accompanied the families of the colonial *memsahibs* (wives of senior officials) of the Raj back to Britain'.[26] Interestingly, on Jewry Street in East London, 'Mr and Mrs Roger set up an Ayah's [sic] home and job centre on the corner of India Street in the 1890's where nannies from Bengal, Burma and China could have lodgings, seek work and arrange passage home.'[27] This ayahs' home was relocated to bigger premises in Hackney in 1921. While it primarily operated as accommodation for Indian ayahs sent there by the white British families, it also became a site that served 'as a refuge for ayahs who had been ill-treated, dismissed from service or simply abandoned'.[28] Rozina Visram further adds that the ayahs' home found the abandoned Indian ayahs 'placements with families returning to India', as families needed ayahs on their travels to India.[29] More lascars were hired from the British colonies before and during the First World War to replace men called up for war service.[30] According to some estimates, 20 per cent of the British maritime labour force was made up of Indian seamen, many of whom were of Bengali origin with surnames such as Miah, Ullah, Uddin and many others.[31] Some of these names are visible at the Tower Hill Memorial in East London. During the First World War, 3,427 were killed, and 1,200 were taken prisoner.[32] The hiring of Bengali seamen continued up to the Second World War, when 'records show that 6,600 seamen were killed ... another 1,000 wounded and 1,200 taken prisoner, many of them Bengali seamen from Sylhet'.[33]

Whilst the lascars were on board, they were known to be treated poorly. Many risked their lives by jumping ship, and took their chances in London's East End.[34] Adams states that the men on the ships 'lived in cramped, overcrowded conditions, without exercise, fresh air or fresh food and without suitable clothing or bedding for cold climates'.[35] In this sense, Ayub Ali was unique in his attempts to unite the community in the 1920s and 1930s for the many who jumped ship. He settled in London in 1920 and, as a seaman and Sylheti, understood the difficulties seamen were experiencing in London. He opened a café called Shah Jolal Restaurant at 76 Commercial Street, East London.[36] The café 'soon became the primary contact point of the Bengali seamen'.[37] Ali provided food and shelter at his lodging house while assisting his compatriots in getting documents to work in England. He also offered other services, such as writing letters to their families and arranging ways to remit their monies back home. The seamen community highly respected him for his work as an intermediary between them and the authorities. He became popularly known as 'Master' because of his education, and 'in the time-honoured village tradition, he acquired the status of a leader, later being made the President of the UK Muslim League'.[38]

According to Claire Alexander, Shahzad Firoz and Naaz Rashid, the number of Bengalis in London increased throughout the 1930s and onwards until the end of the Second World War.[39] During that period, as Alexander et al. argue, 'the first signs of a "community" were apparent, under the leadership of individuals such as Ayub Ali and Shah Abdul Majid Qureshi who, together, established the "Indian Seamen's Welfare League" in Christian Street, Aldgate in 1943'.[40] The Indian Seamen's Welfare League was established as a social welfare organisation to 'provide seamen with social amenities, help with paper work and serve as a means of communication with relatives in India in the event of misfortune during the war'.[41] Adams notes how the membership of the League was largely made up of Sylhetis. Before the Indian Seamen's Welfare League was established, there were several cafés opened 'by former seamen in the late 1930s, followed by the opening of the first full-scale restaurant by Shah Abdul Majid Quereishi in 1938'.[42] These cafés became 'the centres of Bengali gatherings and social interactions'.[43] While most of them were established and run in East London, another well-known Sylheti café was set up by Abdul Mannan in North London in 1944. It was called Basement Café, on 36 Percy Street, where Sylhetis would congregate to find out 'news of jobs, friends and family'.[44] Another Sylheti ex-lascar, Syed Tofussil Ally, opened the British Indian Sailors' Home and seamen's outfitting shop at 32–33 Victoria Dock Road, in Canning Town.[45] Visram highlights how Ally was a 'Sylheti seaman on British ships from 1913 to 1919, [and] had run the lodging-house in Canning Town since 1923'.[46]

The themes around belonging to the nation, or in this instance to the metropole of empire, were prevalent as Britain was constructing its image of its colonial subjects. The preference was to have the 'other' at a distance 'over there', where they were out of sight. If those from 'over there' were 'here', then they were placed into the same category as the undeserving and undesirable of British society: the working class. As Adams notes, the interactions and encounters between the Bengali lascars and the white sailors reveal, quite saliently, how colonialism racialised the body of the other.[47] This situation also reverberates in the present-day context, particularly with the rise of far-right rhetoric. By focusing on empire, and its relations to how it determined much of the migratory experience during colonialism, it is essential to consider how empire never left, even after we entered a supposed postcolonial era. Barnor Hesse and Salman Sayyid contend that Britain upholds the fictitious position in British public culture of a supposed 'termination between imperial past and the nationalist present'.[48] The remainder of this chapter thus explores the historically sanctioned

Bengali language during the empire

When the British settled in Kolkata, it was inevitable that Bengali became the 'officially blessed language of early British India', where Bengalis 'served as a crucible for serious discourses on literature and language, community, and society'.[49] In this context, Anindita Ghosh argues that the concept of civilisation became a 'largely linguistic concept, with language purportedly reflecting the moral and evolutionary status of societies'.[50] In this regard, Persian continued to enjoy 'prominence as the language of state and business, and predated the coming of the Mughals in Bengal', while the practical needs of administration 'made Bengali the language of power and authority'.[51] Determinedly, Ghosh contends that Bengali became the only officially recognised language in the province when English replaced Arabic and Persian in the law courts in 1838, which meant 'Bengali had to be shaped into an effective, standardised prose language'.[52] However, the local intelligentsia was not only producing a standardised Bengali but was also 'purging from it "undesirable"; elements such as the Perso-Arabic and the colloquial'.[53] With Bengali gaining prominence, and the various attempts to 'cleanse' and 'purify' the language, it became evident that this was impossible.

Given that Persian had been the official language in the Bengal for centuries, it is not surprising to find Perso-Arabic elements still reappearing. Ghosh illustrates how Bengali was the language of 'the less educated groups such as a village agent writing a petition, or a clerk keeping the accounts of an estate, who preferred to use Bengali, [which] was strongly marked by an infusion of Persian words'.[54] Standard Bengali also included *tatsama* or Sanksrit loan-words, causing Bengali Muslims to feel marginalised, as the 'Sanskritisation' of Bengali was linked to the 'Hinduisation' of the language. Bengali Muslims in the nineteenth century remained faithful to the Bengali language influenced by Perso-Arabic terms, which came to be known as 'Musalman-Bengali', defined by Ghosh as 'colloquial Bengali, intertwined with popular local myth and legend, ritual and superstition, and very different from the chaste Arabic and Persian in which Islamic religious texts were usually written'.[55] Further, the intersection of these communal and linguistic agendas led to 'the distilling of a specific community identity for the strand, and partly explains the enormous popularity of these works among Muslims of the period'.[56]

The qualification of Bengali as a legitimate 'Islamic' language was made possible as 'verbs were compounded out of Perso-Arabic words, and even used as prefixes and suffixes'.[57] In remaining consistent, the usual 'left to right pattern of the Bengali script was reversed to follow the Persian and Arabic style of writing from right to left', and even 'the printed or manuscript pages of Musalmani-Bengali works were bound in the opposite direction'.[58] This aesthetic, as well as the physical demonstration of religiosity as a community, with a focus on communalism, was enabled through the creation of a communal identity in relation to an imagined and constructed 'other': in this case the Bengali Hindus. The Bengali Muslims 'otherised' the Bengali Hindus, just as the Muslims felt they themselves had been 'otherised' through the Sanksritisation of Bengali, thus adopting the same strategy to reassert their own identity and make Musalmani-Bengali 'their own'. However, with the transformation of Musalmani-Bengali, Ghosh argues that elite Bengali Muslims 'had always identified with Persian, Arabic or Urdu, rather than Bengali, which was perceived as the language of the masses. The linguistic divide here was thus split along lines of class, rather than religion.'[59]

These historical insights and the gestural overview of language development reveal the tensions, but also how these tensions re-emerge before the official Partition of India and the lead-up to the Liberation War of 1971. The first, more potent observation, is before the Partition of India in 1947, the All-India Muslim League was founded in Dhaka in 1906, becoming an essential platform for the Muslim nationalist movement in India. Then, in 1940, when it was announced in the Lahore Resolution that a single state of Pakistan would be created comprising the 'two independent and sovereign states named East and West Pakistan in the two Muslim majority zones of India', Bengali Muslim League leaders raised concerns.[60] Bengali Muslims were worried, as Bengali was not added as a language for East Pakistan. Many Bengali politicians felt Bengali should be the medium of education, arguing that it was the mother tongue of the people of Bengal.[61] These worries continued in the following decades, and one could argue, somewhat ironically, that they brought the Bengali Muslims and Hindus together in unity, becoming a platform to express national consciousness by establishing a distinguished linguistic identity for Bengalis in Bangladesh.

Post-Second World War migration and settling in East London

> You come here, you struggle and then you move on. That's how it works; that's how it will always work.[62]

Having considered the history of Bengalis' arrival in East London prior to the Partition of India, with the creation of West and East Pakistan in

1947 – the latter becoming Bangladesh in 1971, as will be further explored in this section – the first outline considers why the East End has always been a location of settlement for various migrant communities.[63] As one walks through the streets of East London, there are visible signs of the different groups of people who came to the East End to start a new life, escape persecution or find a new place they could call home. Pnina Werbner's arguments on the construction of a new home and how it allows new migrants to retain links with 'back home' are poignant:

> [T]ransnationals are people who move ... in order to create collective 'homes' around them wherever they happen to land. There is no question of simply replicating culture here ... Transnationals are also cultural hybrids, but their hybridity is unconscious, organic and collectively negotiated in practice ... Most translocals have to contend with incredible social and economic hardships, and they draw on culturally constituted resources of sociality and mutual aid for survival. They actively construct 'community' to shield them from racist rejections, but also compete for honour, to have fun, to worship, and to celebrate – together – collective rites of passage or ceremonies of nostalgic remembrance for a lost home.[64]

Over the last few years, an industry has emerged of tour guides showing people the streets of the East End, making it possible to unravel the lives of the various communities who came, built a community and then moved elsewhere. Their contributions, particularly those of the French Huguenots and Eastern European Jews, are still visible through the protection of various building sites declared as heritage sites, street names and names of buildings. In particular, the notion of social and economic hardship is captured in the history of the textile factories where many Jews and later Bangladeshis worked to earn money, both to remit 'back home' and for their families who later joined them in London. The notion of creating a community away from one's homeland is significant. This allowed each community to rejoice in memories and traditions that would otherwise be practised or cherished behind closed doors. The making of a community was essential to the different generations I interviewed. It allowed them to foster a sense of belonging locally and enabled them to engage, negotiate and construct their Bengali identity. Begum argues that the local East End Bengali community reinscribed a particular Sylheti model of homemaking in this new space where the 'home reaches out into wider *uthaan* (courtyard) and *para* (neighbourhood)'.[65] The recreation of this model in the East End provided the possibility of asserting a distinct identity while continuously contesting the process of ' "claiming" and "making" space in East London', thus marking the area as the heartland of the Bangladeshi community in the British Bangladeshi imagination.[66]

The East End's geographical position and its proximity to the docks made this area London's principal industrial quarter. Historically, the East End has always been a location for migrants to settle temporarily because living costs were cheap and 'job prospects made the area particularly attractive'.[67] Today, the area known as Tower Hamlets is a haven for several generations of immigrants.[68] First, there were the French Huguenots, a Protestant community persecuted by the French Catholics who escaped France in the late seventeenth century; many were master weavers who revolutionised the indigenous silk industry, so the area became known as Weaver Town. Afterwards, the Irish arrived in the 1840s during the great potato famine, and 'to this day a large proportion of the white people in Bethnal Green have Irish surnames'.[69] Several decades later, the East End witnessed the 'largest influx of Jews ... after fleeing pogroms following the assassination of Tsar Alexander in 1881',[70] and, like the Bangladeshis who started arriving a few decades later, the Jewish immigrants of the late nineteenth century 'went into clothing sweatshops or set up as tailors'.[71]

One building that now stands as a testament to the different communities' contribution to the area's history and leaves a reminder of their presence is the Brick Lane Jamme Masjid building. In his book *Salaam Brick Lane*, Tarquin Hall talks of his walk through the streets of Spitalfields with Solly, an East End Jew, who points to this building and explains 'it was built as a church by Huguenot silk weavers in 1743 and since then it's been a synagogue and a mosque. As each wave of immigrants settled in the East End, they've made it their own. After the French came the Irish, then the Jews and now the Bangladeshis'.[72] Bengalis started to migrate to London in the late 1940s, not only for better economic opportunities but also because of the Partition of India in 1947. The Partition prompted several difficulties for Bengalis from Sylhet, one of which was the cutting off of Sylhet – now in East Pakistan – from Kolkata – now part of West Bengal in India – thereby 'reducing the opportunities for employment in shipping to such an extent that during the period 1952–55 many former sailors faced destitution'.[73] By the 1950s, the seamen who had jumped off the ships in the London docks had created 'a small, but steadily increasing population of Sylhetis'.[74]

However, it was during the 1950s that the number of Bengalis/East Pakistanis increased dramatically.[75] The 1950s represented the sojourner decade, defined by the 'strong transnational community life that was dense [and] locally oriented', as the migrants 'were deeply embedded in transnational ties and networks based on kinship and village of origin'.[76] Those already settled in East London used these established ties to help those migrating from Sylhet to launch their life in the UK. This was the decade that many felt they would eventually return to their homeland with their savings and never come back to Britain. A large proportion of these savings and remittances were invested in Sylhet, mostly in land and housing.[77] Yet, as Muhammad Anwar points out in his book *The Myth of Return: Pakistanis in Britain*,[78] returning was a myth, and while it continued to remain a myth, research on post-Brexit Britain and British Bangladeshis has shown that there is a growing interest in re-establishing firmer links to 'back home' as a Plan B, should things worsen in the UK.[79]

When the Indian Seamen's Welfare League was established in 1943, it became one of the first major organisations to provide a space for the Bengali seamen. Later, in 1952, the Pakistan Welfare Association was founded, reflecting 'the presence of a network among the migrant Bengalis and [contributing] to the strengthening of connections among community members'.[80] The majority of Bengalis from Sylhet originate from several *thanas* (administrative sub-districts), including Habiganj, Beani Bazar, Maulvi Bazar and Sunamganj – i.e. the same districts 'that had dominated the lascar movements of the past'.[81] Geoff Dench, Kate Gavron and Michael Young argue that post-Partition the *serang* system was dismantled and the seamen who stayed in Britain had no other choice but to reside in the East End and make this their new home.[82] In addition, Aftab Ali, a prominent Indian trade unionist, is said to have advised the Bengali seamen to 'leave their ships at British ports', so that they did not get 'caught up in the Hindu–Muslim riots in Calcutta'.[83]

In the 1960s, however, there were changes to the migration pattern as the British government introduced various Acts to limit the number of people entering the UK. The Commonwealth Immigrants Act of 1962[84] brought forth a system of employment vouchers that imposed restrictions on this right, making it no longer possible to 'enter freely from a British colony or former colony'.[85] Younger Bengali men in East Pakistan took advantage of this voucher system by getting sponsored by their senior kin who had previously worked as seamen to bring them to Britain to 'take the factory jobs'.[86] By 1965, the laws on migration were further tightened by regulations that limited the distribution of vouchers to 'skilled workers and to those applicants who had jobs promised and waiting for them'.[87] This change enabled men already in Britain to arrange for other Bengalis to come to the country. The 1970s was the decade that put an end to 'the sojourner era and [marked] the beginning of a period of family reunification for Bengalis in Britain'.[88] This decade also witnessed family reunification, as Bengali men were bringing their children and wives to Britain, thus debunking the myth of return. The Immigration Act of 1971 imposed further restrictions that limited sponsorship to family members and, eventually, to immediate family only.[89]

The Bengali Language Movement and the creation of Bangladesh

While migration and settlement became an issue for those in Britain, Bengalis in East Pakistan had other worries. In 1952, the Language Movement emerged in East Pakistan to prevent the imposition of the Urdu language by the central Pakistani government. More than six months after the Partition of India, in March 1948, Muhammad Ali Jinnah, considered the founding father of Pakistan, visited East Pakistan and addressed students at Dhaka University. His speech acknowledged and discussed the question of a national language:

> Let me restate my views on the question of a state language for Pakistan. For official use in [East Bengal], the people of the province can choose any language they wish. The question will be decided solely in accordance with the wishes of the people of this province alone, as freely expressed through their accredited representatives at the appropriate time and after full and dispassionate consideration. There can, however, be only one lingua franca – that is, the language for intercommunication between the various provinces of the state – and that language should be Urdu and cannot be any other.[90]

He continues to argue that Urdu 'has been nurtured by a hundred million of this subcontinent, [it is] a language understood throughout the length and breadth of Pakistan and above all a language which, more than any other provincial language, embodies the best that is in Islamic culture and Muslim tradition and is nearest to the languages used in other Islamic countries'.[91] But, in reality, Bengali Muslims had 'always outnumbered the Muslims of other language groups of united India';[92] therefore, the claim that Urdu was the superior language to represent Muslims, especially Bengali Muslims at this time, was flawed.

Philip Oldenburg points out that 56 per cent of the Pakistani population – including both wings – spoke Bengali, thus outnumbering the Urdu speakers yet marked as insufficient to become the lingua franca.[93] The argument emphasising Urdu as more 'Islamic' and placing Bengali as secondary and not 'Islamic' enough was cited by an early social reformer, Reyazuddin Ahmed. He stated that 'Bengali, although the mother tongue of the Muslims, can never be considered the cultural or national language of the Bengali Muslims.'[94] Dhurjati Prasad De points out that this desire to incorporate words and phrases 'denoting Islamic culture and sentiment' into the Bengali language was due to the following three factors:

(1) strong religious sense debarred them from contemplating Bengali as the national language of the community;
(2) there had been a lurking fear of losing the much vaunted Islamic identity which would be devoid of all its meaning if Bengali could be accepted as a medium of expression to the exclusion of Arabic, Persian and Urdu;
(3) the concern for Islamic brotherhood.[95]

Additionally, during the British Raj, Sir Syed Ahmed Khan published a bilingual journal in Urdu and English, whereby the former became a cultural symbol that was crucial in Muslim identity reformation.[96] Although non-Muslims also spoke Urdu, the language became increasingly identified with Muslims owing to its 'dramatically increased use in writings on Islamic religious reform'.[97] Ironically, because of the sudden increase in the usage of the printing press, the Bengali vernacular language – which functioned as an ethnic marker – provided a platform for Muslim scholars in the Bengal to 'contend with religious praxis' and '[become] a medium for communicating ideas about membership in a wider religious community'.[98] De argues that it is with the 'acceptance of Bengali as the vernacular' that the *Mussalmani Bangla* was born, incorporating Arabic, Persian and Urdu words.[99] Interestingly, Urdu's script derives from Persian and Arabic, but the 'grammatical roots lie ultimately in Sanksrit, and thus Urdu and Bengali are closer to one another than Urdu is to Arabic or Persian'.[100]

Retreating to Jinnah's speech at Dhaka University and the central government's refusal to include Bengali as one of the national languages along with Urdu led to a national crisis lasting for five years, from 1947 to 1952. Following Jinnah's declaration, there were attempts to 'de-Sanskritise Bengali, even to the extent of introducing Arabic script for the Bengali language'.[101] This task became a national project, and the central government 'created twenty adult education centres in various locations in East Pakistan to introduce the new script'.[102] This further reinforced the 'othering' and 'foreignness' of the Bengali language by portraying it as a Hindu language, and 'therefore in stark contrast to their vision of the nation'.[103] The de-Sanskritising of Bengali was seen as a neo-colonial project intended to increase the cultural hegemony of West Pakistan. The Bengali language and the various manifestations of the culture obstructed the one-dimensional, Urdu-speaking Muslim identity that the central government was trying to establish. It was an attempt to keep the two wings of Pakistan, East and West, together as the shared and 'common culture of Bengali Hindus and Bengali Muslims as a potential threat to national unity'.[104] However, unlike the Urdu-speaking Muslims, Bengali Muslims did not want to 'dissociate the traditional Bangla script from their language, as, in their opinions, Bangla script did not in any way pose a threat to Bengali Muslim identity'.[105]

Tensions over the language reached their peak on 21 February 1952, when the police shot at a peaceful demonstration in Dhaka. This event has been commemorated and remembered as *Ekushey* (the number 21 in Bengali), and as the birth of the Language Movement, which has generated 'its own language martyrs and symbols, such as the "Shaheed Minar"'.[106] *Ekushey* continues to be celebrated and commemorated in Bangladesh and across the world, including East London. It serves as a reminder of the struggle to preserve the Bengali language and ethnicity, and a 'symbol of resistance and the beginning of the struggle for independence'.[107] The original Shaheed Minar was erected in Dhaka; others were built in Altab Ali Park in Whitechapel, Tower Hamlets, Manchester, Luton[108] and Wales. Most recently, Shaheed Minars have also been erected in places such as Italy,[109] Portugal[110] and North America.[111] This confrontation between the students and the police, which continued for several years, forced the central government, on 29 February 1956, to declare and enshrine Bengali as Pakistan's second national language in its constitution.[112] Messages of protest were inscribed on banners that read 'One letter of the Bengali alphabet is equal to the life of a Bengali.'[113]

Uddin highlights how the clashes in 1952 'marked a turning point in the young nation's history and collective memory'.[114] The Bengalis felt their ethnicity was under attack because 'West Pakistanis viewed customs and traditions observed by Bengali Muslims that were common to Bengali Hindus – such as singing Rabindranath Tagore's songs, wearing *bindis*, and the middle-class custom of having children study the fine arts – as acts of cultural resistance'.[115] These anxieties were causing a hindrance to the nation-state project envisaged by the central government. In this respect, Sadia Toor argues that the implication and the effect of this discourse were 'the designation of Bengali culture and therefore Bengalis themselves as not really "Muslim" – and therefore, by implication, not *Pakistani* – enough, being too in thrall of [*sic*] "Hindu" culture and the arts given their interest and investment', as illustrated in the examples above.[116] After these clashes, by the end of the 1950s, the Awami Muslim League – which hoped to represent East Pakistani Muslims' interests – changed its name to Awami League. This name change 'declared a more inclusive platform, thus welcoming non-Muslim Bengalis into the party, a marked move away from the bonds of religion and minority status that had supported the creation of Pakistan'.[117]

Besides the use of the Urdu language, Islam was being used to justify national solidarity and keep the two wings together. However, as argued by Toor, East Pakistanis' unresolved political demands became increasingly 'couched in the language of "internal colonialism" ', with further suppression of the 'differences and inequalities themselves', leading to atrocities against Bengalis and, consequently, to the nine-month Bangladesh Liberation War in 1971.[118] The war ended in December 1971 with the subsequent establishment of Bangladesh. West Pakistan deemed the secession movement a 'mere product of "Indian" agents and a few "miscreants" ', considering the Hindus to be behind the indoctrination of the Muslims and thus 'responsible for the language movement and the alienation of the Bengalis'.[119] Shifting the blame onto the Bengali Hindus was used to justify the need to keep Pakistan unified and safeguard the Muslims. This undermined the political grievances of the Bengali Muslims and took away agency and self-determination from their desire to separate and create their own nation-state.

Before the Muslim League adopted the nationalist project to create a separate state for the Muslims of India, the Islamisation of the Bengal became a part of what Richard M. Eaton refers to as 'frontier culture'.[120] Islam developed into a 'local' religion. In his discussion on the creation of local traditions of transmission of Islamic knowledge, such as the *puthis* (Bengali Muslim manuscripts), Rafiuddin Ahmed contends that these were crucial for the spread of religion throughout the region, and for the propagation of both revivalist and the so-called 'syncretistic' interpretations of Islam.[121] The syncretisation of Islam as a lived reality in the Bengal was introduced by Asim Roy, who demonstrates how Islam became so entangled in the region that it incorporated other religious elements – among others, Hindu and Buddhist.[122] Benjamin Zeitlyn et al., who use Roy's example to demonstrate aspects of other religions, write about 'the cult of *Pir* (holy man) and their *mazaars* practised throughout the region'.[123] However, the concept of a syncretic Islam is criticised by Gardner, who contends that there is no form of 'pure' Islam, and that within various local cultures and traditions different manifestations of Islam can be found.[124]

For the purposes of this book, I do not delve into the other determinants, including economic and social factors, which also triggered and contributed to the Bengali uprising against the central government. As my research concentrates on language and dress, I have narrowed the focus to the history of events relating to language use as a form of resistance. East Pakistanis sought independence from West Pakistan because of the lack of political representation – an issue the Bengali Muslims were all too familiar with prior to the 1947 Partition. The Muslims of Bengal supported the separation and the creation of a nation for Indian Muslims, as it would function as 'a protective wall against the wealthy and privileged Hindus'.[125] This desire emerged as Bengali Muslims were subject to the domination of Hindus economically, as tenants and labourers under Hindu zamindars or as artisans exploited by Hindu businessmen; politically, as Bengali Hindu leaders drew on all-India political allies to exercise their hegemony from the anti-Partition movement of 1905–1911 and beyond; and intellectually, as Hindus ruled educational institutions.[126] However, the desire for independence and political autonomy from the Bengali Hindus was short-lived because after the Partition, dominance over Bengali Muslims was replaced by the West Pakistanis' rule – thus mirroring the control and authority of the previous hegemonic group: the Bengali Hindus.

Thus, the elections and the non-cooperation movement led by Sheikh Mujibur Rahman marked and crystallised the friction and tension between the two wings. This was due, first, to the general elections in 1970 'giving the [Awami] League an overwhelming endorsement of its six-point election plank calling for an autonomous East Pakistan [which] gave concrete expression to the growing dissent in East Pakistan'.[127] This caused West Pakistan great distress because it required the 'National Assembly to draft the Pakistani constitution', which was postponed, as it would have to 'reflect the League's demand for an autonomous East Pakistan because of the League majority in the Assembly'.[128] This postponement was the precursor of a crisis that was subsequently triggered by Rahman's non-cooperation movement and the increasing demand for independence in East Pakistan.[129]

The changing decades for British Bengalis: Anti-racism and a new home after the 1970s

The liberation of Bangladesh in 1971 coincided with a new set of immigration laws passed in Britain. These new laws restricted and reduced migration flow to immediate family members, consequently putting severe pressure on Bengalis, now known as Bangladeshis, to bring their families to Britain amidst concerns for the newly established state of Bangladesh. Nazil Kibria notes how the nine-month Liberation War became a 'watershed in the development' of British Bangladeshis' community life.[130] This not only transformed the community but 'nationalised' it, and provided a 'homeland state' that previously, with the central government based in West Pakistan, had been non-existent and had functioned as 'a site of oppression and constraint'.[131]

In 1971, according to some estimates, there were about 22,000 people of East Bengali origin living in Britain, with around 3,000 of those living in the East End;[132] these people mobilised and rallied en masse in London for the secessionist movement to secure the independence from West Pakistan. Sarah Glynn describes the substantial impact of the Liberation War in Bangladesh on the community in Tower Hamlets, especially within the political arena. Glynn contends that meetings in Britain 'were held everywhere and action committees were springing up all over the country. There was an overwhelming desire to do something in response to the news coming out from Bengal and the terrible experiences relayed in letters from family and friends still there.'[133] Kibria defines this moment in history as 'a profoundly politicising event that ultimately furthered the integration of Bengalis into British politics. As the Bengali community struggled to support the liberation effort, they formed grassroots organisations and forged relationships with political groups and parties in Britain, especially the Labour Party.'[134] Another substantial movement taking place amidst the fight against racism was that of the Bengali squatters in the 1970s. This decade became the defining moment for the local Bengali families and their struggle to secure better housing, but it was achieved by squatting in dilapidated buildings, and thereby starting the movement to secure safe tenancies.[135]

The migration pattern in the 1980s changed as the entry conditions and visa controls from 1986 onwards became more complex. This legislation created difficulties for British Bangladeshi men who did not bring their families to the UK in the 1970s. Consequently, many were thus involved in legal cases regarding the entry of their family members into the country.[136] And while the War of Independence in 1971 'resonated deeply in London where first generation leaders engaged in fund raising' were campaigning 'against Pakistani institutions and worked for the (inter)national recognition of the "liberation war"', there were other growing concerns for the British Bangladeshis in their new home.[137] During the political struggles of the 1970s, the shift with the British Nationality Act of 1981 introduced an entirely different landscape for former colonial subjects. Nadine El-Enany corroborates this and states that even if 'citizenship of the United Kingdom and Colonies was accepted as a citizenship of sorts, it is difficult to regard it as in any way equivalent to the status of British citizenship as articulated in the 1981 British Nationality Act'.[138] The political landscape had forged a need for Margaret Thatcher's government to consider asserting a more linear projection as to who constituted being British. El-Enany expands on the 1981 Act and its purpose, arguing that 'the 1981 Act drew a hard border around "the motherland", effectively announcing Britain as post-colonial, making it impermeable to its former racialised subjects'.[139] This is projected on to the whole of Britain while, in reality, 'Britain's jurisdiction continues to extend over its remaining colonial territories'.[140]

It is essential to keep in mind how Bengalis were paying attention to the ongoing developments in Bangladesh while they were also paying attention to the rapidly changing citizenship laws in Britain. Towards the end of the 1970s, political orientations changed amongst the first generation, who 'moved away from preoccupations with political struggles in Bangladesh to activism in the UK',[141] as racism and the rise in support for the National Front were gaining prominence in the Spitalfields area. Noting that racism and discrimination against the Bengalis, other Asian communities, and the African and Caribbean communities were present in the early 1970s, Kenneth Leech argues that the killing of Altab Ali in 1978 was the turning point for the Bengali community as well as for the East End.[142] It was this moment in history that led to the organisation and mobilisation of various communities, and gave 'Brick Lane a symbolic role in the national anti-racist struggle'.[143] Leech further argues that 'in 1970 the "skinhead era" arrived in the East End', which witnessed an increase in attacks against Indians, Pakistanis and Bengalis by young people who were members of far-right movements.[144]

The same year, skinhead attacks on two Asian workers at the London Chest Hospital in Bethnal Green on 3 April led to the coinage of the new term 'Paki-bashing'.[145] Racists murdered Tosir Ali in 1970,[146] which, in 1976, led to the creation of the Anti-Racist Committee of Asians in East London to 'draw attention to the inadequacy of the protection offered to Asian people by the police and the authorities'.[147] The racial attacks taking place against non-white individuals were monitored and catalogued by the Spitalfields Bengali Action Group.[148] One of my interviewees, Ismail (interviewed in March 2014), reflected and recollected his memories of experiencing racism while growing up in East London in the late 1970s:

> There used to be a British National Front shop in Petticoat Lane Market. And we used to taunt them. But we were involved; there was a lot of anti-fascist movements as well. I recall one very clear incident. There was me and my friend, we were playing at those times, in terms of what would you do to amuse ourselves. It was a summer's day and we were at the place we called the Ghat. It's basically in Chicksand, just on Chicksand Street. It's got a football pitch, which is a little bit lower down, so it's not the Ghat like the whole. So we were just there and there was a mural on the wall where we used to kill dragonflies there. Me and my friends, we were just jumping on dragonflies. I think we were like ten, eleven. And all of a sudden, these two white men, they just grabbed us and they took us into the block of flats, nearest to the Spelman House. They said 'Go upstairs quickly, and don't come out, hide yourselves. Racists are coming.' Sure enough, we went to the fourth floor and you could see through the landing, they were like a light well – you know, you could look through grids. And we could see there's hundreds of National Front just running down the street, breaking car windows, shops and everything else. These two white men saved us. If they didn't we would have been in a lot of trouble.

The Spitalfields Bengali Action Group found thirty cases of racial attacks from March to May 1976, almost all within the Brick Lane district; in addition, the activities of the National Front were increasing in the area during this time. The continued attacks on the community led to an organised march on 17 October 1977, where more than '3,000 anti-racists marched through the National Front strongholds in Hoxton and Bethnal Green to a multicultural festival in Victoria Park'.[149] However, the killing of Altab Ali transformed the way the Bengali community organised itself to tackle the issue of racism. Ali was a twenty-four-year-old garment worker murdered in a racist attack on the evening of 4 May 1978 on Adler Street in Whitechapel. The park adjacent to where he was murdered, then called St Mary's Park, was renamed Altab Ali Park in 1998 when 'the Tower Hamlets Council approved a name change after a campaign by anti-racist activists'.[150] Altab Ali's murder is considered to be 'the start of a UK-centred struggle against racism, which marked a turning point for the local Bangladeshi community' and triggered the Bengali community's political participation and youth activism in the UK, especially within the Borough of Tower Hamlets.[151] K. Murphy argues that 'not only were the Bangladeshis physically fighting against overt racism from the BNP [British National Party] and NF [the National Front], but there were many reports of more institutionalised and subtle variations of racism from the local police'.[152] This hostile environment created a spatial division between the white and Bengali communities. There was a markedly sharp divide where Bengali people were hardly visible north of the railway bridge and north of the Truman Brewery and Brick Lane.[153]

Another research participant who shared his experience of racism in the 1980s was Mohammed (interviewed in March 2014). We sat at the Osmani Centre, known for acting as a mediator with many gangs that formed on the streets of the East End in the 1990s. Mohammed arrived in Britain aged six or seven, and vividly remembers the targeted racism while growing up in East London. He felt that racism was 'designed to humiliate you, degrade you'. The words he became exposed to and heard regularly as a youngster were 'you smelly Paki', 'go back home, you smell, you stink'. He expanded and noted how his friends, who went to other schools in the area, would receive similar remarks, and 'one of the things they used to do during the home-time was go to the gate and sprint until you get to your home. The reason why they did that, the racists would wait for them and would want to do Paki-bashing. So these boys would have to sprint, and it was amazing.'

It appears that many Bengalis relied on one another to find serenity, away from the daily violence. Mohammed mentioned how the boys, in particular, would wear padded coats and jackets as a form of protection from Paki-bashing. Jahedur, whom I interviewed in February 2014, reiterated Mohammed's description of feeling unsafe going to and from school. Jahedur affirmed how 'even I remember I used to go to school with a baseball bat in my back bag. This was the normal thing – any time you could get attacked.' The fear of an attack was a common concern voiced by many of my research participants. On account of his racist experiences, Jahedur joined the Youth Connection, which was 'a group of basically of young Bangladeshis, who had enough of the racism, and they organised themselves into almost like a club where thousands of people were mainly led by a group called Progressive Youth Organization [PYO], Bangladesh Youth Movement [BYM] and Young Muslim Organisation UK [YMOUK]'.

Shiraj, whom I interviewed in an office at Osmani Centre in East London in March 2014, also shared Jahedur's experience of racism in the 1970s and 1980s. They both grew up in Tower Hamlets after arriving in the UK as young children. Shiraj spoke of the fear he would feel when he went to school and there was always a possibility of his being attacked:

> It was pretty bad. In the late 1970s, early 1980s, there was a lot of racism here and we used to go to school every day with fear that some would probably

get attacked by the racists. Racism was everywhere on the streets and there was probably hardly a week passed without us being called Pakis. So we went through a bad phase. I used to live in Wapping at that time in 1978 and our windows used to get smashed every other week.

When asked further about how he and his family dealt with it and if the police were available to help, he responded:

> We reported to the police. We used to call the police each time and the police used to come, take report. They couldn't, actually they didn't, arrest anybody ... During the bonfire nights, we used to get bomb fires thrown through our letter box in the middle of the night. All these kinds of discrimination we faced. So the way we dealt with it, we started to get together. There was a lot of unity at that time amongst the Bangladeshis, because we were beaten and we stuck together and we try and support each other. So we used to always travel in groups rather than on your own. So you felt safety in groups.

Shiraj experienced racism because he was Bangladeshi and perceived as inferior by his white persecutors. The racism faced by many Bangladeshis prompted them to organise and mobilise politically, allowing them to use their Bangladeshi identity to connect with other Bangladeshis. The term 'Paki' came to connote anyone who came from the Indian subcontinent.[154] However, it appears that one of the reasons why Bangladeshis experienced this level of racism was the challenge to 'Englishness'. Robert Miles points out how 'English nationalism is particularly dependent on and constructed by the idea of "race", with the result that English nationalism encapsulates racism. In other words, racism is the lining of the cloak of nationalism which surrounds and defines the boundaries of England as an imagined community.'[155]

However, the battle with racism changed and reached a critical juncture. The killing of Altab Ali prompted numerous anti-racism rallies outside the park. Bangladeshis collaborated 'with the Socialist [Workers] Party and the Trade Unions and engaged in mass demonstrations and strikes'.[156] The BYM, based and founded in East London, galvanised and cooperated with several organisations, including the Action Committee Against Racial Attacks, Hackney and Tower Hamlets Defence Committee, and the Anti-Nazi League. They all focused on 'organising a huge demonstration and public meetings to show the solidarity, strength and determination of black communities to defend themselves after the death of Altab Ali'.[157] Following the racist murder of Altab Ali, solidarity not only existed amongst activist groups based in London but was extended across various parts of the country. For example, Bradford Asian Youth Movement 'sent delegates to London in 1978 to consolidate and support the organisation of Bangladeshi youth' and their fight against the far right.[158] As recorded by Claire Alexander in an interview with Helal Abbas, a member of the Bangladeshi youth movements at the time of the stabbing of Altab Ali and later the first Bangladeshi leader of Tower Hamlets Council, 'It wasn't just about campaigning, it was about safety. People were living with real fear, fear of being murdered, fear of being beaten up, fear of walking the streets safely ... Altab Ali was a watershed point for us, people felt very bitter, very angry at the injustice, young and old.'[159]

Bangladeshis mobilised to demand their right to live without the fear of being murdered; however, Alom (interviewed in January 2014), from a well-known Bengali cultural group based in Aldgate, believes things changed in the 1980s, and that the community came to the realisation that, in order to make fundamental changes, its members had to join mainstream politics:

> And I think it was from that movement [i.e. the anti-racist movement that had built up in the borough] they also felt they had to be part of the mainstream. If they were going to bring about any meaningful changes within the community, or any impact, they had to get close to power or places of influence; hence they decided to join mainstream political parties. Initially it was the Labour Party, but today, of course, we have people in the Liberal Democrats and the Tory Party. And the whole point was really by being part of mainstream or by joining these political parties, you should be able to bring about changes, for your community. So, yeah, I think ... you asked me if I was involved – I was involved in that kind of campaign where we were asserting the rights of the community. We were saying that we should be treated as any other British citizen. We may be Bengali, we may be what[ever], but regardless we should have the same protection, same access to everything as any other British person; we, in fact, asserted our British identity for equality really.

Considering the presence of violence in the everyday and how this shaped people's lives, it is no surprise that many felt the need to merge themselves into mainstream politics to change the conditions of their communities; it's a form of reclamation to reconcile the needs of the communities via legislation. While political priorities changed, with a focus on the unfolding possibilities presented to a younger generation of Bengalis to stand as councillors, the politics of Bangladesh took a back seat, although they were not entirely forgotten. As a result of these opportunities, the 1980s became the decade of 'the politics of recognition'.[160] Azfar Shafi and Ilyas Nagdee argue that this form of politics emerged through what they coin as the 'Anti-racism from Above', whereby 'to be "recognised" as a unit or constituency by the state, by its institutions – and, increasingly, by forces of the market – enables a turn towards civic politics'.[161] By gradually incorporating the Bangladeshi populace into the local political body, the mass radical political steadfastness of the community was reduced and reinscribed instead by favouring liberal multiculturalism.[162]

The struggles against racism enabled Bengali activists to forge alliances with various left-wing and anti-racist movements – which attempted to tackle not just racism but also 'local issues of discrimination in housing, education, employment, police-community relations, etc.'.[163] This eventually led the activists to become involved and 'active participants in local Labour and SDP [Social Democratic Party] parties, and [they] fielded a number of Bangladeshi local council members throughout the 1980s, particularly in Tower Hamlets'.[164] In their research on the East End, Dench et al. state how 'Tower Hamlets registered a dramatic increase in voter turnout in local elections over the period 1982–90, more than anywhere else in London.'[165] This further illustrates how the Bangladeshi community turned more to their local politics through the voter ballot. Shafi and Nagdee point out how the 'canalisation of Asian political energy into local party politics over the last few decades has led to the decay of independent political self-organisation'.[166] In this respect, Eade and Garbin demonstrate how Bangladeshi entrepreneurs and secular community leaders established alliances with diverse agencies and City businesses to create the new spatial identity of 'Banglatown', seen by Bangladeshi council leaders as an opportunity to attract tourists and boost local Bangladeshi businesses, especially the 'Indian' (i.e. Bangladeshi) restaurants along Brick Lane. This project reinvented locality as an exotic space so that Brick Lane and its surroundings could compete with other ethnic enclaves, especially Chinatown in the West End.[167] Furthermore, the *boishakhi mela* (Bengali New Year) was established in 1998, celebrating the advent of the *boishakh* (monsoon) season. Eade and Garbin provide the following account of the celebration:

> [The celebration was] financed by Cityside, a government-funded regeneration agency working locally in partnership with the council and important City firms. During this festival, Brick Lane is turned into a pedestrian zone with stalls selling homemade food and small handicrafts, and stages where different artistic events are performed (traditional folk music, Bengali dance, drama and pop music with DJs). The organisers of the Baishaki Mela present the event as expressing the desire of British Bangladeshis to both maintain their ties with their country of origin, and to distinguish themselves as an ethnic/cultural 'community' in Britain based on a secular nationalist Bengali heritage.[168]

While some Bengalis engaged with the intense battle against racism, the 1970s and 1980s forced many to look for employment outside East London, as there was a decline in labour-intensive industry, which included sectors such as 'the handling, storage and distribution of cargo in dockland areas like the Isle of Dogs, Wapping and Limehouse; timber industries along the river Lea; furniture making in Shoreditch and Bethnal Green; and clothing and leather production in Spitalfields'.[169] Some went to Luton, Birmingham, Manchester, Bradford and Leeds to work in 'garment factories and corners shops'. In contrast, others 'went to Cardiff, South Shields and Sunderland, the cities and towns that had shipping connections with India and the Far East',[170] while more and more Sylhetis went to the catering trade and 'the "Indian" restaurant business in the UK',[171] which is today dominated by the Sylhetis.[172] What is striking about the Bengali experience of racism and discrimination is that the previous community who settled in the Spitalfields area – the Jewish community – also experienced extensive amounts of racism. The Jewish community, too, organised collectively to fight against it. The racism endured by the Jewish community forced their political self-organisation, captured in the famous Battle of Cable Street in October 1936, where an estimated 100,000 protesters violently prevented a column of fascists from marching through a predominantly Jewish area of London's East End.[173]

The 1990s presented the Bangladeshi community with another dilemma. The year 1993 saw the election of the British National Party's (BNP) first ever councillor, Derek Beackon, in the Isle of Dogs, following a violent racist attack on a seventeen-year-old Bengali student, Quddus Ali, which left him permanently brain-damaged. Beackon's seven-vote by-election victory 'came after a BNP campaign that accused Bengali families of having been given preferential treatment over white families in the allocation of new council housing'.[174] Georgie Wemyss notes other racist attacks on Bengalis in 1994, including those 'on Mukhtar Ahmed and Shah Alam in February 1994'.[175] In the ensuing months, broad-based political mobilisation undertaken by national and local organisations saw Beackon defeated in the full local elections in May 1994. Furthermore, as Wemyss contends, during these eight months, 'the "race politics" of Tower Hamlets and its implications for Britishness were the subject of national and local political and media discourses'.[176] Britishness, I would argue, operated as a key disputing site because there emerged a new discourse whereby Asians were seen as going 'into their cultures to make the new ethnicity'.[177] There was a rupture in their political organising, away from mobilising around political blackness to what Roger and Catherine Ballard refer to as being precipitated by 'a reactive pride in their separate ethnic identity'.[178] This rupture collapsed the experience of racism to one of mere 'ethnic redefinition', as expressed by Ambalavaner Sivanandan, and one that disregarded the interplay of race and class while positing identity as the overarching determiner.[179]

The Bangladeshi community witnessed another shift in the 1990s in the aftermath of the protests and demonstrations against Salman Rushdie's book *The Satanic Verses*, which many scholars argue brought Islam into the public arena.[180] Eade and Garbin contend that, up to the late 1980s, only secular activists were dominating and representing the Bangladeshi community.[181] However, despite the Bangladeshi community's remaining 'largely invisible in Muslim organisations such as the Muslim Parliament, or the later Muslim Council of Britain, Muslim organisations have been active and significant at a local level, particularly since the cutting back of government funding to secular and nationalist cultural and youth organisations'.[182] The swing from secular and nationalist politics to the use of Muslim identity as a political one became prevalent in the 1990s because of 'the growth of religiously oriented and Islamist groups, particularly encouraged by the New Labour Government policies promoting faith communities as a key agent in urban regeneration after the General Election of 1997'.[183] Although the 1990s witnessed the protests against Rushdie's book, and British Muslims observed the unfolding of the genocide against Bosnian Muslims, I would argue that the Muslim identity was only reinforced in the national psyche of Britain after 9/11, and more so after 7/7.

The 1990s also hold a more particular place in British history. Jason Arday notes that the 1990s is projected as 'an inclusive and embracive period that was tolerant of communal and societal difference'.[184] The production of the 1990s as the time of a euphoric Britain that embraced its former colonial subjects as its own is far from the truth. In 1993, Stephen Lawrence was murdered in South-East London, becoming one of the most symbolic cases in the years to come. His case redefined the boundaries of racism when the Macpherson Report was released in 1999, declaring that there *is* institutional racism, with a specific reference to the London Metropolitan Police.[185] In 1999, David Copeland, a 'self-professed Neo-Nazi belonging to the ultra conservative British National and National Socialist Parties', attacked Brick Lane – home to the largest Bangladeshi community in the UK – while also carrying out bombings in Brixton (home to a sizeable African Caribbean community) and the area of Soho (the heart of the queer community).[186] While the last decade of the twentieth century attempted to forge an optimistic multicultural and cosmopolitan outlook for Britain with New Labour's election victory in 1997, it collapsed the radical pushback against racism. It turned Britain's racialised minorities into ethnic enclaves that simply produced 'culture'. Shafi and Nagdee succinctly capture this and expose how 'culture' was used and 'repackaged as "saris, steel pans and samosas", often on the payroll of local authorities'.[187]

The twenty-first century: The emergence of the British Muslim identity

The subject of British Muslims became a concrete fixture after the attacks on the Twin Towers in the United States in 2001. The invasion of Afghanistan further accelerated this in the same year. Nisha Kapoor and Kasia Narkowicz argue that the War on Terror has intensified as the twenty-first century has progressed, and 'discourses aligning British Muslims with terrorism have saturated political and media representations by symbolically excluding from the nation those with legal citizen entitlements'.[188] While there was an acceleration in focusing on 'Muslim' as a variable, 'Paki-bashing' remained a feature for Bengali Muslims in the East End. For example, in Bow a young teenager brutally beat and fatally stabbed Shiblu Rahman, an Asian chef.[189] Although the launch of the War on Terror following the 11 September attacks and the invasion of Afghanistan played significant roles in forging the subject of the British Muslim, the further the invasion of Iraq in 2003 by the very government – New Labour – that had hailed multiculturalism as making Britain a beacon left many British Muslims disillusioned. However, the moment in history that demarcated the British Muslim as a threat, and a more distinctly 'home-grown' threat, was that of the 7/7 attacks. One of the bombs exploded at Aldgate Station in East London.

The bombings in London catalysed the growth of draconian counter-terrorism programmes to monitor and surveil British Muslims, rendering them a 'suspect community'. It is essential, however, to note that contemporary manifestations of Islamophobia and the entrenching of legislation targeting Muslims are not new phenomena. This particular framing of Muslims as an 'other' without the ability to merge into modernity and the 'civilised world' has a long historical trajectory.[190] The London bombings of 7/7 were described by Yasmin Hussain and Paul Bagguley as a major event that shaped the relationship between Muslims and non-Muslims in Britain.[191] These attacks were carried out by "home-grown" terrorists, British Muslims. Non-Muslims in Britain reacted to these attacks with fear, while Muslim communities were framed as 'dangerous'. Reported racist attacks on Muslims and those perceived to be Muslim increased six-fold in the weeks after 7/7 and, in all, up until April 2006, eight Muslim men had been killed in racist attacks in Britain since 9/11.[192] There was another moment in the Bengali East End's political (re)configuration around 2005, two months before the London bombings, when George Galloway, the founder of the Respect Party, won parliamentary seat of Bethnal Green and Bow. Much of Galloway's rhetoric was framed around his anti-war stance, but this shifted to a more religious tone. Galloway used an overtly religious framing, accusing the government of being part of a 'war on Muslims', and as the election approached, 'the slogan of Respect became: "For British Muslims facing the fear of losing their identity, RESPECT is THE only party." '[193] Galloway's success was rooted in how this discourse of Muslim suffering was used, and that, momentarily, 'Muslims found a shared platform with the Left protesting the War in Iraq.'[194]

In the case of the British Bangladeshi Muslims in the East End, these fast-paced, changing political landscapes were shaping the micro-dynamics of power relations on the ground, not just politically but also in their construction of the community's heritage identity. The year after the London bombings, one particular event was moulding the Bangladeshi community's consciousness. In 2003, Monica Ali's *Brick Lane* was published, and protests against the book followed. More demonstrations took place in 2006 when the filming began to make the book into a feature film. Riaz analyses how 'the protests in the summer of 2006 by some of the residents of Brick Lane were not about the literary quality or the supposed inaccuracies of the book, but about the representation of the local people and their culture, which they found offensive'.[195] The identity of those involved in the demonstrations is a vital point, as the majority who demonstrated were Sylhetis. Particular negative associations with Sylhetis inform how the 'Sylheti community often feel that they are treated with disrespect by the Bengalis, and [they] saw Monica Ali's book as the latest proof of this disdain'.[196] The protests were primarily concerned with representation and how the Bangladeshi community was presented to a broader audience. The issues around being Bengali and what it constitutes will reappear in the ensuing chapters looking at dress and language.

While political trajectories continued to shift in Tower Hamlets, this included a new era in local politics, defining a politics of suspension and moving away from national political parties towards representation of the interests of the borough's communities in the local council. In 2010, Lutfur Rahman became the first directly elected executive mayor of Tower Hamlets as an independent candidate. He was re-elected in 2014 as the candidate for his political party, Tower Hamlets First, but was ousted in 2015 following allegations that included 'undue spiritual influence'.[197] However, despite Rahman's five-year ban on participating in local elections following a legal case, he returned to office in 2022 and was re-elected as the council's mayor. In addition to his re-election to office, his newly created Aspire Party also won the majority of seats in the local council. Elected on a left-wing platform, Rahman reinstated the formerly abolished education maintenance allowance that gave college students £30 a week, as well as bursaries exclusively available to young people from lower socio-economic backgrounds to enable them to go to university.[198] What further political shifts will emerge in the East End remains to be seen.

Conclusion

This chapter outlines the history of East London, the Bengal, East Pakistan and Bangladesh. It is by no means exhaustive, but is necessary in order to locate how these histories have shaped the British Bangladeshi Muslim community. Much of the above requires further sober analysis; however, it suffices for the ensuing chapters. Exploring the historical links between Britain and the area of Bengal and why it is significant is a necessary intervention in situating the historical trajectory and how these political sensibilities shaped the community's political and religious engagement in the East End. The key for me, put differently, is to consider how inextricably wedded many of these themes are to people's changing identifications with dress and language. Thus, it was necessary to shed light on the violence and oppression experienced following the creation of the two wings of Pakistan and then the creation of Bangladesh. There was also discussion of the history of the Indian subcontinent in tandem with various legislative developments in Britain that were impacting the Bengalis migrating to Britain and their multiple ways of managing the families they left behind. Simultaneously, while these new pieces of legislation and Acts were being introduced, Bengali men were disillusioned and disenfranchised by the hostility with which they were confronted and the onslaught of racism prompted by their attempts to settle into their 'new' home, with many realising that they were not going to 'go back'. While forging new(er) identities, many had to contend anew with their religious identities and major events shaping previous (re)configurations. As such, these historical transformations and moments, as expressed by many of the research participants, shaped and provided a point in time for many to reformulate their own understandings of themselves, and their relations with others and within British society, vis-à-vis dress and language.

Notes

1 C. Adams, *Across Seven Seas and Thirteen Rivers: Life Stories of Pioneer Sylheti Settlers in Britain* (London: Thap, 1987), p. 66.
2 J. Eade, 'Bengalis in Britain: Migration, state controls and settlement', in J. Chatterji and D. Washbrook (eds), *Routledge Handbook of the South Asian Diaspora* (Abingdon: Routledge, 2013), pp. 280–294.
3 The use of the term 'Bengali' here refers to the whole of the population of the pre-1947 state of Bengal. After the Partition of India, the eastern part of the state became East Pakistan, and the population of the region East Pakistani. The term 'Bangladeshi' refers to the population of the independent nation of Bangladesh, created when the former East Pakistan gained independence from Pakistan in 1971. There are also a significant number of Bengalis in West Bengal, India.
4 See Y. Samad, 'The politics of Islamic identity among Bangladeshis and Pakistanis in Britain', in T. O. Ranger, Y. Samad and O. Stuart (eds), *Culture, Identity and Politics: Ethnic Minorities in Britain* (Aldershot: Avebury, 1996); S. Rozario and S. Gilliat-Ray, *Genetics, Religion and Identity: A Study of*

British Bangladeshis (2004–7), Working Paper Series 93 (Cardiff: School of Social Sciences, Cardiff University, 2007); S. Glynn, 'Bengali Muslims: The new East End radicals?', *Ethnic and Racial Studies* 25:6 (2002), 969–988.
5 R. Visram, *Ayahs, Lascars and Princes: The Story of Indians in Britain 1700–1947* (Abingdon: Routledge, 1986).
6 See K. N. Chaudhuri, *The Trading World of Asia and the English East India Company 1660–1760* (Cambridge: Cambridge University Press, 1978).
7 M. H. Fisher, 'Working across the seas: Indian maritime labourers in India, Britain, and in between', *International Review of Social History* 51:S14 (2006), 21–45 (p. 33).
8 A. A. Ullah, 'In search of lascars', *Daily Star*, 23 December 2013, www.thedailystar.net/in-search-of-lascars-3533 (accessed 15 May 2023).
9 S. Gilliat-Ray, *Muslims in Britain: An Introduction* (Cambridge: Cambridge University Press, 2010), p. 30.
10 M. H. Fisher, *Counterflows to Colonialism: Indian Travellers and Settlers in Britain, 1600–1857* (New Delhi: Orient Blackswan, Permanent Black, 2004), p. 4.
11 H. Ansari, *The Infidel Within: Muslims in Britain since 1800* (Oxford: Oxford University Press, 2018), p. 43.
12 Fisher, 'Working across the seas', p. 32.
13 Ansari, *The Infidel Within*, p. 35.
14 A. Riaz, *Islam and Identity Politics among British Bangladeshis: A Leap of Faith* (Manchester: Manchester University Press, 2013), p. 23. The narrative continues: 'Perhaps the most famous child of Bengali-British parentage was Albert Mahomet. He was born in 1858 at Sophia Street in Bow, East London, to an English mother and an ex-seaman from Calcutta. Mahomet grew up in a world of crime and poverty that claimed many of his siblings. Eventually, he moved to the city of Wells and became a respected Methodist preacher and photographer.'
15 Ibid., p. 20.
16 Ibid., pp. 20–21.
17 A. A. Ullah and J. Eversley, *Bengalis in London's East End* (London: Swadhinata Trust, 2010), p. 21.
18 K. Gardner and A. Shukur, '"I'm Bengali, I'm Asian and I'm living here": The changing identity of British Bengalis', in R. Ballard (ed), *Desh Pardesh: The South Asian Presence in Britain* (London: Hurst, 1994), pp. 142–165 (pp. 146–147).
19 Adams, *Across Seven Seas and Thirteen Rivers*, p. 128.
20 J. Eade and D. Garbin, 'Changing narratives of violence, struggle and resistance: Bangladeshis and the competition for resources in the global city', *Oxford Development Studies* 30:2 (2002), 137–149 (p. 138).
21 K. Gardner, *Global Migrants, Local Lives: Travels and Transformation in Rural Bangladesh* (Oxford: Oxford University Press, 1995).
22 Riaz, *Islam and Identity Politics among British Bangladeshis*, p. 21.
23 Ibid.

24 D. Robinson-Dunn, 'Lascar sailors and English converts: The imperial port and Islam in late 19th-century England' (2003), History Cooperative, http://webdoc.sub.gwdg.de/ebook/p/2005/history_cooperative/www.historycooperative.org/proceedings/seascapes/dunn.html (accessed 23 February 2023).
25 Ibid.
26 D. Jones, 'Exploring Banglatown and the Bengali East End' (London: Tower Hamlets Council, 2004), https://sylhetiproject.files.wordpress.com/2018/11/bengali-history-walk.pdf (accessed 27 March 2024).
27 Ibid.
28 R. Visram, *Asians in Britain: 400 Years of History* (London: Pluto Press, 2002), p. 51.
29 Ibid.
30 Ansari, *The Infidel Within*.
31 Ullah, 'In search of lascars'.
32 Adams, *Across Seven Seas and Thirteen Rivers*.
33 C. Alexander, S. Firoz and N. Rashid, *Bangla Stories: The Bengali Diaspora in Britain. A Review of the Literature* (London: London School of Economics, 2010), www.banglastories.org/uploads/Literature_review.pdf (accessed 24 February 2023).
34 Visram, *Asians in Britain*.
35 Adams, *Across Seven Seas and Thirteen Rivers*, p. 16.
36 Visram, *Asians in Britain*, p. 257.
37 Riaz, *Islam and Identity Politics among British Bangladeshis*, p. 26.
38 Visram, *Asians in Britain*, p. 257.
39 Alexander et al., *Bangla Stories*, p. 7.
40 Ibid.
41 Visram, *Asians in Britain*, p. 264.
42 Adams, *Across Seven Seas and Thirteen Rivers*, pp. 43, 163.
43 Riaz, *Islam and Identity Politics among British Bangladeshis*, p. 26.
44 Visram, *Asians in Britain*, p. 257.
45 Ibid., p. 256.
46 Ibid.
47 Adams, *Across Seven Seas and Thirteen Rivers*.
48 B. Hesse and S. Sayyid, 'Narrating the postcolonial political and the immigrant imaginary', in N. Ali, V. S. Kalra and S. Sayyid (eds), *A Postcolonial People: South Asians in Britain* (London: Hurst, 2006), pp. 13–31 (p. 21).
49 A. Ghosh, *Power in Print: Popular Publishing and the Politics of Language and Culture in a Colonial Society, 1778–1905* (New Delhi: Oxford University Press, 2006), p. 7.
50 Ibid.
51 Ibid., p. 10.
52 Ibid., p. 30.
53 Ibid.
54 Ibid., p. 43.

55 Ibid., p. 42.
56 Ibid., p. 259.
57 Ibid., p. 265.
58 Ibid.
59 Ibid., p. 266.
60 H. Rashid, 'A move for united independent Bengal', in S. Islam (ed.), *History of Bangladesh 1704–1971*, Vol. I, *Political History* (Dhaka: Asiatic Society of Bangladesh, 1992), pp. 400–421 (p. 403).
61 S. Hamid, *Language Use and Identity: The Sylheti Bangladeshis in Leeds* (Bern: Peter Lang, 2011), p. 18.
62 T. Hall, *Salaam Brick Lane: A Year in the New East End* (London: John Murray, 2005), p. 46.
63 I will be using the term 'British Bangladeshi' when discussing and describing the British Bangladeshi community, and have, so far, used the term 'Bengali' to describe Bengalis from the Bengal (Indians of West Bengal and Bangladesh) – prior to the creation of nation-states. I will also, later in the chapters, problematise the term 'Bengali', and what it means and has come to mean to my interviewees.
64 P. Werbner, 'Introduction: The dialectics of cultural hybridity', in P. Werbner and T. Modood (eds), *Debating Cultural Hybridity* (London: Zed Books, 1997), pp. 1–26 (p. 12).
65 S. Begum, 'From Sylhet to Spitalfields: Exploring Bengali migrant homemaking in the context of a squatters' movement, in 1970s East London' (PhD dissertation, Queen Mary, University of London, 2021), p. 21.
66 C. Alexander, 'Making Bengali Brick Lane: Claiming and contesting space in East London', *British Journal of Sociology* 62:2 (2011), 201–220.
67 Ullah and Eversley, *Bengalis in London's East End*, p. 84.
68 G. Wemyss, 'White memories, white belonging: Competing colonial anniversaries in "postcolonial" East London', *Sociological Research Online* 13:5 (2008), 50–67.
69 G. Dench, K. Gavron and M. Young, *The New East End: Kinship, Race and Conflict* (London: Profile, 2006), p. 14.
70 Ullah and Eversley, *Bengalis in London's East End*, p. 84.
71 Dench et al., *The New East End*, p. 16.
72 Hall, *Salaam Brick Lane*, p. 44.
73 Alexander et al., *Bangla Stories*, p. 7.
74 Adams, *Across Seven Seas and Thirteen Rivers*.
75 C. Peach, 'Estimating the growth of the Bangladeshi population in Great Britain', *New Community* 16:4 (1990), 481–491.
76 N. Kibria, *Muslims in Motion: Islam and National Identity in the Bangladeshi Diaspora* (New Brunswick, NJ: Rutgers University Press, 2011), p. 83.
77 Gardner and Shukur, 'I'm Bengali, I'm Asian and I'm living here', p. 147.
78 M. Anwar, *The Myth of Return: Pakistanis in Britain* (London: Heinemann Educational, 1979).
79 V. M. Redclift and F. B. Rajina, 'The hostile environment, Brexit, and "reactive-" or "protective transnationalism"', *Global Networks* 21:1 (2021), 196–214.

80 Riaz, *Islam and Identity Politics among British Bangladeshis*, p. 26.
81 Kibria, *Muslims in Motion*, p. 80.
82 Dench et al., *The New East End*, p. 39.
83 Ibid.
84 The Commonwealth Immigrants Act of 1962 required workers from South Asia and the Caribbean to obtain employment vouchers before seeking entry to the UK. However, with cheap labour still in high demand, mill and factory managers were easily persuaded to issue such vouchers to existing workers' kin. Therefore, instead of calling a halt to immigration, the Act actually encouraged chain migration. A. Shaw, *Kinship and Continuity: Pakistani Families in Britain* (London and Amsterdam: Routledge and Harwood Academic, 2000).
85 Dench et al., *The New East End*, p. 43.
86 Gardner and Shukur, 'I'm Bengali, I'm Asian and I'm living here', p. 148.
87 Dench et al., *The New East End*, p. 43.
88 Kibria, *Muslims in Motion*, p. 83.
89 Ibid., p. 84. See also N. El-Enany, *(B)ordering Britain: Law, Race and Empire* (Manchester: Manchester University Press, 2020).
90 S. M. Uddin, *Constructing Bangladesh: Religion, Ethnicity, and Language in an Islamic Nation* (Chapel Hill: University of North Carolina Press, 2006), p. 124.
91 Ibid., pp. 1–3.
92 R. Islam, 'The Bengali language movement and the emergence of Bangladesh', in C. Maloney (ed.), *Language and Civilization Change in South Asia*, Contributions to Asian Studies 11 (Leiden: E. J. Brill, 1978), pp. 142–154 (p. 144).
93 P. Oldenburg, 'A place insufficiently imagined: Language, belief, and the Pakistan crisis of 1971', *Journal of Asian Studies* 44:4 (1985), 711–733 (p. 717).
94 D. P. De, *Bengal Muslims in Search of Social Identity, 1905–47* (Dhaka: University Press, 1998), p. 98.
95 Ibid.
96 Uddin, *Constructing Bangladesh*, p. 59.
97 Ibid.
98 Ibid., p. 60.
99 De, *Bengal Muslims in Search of Social Identity*, p. 105.
100 Oldenburg, 'A place insufficiently imagined', p. 717.
101 Uddin, *Constructing Bangladesh*, p. 125.
102 Ibid.
103 Ibid.
104 Ibid.
105 Hamid, *Language Use and Identity*, p. 23.
106 S. Toor, 'Bengal(is) in the house: The politics of national culture in Pakistan, 1947–71', in M. N. Chakraborty (ed.), *Being Bengali: At Home and in the World* (Abingdon: Routledge, 2014), p. 210. The Shaheed Minar is a national monument erected in Dhaka, Bangladesh, to commemorate the memories and lives of those who died during the Language Movement in 1952.
107 Uddin, *Constructing Bangladesh*, p. 125.

108 Alexander et al., *Bangla Stories*.
109 Diplomatic correspondent, 'Permanent Shaheed Minar set up in Rome', *Daily Star*, 20 February 2011.
110 J. Mapril, 'A Shahid Minar in Lisbon: Long distance nationalism, politics of memory and community among Luso-Bangladeshis', *South Asia Multidisciplinary Academic Journal* 9 (2014), 1–17.
111 Staff correspondent, 'Toronto gets permanent Shaheed Minar', *Daily Star*, 21 February 2022.
112 Toor, 'Bengal(is) in the house', p. 210.
113 M. Monsur, 'Politics of language planning in Pakistan and the birth of a new state', *International Journal of the Sociology of Language* 1996:118 (1996), 63–80 (p. 76).
114 Uddin, *Constructing Bangladesh*, p. 120.
115 Ibid.
116 Toor, 'Bengal(is) in the house', p. 210.
117 Uddin, *Constructing Bangladesh*, p. 121.
118 Toor, 'Bengal(is) in the house', p. 229.
119 Oldenburg, 'A place insufficiently imagined', p. 729.
120 R. M. Eaton, *The Rise of Islam and the Bengal Frontier, 1204–1760* (Berkeley: University of California Press, 1993).
121 R. Ahmed, *The Bengal Muslims 1871–1906: A Quest for Identity* (New Delhi: Oxford University Press, 1981).
122 A. Roy, *The Islamic Syncretistic Tradition in Bengal* (Princeton: Princeton University Press, 1983).
123 B. Zeitlyn, M. K. Janeja and J. Mapril, 'Introduction. Imagining Bangladesh: Contested narratives', *South Asia Multidisciplinary Academic Journal* 9 (2014), 1–16 (p. 3).
124 K. Gardner, 'Desh-bidesh: Sylheti images of home and away', *Man* 28:1 (1993), 1–16.
125 G. W. Choudhury, *The Last Days of United Pakistan* (Bloomington: Indiana University Press, 1974), p. 10.
126 Oldenburg, 'A place insufficiently imagined', p. 723.
127 V. P. Nanda, 'Self-determination in international law: The tragic tale of two cities – Islamabad (West Pakistan) and Dacca (East Pakistan)', *American Journal of International Law* 66:2 (1972), 321–336 (p. 323).
128 Ibid.
129 Ibid.
130 Kibria, *Muslims in Motion*, p. 85.
131 Ibid.
132 S. Glynn, 'The spirit of '71: How the Bangladeshi War of Independence has haunted Tower Hamlets', *Socialist History Journal* 29 (2006), 56–75.
133 Ibid., p. 70.
134 Kibria, *Muslims in Motion*, p. 85.
135 S. Begum, *From Sylhet to Spitalfields: Bengali Squatters in 1970s East London* (London: Lawrence Wishart, 2023).
136 Gardner, *Global Migrants, Local Lives*.

137 Eade and Garbin, 'Changing narratives of violence, struggle and resistance', p. 140.
138 El-Enany, *(B)ordering Britain*, p. 90.
139 Ibid., p. 126.
140 Ibid.
141 Ullah and Eversley, *Bengalis in London's East End*, p. 53.
142 K. Leech, *Brick Lane, 1978: The Events and Their Significance*, 2nd edn (London: Stepney Books, 1994).
143 Ibid., p. 7.
144 Ibid.
145 Ibid. The term 'Paki' is not a mere abbreviation of 'Pakistan' or 'Pakistani'. Instead, it is a term that is 'used to refer to south Asians at large, as a blanket label, is in itself racist, because it ignores the multiplicity – ethnic and religious – of the many communities thus targeted. And the attendant stereotypical projections of the south Asian as "meek" and "subservient" have a long colonial history.' F. Rajina, 'KSI and the P-word: How the YouTuber's use of the slur slots into a long history of anti-Asian discrimination in the UK', *The Conversation*, 11 April 2023, https://theconversation.com/ksi-and-the-p-word-how-the-youtubers-use-of-the-slur-slots-into-a-long-history-of-anti-asian-discrimination-in-the-uk-203299 (accessed 27 March 2024).
146 Ullah and Eversley, *Bengalis in London's East End*, p. 56.
147 Leech, *Brick Lane, 1978*, p. 7.
148 Ullah and Eversley, *Bengalis in London's East End*, p. 56.
149 M. Jorda, 'Search goes on to find new clues to murders', *East Ender*, 20 May 1978.
150 J. Visser, 'Anti-racist activism in London: Exploring multidirectionality at commemorations of the Battle of Cable Street and the murder of Altab Ali', *Journal of Intercultural Studies* 41:5 (2020), 623–637 (p. 626).
151 C. Alexander, 'Contested memories: The Shahid Minar and the struggle for diasporic space', *Ethnic and Racial Studies* 36:4 (2013), 590–610 (p. 603).
152 K. Murphy, 'Do the police really want to know?', *Evening News*, 5 July 1978, cited in A. Hoque, 'The development of a Br-Islamic: Third generation Bangladeshis from East London (Tower Hamlets)' (PhD dissertation, Goldsmiths, University of London, 2010), p. 197.
153 Leech, *Brick Lane, 1978*.
154 Rajina, 'KSI and the P-word'.
155 R. Miles, 'Recent Marxist theories of nationalism and the issues of racism', *The British Journal of Sociology* 38 (1987), 24–43 (p. 38).
156 Hoque, 'The development of a Br-Islamic', p. 197.
157 A. Ramamurthy, 'The politics of Britain's Asian Youth Movements', *Race Class* 48:38 (2006), 38–60 (p. 44).
158 Ibid.
159 Alexander, 'Contested memories', p. 602.
160 A. Shafi and I. Nagdee, *Race to the Bottom: Reclaiming Antiracism* (London: Pluto Press, 2022), p. 67.
161 Ibid.

162 Ibid., p. 88.
163 Alexander et al., *Bangla Stories*, p. 12.
164 Ibid.
165 Dench et al., *The New East End*, p. 212.
166 Shafi and Nagdee, *Race to the Bottom*, p. 94.
167 Eade and Garbin, 'Changing narratives of violence, struggle and resistance'.
168 Ibid.
169 S. Carey and A. Shukur, 'A profile of the Bangladeshi community in East London', *Journal of Ethnic and Migration Studies* 12:3 (1985), 405–417 (p. 408).
170 Ibid., p. 406.
171 Ibid., p. 410.
172 C. Alexander, S. Carey, S. Hall, J. King and S. Lidher, 'Beyond Banglatown: Continuity, change and new urban economies in Brick Lane' (2020), Runnymede Trust, www.runnymedetrust.org/publications/beyond-banglatown (accessed 27 March 2024).
173 D. Rosenberg, *Battle for the East End: Jewish Responses to Fascism in the 1930s* (London: Five Leaves, 2011).
174 G. Wemyss, 'The power to tolerate: Contests over Britishness and belonging in East London', *Patterns of Prejudice* 40:3 (2006), 215–236.
175 Ibid., p. 216.
176 Ibid.
177 A. Sivanandan, *Communities of Resistance: Writings on Black Struggles for Socialism* (London: Verso, 1990), p. 91.
178 R. Ballard and C. Ballard, 'The Sikhs: The development of South Asian settlement in Britain', in J. L. Watson (ed.), *Between Two Cultures* (Oxford: Basil Blackwell, 1977), p. 54.
179 Sivanandan, *Communities of Resistance*, p. 92.
180 See B. Parekh, 'The Rushdie affair and the British press: Some salutary lessons', in Commission for Racial Equality and Policy Studies Institute, *Free Speech: Report of a Seminar Organised by the Commission for Racial Equality and the Policy Studies Institute* (London: Commission for Racial Equality, 1990), pp. 59–79; T. Asad, *Genealogies of Religion: Discipline, and Reasons of Power in Christianity and Islam* (Baltimore and London: Johns Hopkins University Press, 1993); Ansari, *The Infidel Within*.
181 Eade and Garbin, 'Changing narratives of violence, struggle and resistance', p. 142.
182 Alexander et al., *Bangla Stories*, p. 13.
183 Ibid.
184 J. Arday, *Cool Britannia and Multi-Ethnic Britain: Uncorking the Champagne Supernova* (Abingdon: Routledge, 2019), p. xii.
185 A. Thomas-Johnson, *Becoming Kwame Ture* (Cape Town: Chimurenga, 2020).
186 M. Chakravorty, 'Brick Lane blockades: The bioculturalism of migrant domesticity', *MFS Modern Fiction Studies* 58:3 (2012), 503–528.
187 Shafi and Nagdee, *Race to the Bottom*, p. 88.
188 N. Kapoor and K. Narkowicz, 'Unmaking citizens: Passport removals, preemptive policing and the reimagining of colonial governmentalities', *Ethnic and Racial Studies* 42:16 (2019), 45–62 (p. 52).

189 V. Dodd, 'Teenager faces 13 years for racist killing of Asian', *Guardian*, 15 December 2001.
190 E. Said, *Orientalism* (New York: Pantheon, 1978).
191 Y. Hussain and P. Bagguley, 'Securitized citizens: Islamophobia, racism and the 7/7 London bombings', *The Sociological Review* 60:4 (2012), 715–734.
192 A. Kundnani, *The End of Tolerance: Racism in 21st Century Britain* (London: Pluto Press, 2007).
193 Riaz, *Islam and Identity Politics among British Bangladeshis*, p. 47.
194 N. Ahmed, 'Class, ethnicity and religion in the Bengali East End: A political history', *Ethnic and Racial Studies* 39:13 (2016), 2416–2418 (p. 2417).
195 Riaz, *Islam and Identity Politics among British Bangladeshis*, p. 50.
196 Ibid.
197 A. McColgan, 'Undue spiritual influence: A historical analysis', *King's Law Journal* 28:2 (2017), 279–308.
198 Tower Hamlets Council, 'Education Maintenance Allowance (EMA) and University Bursary schemes' (2022), Tower Hamlets, www.towerhamlets.gov.uk/lgnl/education_and_learning/school_finance_and_support/EMA-and-University-Bursary-awards/EMA-and-University-Bursary.aspx (accessed 21 May 2023).

2

Shaping of identity: The relationship with South Asian clothes

The nineteenth-century Bengali poet Michael Madhusudan Datta once shocked his friends and acquaintances by attending a Raja's party in full European dress. When the Raja asked him why he was not wearing the customary *dhoti* (waist-cloth) and *chadar* (shawl), the poet replied with a laugh: 'If I came wearing them I'd have to help carry pitchers and napkins; but these are the clothes of the Ruling Race; so there's no fear of that.' On another occasion, Datta was seen emerging from a lake, this time dressed in a *dhoti*. When a friend taunted him, 'Where is your hat and coat now?', the poet replied, 'Man is many-formed: he takes on different forms according to the situation in which he finds himself.'[1]

Introduction: Dress or clothes?

Religious and ethnic identities, as mentioned in the previous chapter, are manifested in multifaceted ways. Here, the focus will be on the relationship between the formulations of identity, whether individual or collective, and the types of dress(es) one chooses to adopt and wear. First, this chapter elaborates on the kinds of dress the research participants chose at specific points in their lives and why they made these choices. It focuses on how Bangladeshis negotiate and interact with different forms of attire, particularly the *sari*, the *shalwar kameez*, the *lungi* and the *funjabi*.[2] Readers will be guided by exploring the *sari* and *shalwar kameez* before probing into the *lungi* and *funjabi*. Finally, the chapter will consider the research participants' insights and thoughts to decipher their relations to these different attires. Wherever possible, there will be references to how the geography of the East End enables a particular comfort or discomfort with the garments. As there were generational differences in the responses to how these clothing items are positioned in their lives, much of the analysis is informed by how the respondents spoke about their relation to the clothing. The chapter interrogates when such outfits are worn, how such a choice is made and the wearers' interpretation of the clothes. It also tries to gauge the growing invisibility of the garms in the public sphere.

The terms 'clothes' and 'dress' are used interchangeably throughout the chapter. However, according to Emma Tarlo, 'clothes' are deemed detachable, 'thereby denying the very permanence they sometimes seem to suggest',[3] whereas 'dress' includes body modifications and supplements, thus giving it a broader application. During the interviews, the primary focus was on the clothes and on the functions meanings ascribed to the different attires by the research participants. In the proceeding pages, I examine what the clothes symbolise and how they help the individuals interviewed to understand their own sense of self in relation to others. Tarlo suggests that it is not that clothes do not hold any particular meaning, but that their 'peculiar proximity to our bodies give them a special potential for symbolic elaboration'.[4] Elizabeth Wilson makes the following argument to illustrate Tarlo's point:

> A part of this strangeness of dress is that it links the biological body to the social being, and public to private. This makes it uneasy territory, since it forces us to recognise that the human body is more than a biological entity. It is an organism in culture, a cultural artefact even, and its own boundaries are unclear ... Dress is the frontier between the self and the not self.[5]

According to Mary Ellen Roach-Higgins and Joanne B. Eicher, dress is defined as 'an assemblage of modifications of the body and/or supplements to the body'.[6] They further argue that this includes obvious features placed on the body (the supplements), such as garments, jewellery, accessories and other categories of items. Ethnic dress, on the other hand, is specifically worn 'by members of one group to distinguish themselves from members of another by focusing on differentiation. Ethnic dress visually separates one group from another. It can also involve other sensory aspects of dress.'[7]

Clothing can be seen as a vehicle to identify an ethnic or religious group, and ethnic and religious dresses can be seen as an expression of pride in and love for one's heritage and group cohesion. Further, they indicate the individual's identity expression and demonstrate that 'group inclusion and exclusion are made apparent through modifying and supplementing the body'.[8] Eicher and Barbara Sumberg further argue that ethnicity creates 'insiders verses outsiders, with boundaries that separate outsiders and insiders and symbols that identify members of a group as being distinct from other groups. This "we-ness" includes a common heritage with shared language, similar dress, manners, and lifestyle.'[9] In this sense, in any culture, clothes are an essential aspect, as they function as an outward, prominent symbol of the culture concerned. They are also one of the first elements of a culture people can utilise to distinguish one group from another, which can be referred to as 'personal identity'. Dress, therefore, functions as a visible marker of ethnicity and is used as a means to communicate one's belonging to or membership of a group.

Although any form of ethnic dress is, theoretically, perceived to function as a marker of one's ethnic identity, demonstrating the common or shared heritage and background of a particular group of people, it can also be merged into the construction of a national dress and a marker of who belongs to the nation. This belonging is demonstrated in Gerald D. Berreman's study undertaken in a northern city in India where Muslims were identifiable through the *burkha* and, therefore, outside the construction of the nation-state, while Hindus were identified through the *sari* and representatives of the nation-state. He noted that during the 1969 Hindu–Muslim riot in Ahmedabad, the would-be killers identified 'their victims through dissimilar Hindu and Moslem [sic] ways of dressing', with Hindus and Muslims alike consequently 'wearing western clothes as a measure of safety'.[10] The wearing of western clothes posits the neutrality of the state, as the clothes represent neither an ethnicity, a religious identity nor a national identity. Here, one can note how the descriptors 'Hindu' and 'Muslim', which are terms used to identify one's subscription to a religion, are, in this instance, utilised as a way to demarcate ethnic identities, with the former having the privilege of incorporation into the national imagining, while the latter is perceived as the outsider.

To further complicate how these classifications finesse and shift in the UK context, it is essential to draw on the interviews with the research participants to understand how different garments are indexed. This is explored by considering how the garments are contested within different social domains. Many of the contestations analysed later in the chapter are rooted in the struggle for social acceptance, but above anything else they emphasise their wearers' affinity to their faith. Furthermore, this speaks from a position of the salience of being othered, which has found emphasis more in the Muslim aspect more than other elements of the research participants' identities.

The *sari* and the *shalwar kameez*

Women of North India and Pakistan have traditionally worn the *shalwar kameez* in the Indian subcontinent,[11] and these women were 'Hindu, Muslim and Sikh, originally sharing a regional territory and a common cultural base'.[12] It appeared on the streets of Britain from the mid-1960s onwards, marking the time as one of 'rapid growth of Asian communities as family groups consolidated themselves'.[13] The presence of the *shalwar kameez* created the emergence of stereotypes regarding South Asian women, who 'were classified as orthodox women who were rigid in maintaining their "backward" cultures, when they should, as seen from the outside, have been adopting local styles'.[14] Parminder Bhachu further states that wearing the *shalwar kameez* in the public space put forward South Asian women as a visible 'other', as a result of which they experienced racism, being taunted in public and labelled as 'Pakis'. Bhachu interviewed Geeta – one of the first women to open a boutique in London for British South Asians – who discusses how the *shalwar kameez* was viewed as a 'Paki' dress in England. While factoring this in, Geeta speaks of the strategies she developed 'to negate this racism and to emphasise cultural pride in the face of the destructive effects of British imperialism'.[15] Geeta states:

> The *salwaar-kameez* used to be a Paki dress. We are told that all the time. Today, every high street store has outfits that are and look like a long *kameez* with *kaajs* on the side and trousers, sometimes straight-cut ones. The *salwaar-kameez* has come a long way. There was a lot of racism. Gone are the days when people used to say 'you smell of curry'. They are eating curry all the time. Every time I go to the supermarket, I see chicken tikka masala, or some onion bhaji or some curry something or the other in their trolleys.[16]

Geeta's point about the availability and visibility of the *shalwar kameez* is intriguing. The visibility is made possible by mapping the garment onto celebrities' bodies, making it a more palatable outfit.[17] Indeed, the *shalwar kameez* and its visibility via upper-class women such as Princess Diana and Jemima Khan reveal how ethnic wear travels through social space and is affirmed through social and cultural capital positionings. Situated at the site of this convergence, the ways in which the *shalwar kameez* shapes people's understandings of it in social spaces in the everyday becomes a contestation between what constitutes 'appropriate' clothing (read: in line with Islamic expressions) and what is acceptable socially in non-Muslim spaces.

Compared to the *shalwar kameez*, the *sari* is an unstitched long piece of cloth that is draped in various styles, and its length varies from four to nine yards. The word *sari* derives from Sanskrit, meaning 'a strip of cloth'.[18] The *sari* can be draped in multiple ways; Ṛta Kapur Chishti has documented varying *sari* drapes and notes how they have subtle differences and regional affiliations.[19] The *Nivi*-style drape is the most popular, and Arti Sandhu contends that this is because the draping 'emerged towards the end of the nineteenth and into the mid-twentieth century as a sign of emancipated womanhood amongst the elite and middle classes and as part of a wider mobilisation of clothing and textiles for political resistance, activism and self-identification in India'.[20] Sandhu posits that the *Nivi* style provided the possibility of a hybrid sartorial expression, bringing together 'tradition' (read: Indian) with 'western elements' (read: blouse and petticoat).[21] Much of the conversation with my research participants regarding the *sari* and the *shalwar kameez* revolved primarily around modesty and the perceived attachment that the garments had to specific religions: Islam and Hinduism.

(Im)modest(y) and religion

I met with Farhana (interviewed in June 2014) in a café in Bethnal Green. She was already inside the café in her floral, summery dress. Unfortunately the music was too loud, so we decided to go to the nearby park. Once settled on a bench, we spoke about her growing up in East London and what the garments associated with expressions of Bengaliness meant to her. She stated that 'people can wear whatever they want, really. It's not defined by a dress code.' She further elaborated and explained how she differentiates the wearing of the *sari* from that of the *shalwar kameez*:

> The *sari* is something that is specific to the Indian subcontinent and Bangladesh, and Bengali culture … the *shalwar kameez* is much more of an Islamic kind of dress, as far as I'm concerned, also from the subcontinent, but more of an Islamic way of dressing, really. Whereas the *sari*, Hindus, Muslims, whoever, wore it, and there was no, sort of, distinction as such, in terms of religious identity … it was a cultural, sort of, dress, for many women.

Farhana consciously distinguishes between the two dresses and emphasises the role of the *sari* as a marker of one's ethnic identity and the *shalwar kameez* as a marker for one's religious identity. The *sari* here is captured as the normative dress of the Indian subcontinent and is not indexed through a religious lens. This differentiation is noted in Tarlo's work, where a daughter of a priestly Brahmin[22] family is not allowed by her father, who officiates as a priest, 'to wear the *shalwar kamiz* on the grounds that it is "Muslim dress"'.[23] Even though the *shalwar kameez* breaks the rule around the sanctity of the unstitched cloth for upper-caste practising Hindus, instead it is Islamophobic sentiments dictating why the daughter cannot wear the *shalwar kameez*. Furthermore, if we consider the process of racialisation attributed to Bengalis leading up to the Liberation War of 1971, West Pakistanis coded Bengali Muslims as having too much proximity to 'Hindu' traditions, including the wearing of the *sari*. Nazia Hussein notes how the 'new woman' of Bangladesh 'embodied cultural practices, such as *bindi* and *sari*, [and] marked Bangladesh's independence movement from Pakistan, seeking to establish a secular fusion identity combining religious (Islamic) and cultural practices'.[24] In that sense, although clothes are a personal choice, they are nevertheless 'completely social because they are socially acquired "selections" from socially constructed ways of attributing identities on the basis of social positions individuals fill'.[25] In addition to this, Erving Goffman argues that there is a difference between personal and social identities, where the former refer to self-attributions and the latter to widely shared categorisations of individuals as social objects.[26]

While we continue speaking, Farhana also points out how the *shalwar kameez* is not a gendered dress, since, as she explains, 'it's like a unisex dress, you know, there's no sort of sense of gender about it ... and so, for me, Islam sort of tries to show, not show the body really, or parts of the body, where the *sari* is a very feminine garment'. Here, Farhana is placing her identification with the *shalwar kameez* – mainly through her understanding of the meanings and symbolism attributed to it through a religious lens. Despite the coding of the *shalwar kameez* as a 'Muslim' garment in India, Tarlo found that it was associated with well-educated people, and noted how the father of one of her contributors wanted his daughter to look like an 'educated city girl'. However, the contributor's uncle, a priest, 'felt it indecent for a respectable Hindu girl to wear a *shalwar kamiz* which was suitable only for Muslims or fancy city people'.[27]

Meanwhile, in Bangladesh – a Muslim-majority country – the distinctions around sartorial choices are articulated through class positionings while contorting the dresses to meet the modesty requirements as set by cultural, social and religious norms. In that regard, the *shalwar kameez* is deemed the more appropriate garb for work and everyday wear.[28] Hussein further contends that the 'new women' of Bangladesh balance 'their role as symbols of good (respectable) yet "modern" womanhood, participating in paid employment and well versed in a contemporary consumerist and trendy lifestyle'.[29] Such ambiguities, dichotomous oppositions of 'modernity' and 'tradition', were produced at the intersection between economic capital and social capital, locating narratives of being 'progressive'. Victoria Redclift's research on the Bihari community in camps in Bangladesh highlights how, on account of the popularity of the *shalwar kameez* among urban Bengali women, the Bihari ' "Urdu speaking outsiders" have re-appropriated the item' because following 'contemporary urban Bengal culture' carried a particular cultural and social capital with it. This facilitated an easier way to integrate into wider Bangladeshi society and avoid being discriminated against.[30]

Despite these contested meanings attributed to the *shalwar kameez* in India and Bangladesh, the dynamics operate differently in East London. As argued by Stuart Hall, identities 'emerge within the play of specific modalities of power, and thus are more the product of the marking of difference and exclusion, than they are the sign of an identical, naturally-constituted unity – an "identity" in its traditional meaning (that is, an all-inclusive sameness, seamless, without internal differentiation)'.[31] Of note is that, while identities do exist with the meanings ascribed to them by members of a group, these meanings vary among the members. The concept of contestation in the present chapter will capture these multiple meanings.

In line with Gerd Baumann's argument on 'the processes by which *culture* and *community* become objects of debate and terms of contestation', the research participants negotiate their received traditions and meanings from their parents.[32] I wore jeans and a *kameez* top when I arrived at East London Mosque to interview Shiraj (interviewed in March 2014). A concerted effort was made to wear appropriate clothing to enter the mosque, which requires one to dress modestly, including the covering of the body and a scarf to cover the hair. I wore a scarf around my neck but did not use it to cover my hair, as I was going in to interview Shiraj and not to pray. Someone picked me up from the reception area, and he took me to an empty office room on the third floor. While I waited to interview Shiraj, his colleague offered to make me a cup of tea and returned after a few minutes. After Shiraj arrived, smartly dressed, he sat down and put his phone on silent. When we started talking about clothes and how they shape identities – particularly the *sari*. Shiraj stated how he had noticed a reduction in girls wearing it. He agreed with its decline and notes:

> I don't think *sari* is a good form of dress. It reveals some parts of the body which is supposed to be covered, according to Islamic faith. *Shalwar kameez* is much better than *sari*, in that sense. People wear *sari* at home. My wife wears it sometimes at home but I've seen more and more girls are moving towards *shalwar kameez* than *sari*s nowadays.

Though the *sari* can be revealing, depending on how one wears it, it is possible to ensure that the whole body is entirely covered by pinning the part of the *sari* swirled over the shoulder to the blouse. When I asked Shiraj if the *shalwar kameez* was a visible dress on the streets of East London in the 1970s and 1980s, he asserted: '(The) *sari* was very popular. I hardly saw any of my aunties and people of my mother's age wearing *shalwar kameez*, and now you will see that's quite common.' Shamim (interviewed in November 2013) reaffirmed how his mother, who had been working for the National Health Service for twenty-five years, still wore the *sari*, and noted how his mother saw no need to wear trousers or other clothes to go to work. This practice of wearing the *sari*, it seems, was common among a particular generation of Bangladeshi women who were the first to move to the UK with their husbands and continued to wear it. When I spoke to Dr Fahima (interviewed in September 2014) about the *sari*, she expressed the distinct meanings attributed to the garments and how they were, quite strictly, associated with the marital status of the woman:

> Yeah, I wear the *shalwar kameez* as well, and you know, there was this whole thing in the past where even women, you know, if they wore *shalwar kameez*

over a *sari*, they would be frowned upon and say: 'Yallah dekhrayni shalwar kameez findi layse goro beti!' [Lord, look at how she is wearing the *shalwar kameez* at home!]. There are the kind of people obviously from my mum's generation, they wouldn't dream of wearing *shalwar kameez*, they'd still be wearing their *sari*s ... my mom always wore a *sari*, even my *hori* (mother-in-law) wears a *sari*, she came here and she was quite comfortable ... Even though, religiously *sari*s are very immodest garments, they can be very immodest, it's a cultural thing, and when we grew up, there is this kind of thing where we wear *shalwar kameez* until a certain age, then you move over to wearing a *sari* through marriage, isn't it?

Dr Fahima, whom I interviewed in a café at her workplace in Central London, spoke in detail about how she ties the *sari* to ensure she wears it 'very modestly' and that her entire body is covered. Many of the ways in which she drew these boundaries around modesty were to ensure it was congruent with her *hijab* also. In this respect, Hall's definition of identity as an ongoing process 'of "becoming" as well as of "being"'[33] is a valuable analysis to conceptualise the changes in the ways British Bangladeshi women relate to the *sari*. On the other hand, Dr Fahima's mother and mother-in-law appear to have a more concrete idea of what the different garments signify for a woman. In that regard, Dr Fahima's identification with the *sari* was instructed and constructed through her religious understanding of modesty, as opposed to the social status one acquires through the dress. Moreover, she recognises the historical trajectory of the dresses and draws our attention to how *identification*, rather than *identity*, is a complex (and frequently ambivalent) process. In contrast, the term 'identity' designates 'a *condition* rather than a *process*'.[34]

Rachel Dwyer makes a compelling argument using Bollywood as an example to illustrate the differing roles of the *shalwar kameez* and *sari*. Dwyer argues that adopting the latter, almost a form of rite-of-passage, transforms a girl into a mature woman through marriage. In contrast, the former depicts and retains innocence and girlhood:

> First we must look at the heroine, who is a perfect woman at least by the end of the movie if not the beginning. Usually well known as a star, she must be beautiful, young, virginal and innocent but ready to fall in love. She may begin the film by wearing western clothes or a loose interpretation of the *salwaar-khamees*, but by the end of the film will most likely wear a *sari*, if only for her wedding which ends the film.[35]

Although the *sari* is worn by women from various national, ethnic and religious backgrounds, and does not expressly hold a religious reference, the focus on how much skin is on show causes unease for the research participants interviewed. It is the revealing of skin that many view as rendering the garment 'un-Islamic'. Moreover, the various conceptions of modesty and the relationship between women's dress and their appearance in public is a factor that was also prevalent during the British Raj. Before the nineteenth century, and unlike their European counterparts, Indian women 'of all statuses did not wear undergarments that confined or constricted their breasts, stomachs, and/or hips. When Indian women wore bodices or blouses (*choli*), in the later nineteenth century, they were made to be form-fitting and to accentuate the shape of their breasts.'[36] A woman with her waist exposed and a semi-opaque cover over her hips is noticeable in a nineteenth-century 'painting by Varma, of two figures, Shantanu and Matsyasughandi, from an Indian myth' (Figure 2.1).[37]

Falguni Sheth argues that 'the current version of the *sari* has been familiar in Western (mostly British) contexts for at least 200 years', and that since the late nineteenth century it has 'seen a series of changes that have rendered it more suitable to the "Western" gaze'.[38] The addition of multiple garments by the British to make the *sari* more 'modest' is an example of the civilising mission in India, which was shaped by British intervention to regulate the clothing practices of the population over whom it ruled. Tarlo contends that 'the widespread adoption of the blouse was probably the most noticeable effect of British influences on Indian women's dress'.[39] J. Devika, for example, shares an instance of a woman berated for choosing to add a blouse to her *sari*:

> One example comes from an anecdote of the spouse of an early twentieth-century Keralan reformer, who wished to integrate the blouse into her *sari*, enhancing her sexual appeal, which was thought to be diminished by wearing the *sari* without the blouse. Her husband approved. Her mother berated and beat her for behaving like a 'Muslim' and a promiscuous 'dancing girl'.[40]

The covering of her chest 'with a blouse is to become more seductive by a form of allure through opacity, which is associated (in the part of the region from where the story originates) with the sexually promiscuous practices of Muslims and not Hindus'.[41] The above story and the British colonial emissaries' outlook on modesty, with the introduction of various supplementary garments to the *sari*, indicate how modesty and its signifiers vary and are very much dependent on political, social, religious and cultural understandings of what clothes ought to be. Contemporarily, the *sari* is worn with a long petticoat and blouse, modified under British rule to help increase 'modesty' and, by correlation, to 'reduce' the sexual promiscuity of the women who wore *saris* by fashioning various auxiliary garments that would help conceal, veil and shroud their bodies. The *sari* is also projected as a sexy and sensual garment because the waist, midriff and upper back are exposed. However, I would argue that this particular characterisation emerged as the result of pop culture consumption, via Bollywood in particular, where

Figure 2.1 Shantanu and Matsyagandha. *The Boat-Woman and the Noble.* Painting by Ravi Varma. Another painting by Varma portrays a different version of the *sari*, worn without a blouse or petticoat.

there is an explicit and overt sexualisation of the *sari* despite the voluminous amount of material and the complexity involved in affixing it to the body.

Dr Fahima and Nasima (interviewed in June 2014) regard the *sari* as an 'Indian thing' and specifically 'Hindu' attire, which, according to Nasima, Bangladeshis inherited because they belonged to India before the Partition. This particular framing is observed by Dwyer, noting that the *sari*, amongst Muslims, 'is increasingly seen as "Hindu" and inappropriate for Muslim women'.[42] Dwyer also persuasively speculates that this is due in part 'to the conflation of Indian and Hindu, which has been gathering momentum in recent decades with the rise of Hindu nationalism'.[43] Dwyer's observation corresponds with Berreman's consideration of how the nation – India in this instance – is conceptualised by placing the Muslim at the periphery while the Hindu woman is made legible through the *sari*. This formulation is then reinscribed in the diaspora using a similar mode of thinking. However, it is notable that this is also being rearranged into a specific order informed by the lens of the War on Terror.

Other research participants, such as Shaju (interviewed in December 2014), whom I met in a café at St Pancras International Station, further reiterated the relationship between the *sari* and the failure to fulfil the religious requirement to practise modesty. After reflecting on the role of dress and identity, especially the *sari*, he captures how it is relegated to specific domains and explains that 'if you're at home, then wear it, or if you're going to a wedding or something, I think it needs to be moderated sometimes. I think it has been [like that] since the last ten years.' When I enquire further about how he believes this moderation has been implemented, he responds:

> Well, before, you had the old hip showing and all that stuff. I think that's wrong because we're Muslims, [and we] shouldn't be imitating [it]. And the *sari* comes from Hindu culture, isn't it? I think people should wear clothes which they prefer at home. If those clothes go against – if you're Muslim, that is – your faith, in terms of revealing part of your body which you shouldn't, or kind of exposes the figure, which is almost the same. I think we Muslims are encouraged to cover; to women there is that emphasis on … showing or wearing something which is too revealing. *Shalwar kameez* is a bit more tolerable, but I'm looking at the *sari*, and it's something which really captures your attention. It does.

Shaju's positioning considers the religious injunction to remain modest as more essential. He approves of the *shalwar kameez*, which covers the whole body, and is thus more befitting of religious demands than the *sari*. From this point of view, it is evident that clothes are more than just an aesthetic expression. Shaju was born and brought up in Tower Hamlets, and, as presented by Ashraf Hoque in his thesis on young Muslims of Luton, is one of many young Muslims in Britain who 'are in the process of creating a "culture" of their own; one that embraces the validity of Islam in shaping their identity yet without the "cultural baggage" associated with the Islam of their parents'.[44] In that sense, Shaju's views do not differ considerably from those of Nasima, Shiraj and Dr Fahima. However, they also encapsulate their cultural self-definitions vis-à-vis their religious leanings. Moreover, the moulding of cultural and religious identities encapsulates the messiness of how such identities are constantly shifting and finessing according to contemporary socio-cultural and religious meanings attributed to the garments. Further, this demonstrates how deculturation does not entirely diminish a cultural identity but merely micro-manages it through an individual's faith.

In her analysis of the wet sari, Dwyer notes how 'the Indian cinema has a specific erotics of clothing'.[45] The cinematic projections of the *sari* to its audience are showcased through the sensuous nature of the *sari* rather than by showing naked bodies, which are usually associated with shame and fear. Clothes, then, offer 'an alternative epistemological foundation, a form of political, visual and tactile communication that reveals aspects of the inner psyche, community practice and broader political change. Anthropological studies on dress reveal that dress is a site of convergence for transnational, global and local forces.'[46] The convergence of these various forces is evident when Tarlo interviews Humera, whose father expected her to wear the *shalwar kameez* in her teens:

> The shalwar kamiz for the sub-continental psyche represented religion at one level, culture, respectability and *udab* (etiquette) which was very important both in the Islamic tradition and in the Pakistani tradition as well. I always rebelled against that and thought, 'I'm not wearing it.' Of course I did sometimes wear it for special occasions, but otherwise not. It was an ongoing source of conflict.
>
> It [the shalwar kamiz] wasn't relevant to me. Also you have to remember that the shalwar kamizes available in the sixties and seventies were horrible. There was that too. I don't think I thought much about it consciously at the time, but if I thought hard about it, I think subliminally I felt that it singled you out. Also, in my mind it represented a type of person who was 'traditional' and all that and I didn't see myself like that. I didn't want to be put in that box.[47]

Humera's internal cultural dissent illustrates how her parents drew particular boundaries around what the *shalwar kameez* represented. However, it also points to how the garment was positioned in wider British society: an othered piece of clothing. The consciousness of being located as an other in Britain proved to be one of the reasons for many to avoid wearing the garment. In that regard, the *shalwar kameez* was affixed to a specific geographic location. It did not necessarily have the same socio-religious implications that it did in the Indian subcontinent. In contrast, the *sari* was viewed as cultural attire and had no religious legitimacy because it clings to the body and reveals the midriff. Shiraj stressed that he had witnessed a shift towards the wearing of the *shalwar kameez*, and that this might be due to other factors and not solely based on religious norms. Shaheda (interviewed in May 2014) stated that she only wore the *sari* occasionally because she did not like it, and 'because it's difficult to maintain', opting for the *shalwar kameez* at home. While the latter has been indexed as aligning with Islamic sensitivities around modesty, I want to turn to a case that challenges this notion and attempts to reclassify the *shalwar kameez* in an alternative domain within the broader British context.

The case of Shabina Begum and the boundaries of religion and ethnicity

The case of Shabina Begum was curious, surrounding what qualifies as religious dress with additional layers of complexity.[48] In September 2002, Shabina Begum arrived at Denbigh High School in Luton, where she was a pupil, wearing the *jilbab* with the *hijab*, not her school uniform. She was accompanied by two young men, one of whom was her brother, who spoke to the school's assistant headteacher, insisting that Shabina should be allowed to wear the *jilbab* in school as this was the only garment that met her religious requirements. He talked of human rights and threatened legal proceedings if the school failed to grant those rights. The assistant head, who reported feeling threatened by their attitude and approach, told the girl to go home, get changed and return to school in the prescribed uniform. Instead, the two young men encouraged Shabina to leave the office, arguing that they were 'not prepared to compromise on this issue. Their objection to the existing uniform was that it was insufficient for covering the contours of the female body and was therefore inappropriate for maturing Muslim girls.'[49]

Denbigh High School's uniform policy included the option to wear the *shalwar kameez*, introduced in 1993 'following consultation with parents, students, staff and the imams of three local mosques, all of whom had approved the uniform and considered it suitably modest to meet Islamic dress requirements'.[50] Shabina's case reached the High Court in 2004. The school, in the meantime, 'consulted the imam of the Central Mosque in Luton and the Chairman of the Religious Affairs Department of the London Central Mosque in Regents Park, both of whom confirmed that shalwar kamiz was not "un-Islamic" and did conform to the "Islamic dress code" '.[51] Prior to making the demand to wear the *jilbab* to school, Shabina had worn the *shalwar kameez*-and-*hijab* option, where the latter had to be navy blue to match the school's uniform colour.⁵² The *shalwar kameez* was also worn by some 'Muslim, Hindu and Sikh female pupils'.⁵³

Furthermore, Tarlo cites a letter dated 18 December 2002, in which the London Central Mosque wrote:

> [L]ooking around the world we see an amazing variety of garments which meet these requirements [of the Islamic dress code]. Also the clothes of women differ from country to country, and in some countries, from region to region. Hence we don't see any un-Islamic act for [*sic*] wearing a Shalwar Kamiz ... Finally may I add that whatever I have described in the foregoing paragraphs are the general consensus of the vast majority of the Muslim scholars.⁵⁴

However, despite this affirmation by the imams, Shabina's brother claimed the *shalwar kameez* was 'a "Pakistani cultural dress" which had no religious basis'.⁵⁵ Another argument made by Shabina was that not only was the *shalwar kameez* a part of 'Pakistani culture' but it 'could also be worn by Hindus and Sikhs'.⁵⁶ This particular characterisation of the *shalwar kameez* as encompassing a cultural expression extending to other religious communities is presented, therefore, as diluting the garment's Islamic certainty. The viability of this framing is flawed, as the *jilbab*, a form of a long dress with full sleeves, is also worn by other religious communities, including Catholic nuns. Therefore, the notion of creating a religiously coded culture that sits within a universal framing of Islamic expression that unifies the *ummah* rather than dividing via 'cultural' signifiers is a critical perspective. In the absence of 'culture', there is an emphasis on creating not only a universal Islam, or Islamic expression via dressing, but one cementing a linear Islamic aesthetics that can exist outside the bounds of 'culture'.

Dr Imran (interviewed March 2014), whom I interviewed in a café in London, spoke of an '*ummah* culture' where the *sari* was perceived as 'un-Islamic'; to feel like a member of the *ummah*, he argued, a woman would have to wear 'the *burqa* or they wear *chador*'.⁵⁷ In this regard, the '*ummah* culture' allows Muslims from across the globe, wherever they are, to feel they belong to a perceived global Muslim community. However, according to Shabina's brothers, the prescription is that it is incumbent upon Muslims to adhere to a single, agreed form of clothing to be accepted. The idea of 'pure' Islam, where all Muslims dress the same, appears to designate a perceived shared, monolithic culture, signifying an innovative departure from all things related to *ethnic* culture. Shabina's case reverberates with Rogers Brubaker and Frederick Cooper's second outline of how 'identity' is used as a 'specifically *collective* phenomenon', as Shabina and her brothers were trying to denote 'a fundamental and consequential *sameness* among members of a group'.⁵⁸ In the process of creating this *sameness* within their perceived ideas of how Muslims ought to self-identify through dress, they were dispelling their South Asian identity and prioritising their religious identification. However, this attempt at creating a de-cultured Islamic aesthetic in the UK is impossible, as Muslims have regularly contested and reconfigured these notions. Even the production of a supposed de-cultured Islamic aesthetic has to engage with *a* form of cultural expression. Attempting to present a totalising logic negates the diversity of Muslims and relies more on concretising the Muslim subject.

Another theme concerning these two garments is how they are relegated to only special occasions and not worn daily. This was affirmed by Nafisah (interviewed in May 2014), who wears the *sari* and/or *shalwar kameez* when she goes to weddings or family functions. She shares:

> I would always wear Asian clothes, and even when I graduated I wore like an Asian dress and stuff like that; I think it's part of the cultural identity. I can never see myself going to a family wedding – Asian family wedding – wearing a dress or, you know, it would never feel right, it would feel like I'm losing out, or that I'm not being part of it.

Hall describes identities as 'the names we give to the different ways we are positioned by, and position ourselves within, the narratives of the past'.[59] Although Nafisah does not expressly link her decision to wear the garments to a 'past', she is nonetheless attributing it to the retention of a form of cultural identity within her familial spaces. In contrast, they are worn less in non-familial spaces because those spaces are encoded to cater for the white normative society where the 'other' has to carry the burden of conviviality.[60]

The differences between the *shalwar kameez* and the *sari* supposedly mark the boundaries between the religious and cultural spheres. However, Shabina Begum's case generates a far more complex framing than the simplistic binary of culture versus religion. Meanings attached to the different attires change with time and space and encode new significations. The research participants valorised the *shalwar kameez* more than the *sari*, using religion to ground their thoughts. The *sari* memorialises one's culture and ethnic origins, while the *shalwar kameez* animates a more modest projection but embodies an additional symbol of ethnic identity without compromising one's religious convictions. Interestingly, Dwyer points out that western readers may find it surprising that 'western clothes are seen as more figure revealing than the *sari*', since each carries its code of modesty.[61] She states:

> These codes are not just signs of cultural difference; these garments carry inherent codes within them so that the woman who wears a *salwar khamees* without any form of veil, draped in whatever manner or a woman who commits the social *faux pas* of letting the sari slide off her shoulder are seen as drawing more attention to her breasts than [a] woman wearing a tight shirt in a western-style.[62]

Though the codes mentioned above by Dwyer are specific to India, they nonetheless point to the fact that context and the setting situate and entrench the codes. Clothes and dress thus become a 'situated bodily practice' contoured by cultural norms and expectations within a given context.[63] The majority consensus amongst the research participants seems to indicate a change in what is socially accepted, which is heavily drawn from the use of religion as the arbitrator. Although not the same, there appeared to be an agreement that the less skin on show and the baggier the outfit, the more aligned the garment is with Islamic sensibilities. This breaks away from how the *sari* and *shalwar kameez* are deployed in Bangladesh, where the latter is intimately tied to class/social mobility and performs to an urban, progressive aesthetic. In contrast, the *sari* has experienced reduced visibility.[64]

In the UK context, the *sari* was specifically associated with the generation of Bangladeshi women, usually married, who were brought to the UK from Bangladesh. They became the bearers of tradition and culture. These women continued to wear traditional *sari*s and adopted more sober ones, usually after being widowed, to locate their social status and age. As a result, the *sari* is 'heavily laden with cultural meanings of nostalgia, tradition, womanhood, nationalism and social status'.[65] However, those meanings shifted and became associated with newer paradigms while placing the *sari* in the wider UK context. Tarlo notes that because the first generation of Bangladeshi women in London was, in effect, 'restricted to an ethnically, linguistically and religiously coded space', these women did not seek respectability from fellow Londoners.[66] Instead, they were seeking respectability from other Bengalis and to 'not attract too much unwanted attention, gossip or speculation. To achieve this, black outer garments and headscarves were perceived as a safe option because they deflected attention, although most had not felt them necessary when they lived in Bangladesh.'[67]

On the other hand, the *shalwar kameez* assumes a different role as it not only fulfils the religious requirements of modesty but also functions as a garment vital enough to be incorporated into state schools' uniform policies. Shamim (interviewed in November 2013) concurred with Nafisah's point that the *shalwar kameez* and *sari* have become novelties exclusively worn for special occasions. He emphasised how this is most visible while celebrating both Eids in Tower Hamlets. However, the only other sphere in which the *shalwar kameez* is visible daily is that of local secondary schools, where young girls wear it as uniform. Nonetheless, the controversy regarding Begum's case and the positing of the *shalwar kameez* as an inadequate garment to represent supposed 'Islamic sensibilities' challenged how different Muslims conceptualised modesty differently. But Begum's challenge discloses the existence of socio-cultural and religious relations that continuously negotiate the rapidly changing demands of Muslims, sometimes by Muslims themselves. The *shalwar kameez* and the *sari*, therefore, are not simply regulated by the garments' location in the subcontinent and their dichotomous positioning via the urban versus the rural, which reveals how Bangladeshi Muslims in the UK are cultivating their relations more via the political as the core site. Put differently, the Bangladeshi body politic is being purged of its cultural expressions and reinscribed with a uniform religious expression. In this expression, acutely revealed through Begum's case, even the *shalwar kameez* begs further scrutiny.

The male embodiment of clothes: The *lungi* and the *funjabi*

The *lungi* is a sarong-like garment, usually worn in a hot climate where wearing trousers would otherwise be very unpleasant. It is the national dress for men in Bangladesh. The *lungi* is designed in a skirt style, sometimes easily confused with the *dhoti* (famously worn by Gandhi), which comprises linear-like sheets. The *funjabi* (pronounced with an 'f' by Sylhetis and also known as the shalwar Punjabi suit) consists of wearing a *kameez* (a long tunic) or *kurta* (a tunic). However, in Bengali, *funjabi* refers to the top garment only. It can be worn with slim *shalwar* pyjamas (pronounced *fyjamas* by Sylhetis), jeans or any other type of trousers. It is important to note that while Bangladesh utilises the *lungi* as a national dress, no male head of state has ever worn it to any state function. This is because, in Bangladesh, this attire is the dress 'of the working class'.[68] However, its value and meanings are remade in the diaspora in East London and are not necessarily informed by class as a variable.

During my fieldwork, I realised how some male participants struggled to respond to the questions regarding clothes. For example, when I asked 'How important are clothes to maintain one's identity?', many male participants responded with references to female clothes only. And when I mentioned the *lungi*, many would sit up straight and feel shy because it is an intimate piece of clothing that functions like the kilt without any undergarments worn within the domestic sphere. Others sat in silence, trying to figure out how they felt about clothes and why they chose to wear what they did. This was interesting for me, as a researcher, as it indicated how much of the canon regarding clothes, particularly in reference to the British Muslim community, tends to revolve around women and their sartorial choices. There is little focus on British Muslim men and their own dress choices. From the reactions I received, I can assume that this was possibly the first time the male participants were asked what clothes meant to them.

As with the women in India, when the British arrived in the country for the first time, they were invariably shocked by the 'nakedness' of the loin-clothed Indian boatmen.[69] In East London, it is noteworthy to mention that the *lungi* came to be confined to the private sphere – i.e. the home – and was only brought into the public sphere for Friday prayers, known as *jummah* in Arabic. The interview quotes below reveal how the generation of Bangladeshi men who arrived in the UK wear the *lungi* in public. I interviewed Sohaib (interviewed in January 2014) in Whitechapel at the Pie Factory opposite East London Mosque. The restaurant, where the food is halal and which is run by Muslims, is reviving the East End's working-class traditional staple food of pie and mash, sharing its history and recipes on the walls. It is restoring an old East End tradition and adding flavours from the South Asian palate, such as a spicy pie, chicken tikka pie and many other options. Sohaib, a Bangladeshi who came to the UK as a child with his parents, was dressed in a suit, and once we had ordered we started the interview. When we discussed how men identify with traditional Bengali clothes, he stated 'So I wear the *funjabi* and the *fyjama* and the *lungi*; not *lungi* so much. Some people do, for *jummah*; some of the elders, they wear *lungi* with the *funjabi*. But it's not – maybe it's because of the cold in this country … but I think it's just not done around here. I wouldn't want to be the odd one out.'

Sohaib's response indicates that the *lungi* is adopted by a specific generation of Bengali men, mostly those in their fifties and sixties, who continue to wear it for *jummah*. His final comment also suggests that the *lungi*, even once it enters the public sphere, is worn by a generation more attached to it. He emphasises that he would not want to be 'the odd one out'. Goffman has argued that people always desire to 'fit in' and minimise visible othering.[70] In this instance, this othering does not concern the dominant white gaze but is more in relation to peers, i.e. fellow Muslims and, specifically, other Bangladeshi Muslims. I mentioned earlier that the *lungi* is a sarong-like garment and, in the UK context, it would be defined as a 'skirt'. There is something to be said here about how masculinity needs to be asserted amongst peers because of the dominant acculturation of how the *lungi* is projected as an 'effeminate' garment.

While this is the case, I contend that the *lungi* can operate differently in East London. With the high demographic of Bangladeshis in East London, the *lungi* can be incorporated into the public domain by expanding the notion of the domestic space. For example, the first generation who arrived in the area and settled there are already familiar with the local landscape, a familiarity characterised by face-to-face relations rooted in close personal and emotional ties, especially kinship. Shabna Begum, who traces the history of the Bengali squatters in 1970s East London, argues that for 'Bengali migrants, home extended to zones outside of the physical space, which in Sylhet is known as *para*', extending the sense of home and the domestic sphere.[71] In that sense, I would argue that Sohaib recognised the presence of *para* for a specific generation of Bangladeshis and how they also made it home. However, in its current articulation, the *para* is being remade by a younger Bangladeshi cohort for whom the public and the private are demarcated differently.

I interviewed Khalid in January 2014 at a café in Canary Wharf. He had just finished work and was dressed in smart trousers and a shirt with a brown blazer. We found a quiet spot in the café, and when we started speaking about the *lungi*, he smiled. He mentioned how his dad sometimes wears the *lungi* with a *funjabi* for *jummah*, but he has never done so. The following exchange illustrates this:

> Me: Do you not wear *lungi*?
> Khalid: I don't know. I very rarely wear it [laughs]. *Lungi*s are amazing, they're really amazing.
> Me: But yet you don't wear it?
> Khalid: Yeah, I don't wear it because I'm uncomfortable. I'm used to wearing shorts in the house. No, I do *akhta* (sometimes). I'm not against it. I do wear *lungi* sometimes at home. Absolutely, only at home. Never –
> Me: Never to the *jummah*?
> Khalid: Never ever. Put it this way – when David Beckham wore his sarong, he got plastered for that, he got absolutely laid for that; if I spend time in my house in my *lungi*, people are going to think I'm a crazy guy. Again, you're thinking about what other people are going to think of you.

Khalid emphasises 'what other people ... think of you', much like Sohaib, who spoke about not wanting to be the 'odd one out', demonstrating how perception is central to their clothing decisions. The possible presence of mockery thus informs how the *lungi* is navigated in public space, ensuring there is no room to be stigmatised. In Bangladesh, the *lungi* is very much associated with the working class and does not carry the stigma it does in the diaspora. In their research on clothes consumption for Eid-al Fitr in Bangladesh, M. Rahat Khan and Kritika Sharma found that the *lungi* and *sari* were garments that the rich shopped for to gift to the poor.[72] I noticed how, during our conversation, Khalid blushed while speaking about the *lungi*. When we finished the interview, he mentioned that he had never been asked about his clothes before, and that the question about the *lungi* made him feel uncomfortable. This is a poignant point because Khalid spoke openly and honestly about Muslim women's clothing but felt uneasy while discussing his own sartorial choices. The continuous preoccupation with Muslim women and their clothes in the media explains why many men are more at ease with this topic of conversation. On the other hand, Mohammed (interviewed in March 2014) spoke fondly of the *lungi* but also confined it to the private sphere, specifically to be worn at home. He noted:

> [There] was an East London mosque run – Run 4 Your Mosque – so what I said was: I'm gonna do something different. So I wore my *lungi* and did the running, you know, and we did another thing; another one of my friends, he actually said for charity he would wear *lungi* from Scotland to London, and he did it. But I think the *lungi*s would be a clothing within the home.

Mohammed grew up seeing the *lungi* worn indoors but did not elaborate on whether it should be worn outside. Interestingly, the use of the *lungi* as part of a charity campaign indicates its temporary and gimmicky position and appearance in the public sphere: it is a type of 'craze' that charity campaigns will do to attract attention, since it is seen as an odd thing to wear. It is worth noting that the temporary nature of a charity campaign and the wearing of attire deemed appropriate only for the home illustrates that 'action transforms space', and the acknowledgement of space 'can illuminate the situated nature of dress'.[73] Ismail (interviewed in March 2014) stated his love for the *lungi* and how he and his friend had tried to revive the wearing of the *lungi* in creating 'the *lungi* movement', because he thinks 'that's the best thing ever invented for men. It's just amazing'. When I asked him if he wears it at home, he responded, 'I wear it. And I wear the *genji* (vest top) as well. Anyone that goes [to] Bangladesh, they always bring me *lungi* and *genji*, that's all I ever ask for. But I think I tried it with my sons but it's not happening – they just want their PJs. But it's gone. It's a shame.'

Ismail shares how he wore the *lungi* and the *funjabi* to *jummah* as a child, but now, as an adult, he attends *jummah* with a *funjabi* and wears it with trousers rather than the *lungi*. There is an apparent stigma attached to the *lungi* more than there is with the *funjabi* – something I explore further later. The *lungi* undermines the presentation of masculinity, further reiterated by Faruk (interviewed in April 2014), who noted 'I don't wear *lungi*, I just feel uncomfortable in a *lungi* … [laughs] I won't go into the actual reason why I don't wear it. It's quite embarrassing, I don't want to say – it feels like a kilt [laughs].' On the other hand, Shaju (interviewed in December 2014) expressed his love for the *lungi* and explained 'I wear it at home. If there wasn't a stigma attached to it and if the weather was nicer I'd wear it all day. It doesn't make sense, does it? If it's comfortable, wear it.'

As the above comments demonstrate, the *lungi* carries a sense of embarrassment and stigma. This is certainly because the diaspora places a specific gendered meaning on the garment. In that sense, the stigma is reduced as long as members of the Bangladeshi community possess the attributes projected as 'normal' and 'ordinary' by the majority within the group.[74] This makes it possible to reduce the encounter with stigma, even though, for an older generation of Bangladeshis, the area is incorporated into their *para* and they can be seen wearing the garment for *jummah*.

Shaju's reference to the stigma attached to wearing the *lungi* outside the private sphere – in this case his home – helps us understand how social locations can avert or produce stigma. To understand why we choose what we wear in the public sphere, we must contend with how dress is a silent testimony that quietly locates our belonging to society, marked by the dominant culture. Carole Turbin points out:

> Because dress is not a simple cultural expression of society or individuals but a form of visual and tactile communication linked to the body, self, and communication, it is paradoxical and double-edged, both public and private, individual and social. Dress adorns the surface and at the same time masks and/ or reveals (sometimes unwittingly) the inner psyche. Dress is inherently and simultaneously both public and private because an individual's outwardly presented signs of internal or private meaning are significant only when they are also social, that is comprehensible on some level to observers.[75]

Goffman notes that expected identity norms are a general feature in every society and community.[76] So, in order to avoid the stigma, the wearing of the *lungi* is concealed in the home or, if it appears in the public sphere, it is temporary for a cause or campaign. Nevertheless, the elders, referred to as *murobbis* in Bengali, continue to wear it in public regularly because, for them, stigma is not what they use to mark their boundaries. Instead, their positioning as the *murobbis* gives them a respected status within the wider Bangladeshi community in the area, minimising the encounter with stigma. I would also add that this is the generation that fought hard to make the East End their home, and expanding the home from beyond the house means they feel that the wider *para* is also where they can continue to assert their identities.

I met with Shaheda (interviewed in May 2014) in a café in Bethnal Green. She wore a *hijab* and *jilbab* and had her work lanyard around her neck, as she had come from her job. After ordering some hot drinks, we spoke about the research briefly, and when I asked her what dress meant to her and how it shaped her identity, she remained quiet for a few minutes. Then, she took a sip of her drink, spoke of dress and its relevance, and stated how wearing traditional cultural dresses is not necessarily essential to express one's Bengaliness. She exclaimed how it is 'symbolic, especially to the first generations, they think that if you were wearing that, then you're more respectful of your culture and you know where you come from more than if you're not wearing that because for some reason they think whatever is on show, that's what you are'. While speaking about the importance of dress for the *murobbis* because it asserts a strong heritage identity, Shaheda also explored how she noticed a change in her dad's wardrobe, which she saw as being in tandem with his increasing religiosity. She explains:

> My dad more so [i.e. became more religious] after he got married to my mum, especially by the time my second brother came along. Before, he was [in] the full flare, wearing, you know, long hair … everything … but after being with my mum she kind of brought him more onto the more religious path and now, he's, you know … always wearing the *funjabi*, he's got the whole, you know, beard. Whenever he's talking to someone, religion always crops up.

Shaheda provides insight into her father's relationship with Islam and how it changed after marrying her mother. He 'activated' his Islamic identity by wearing the *funjabi*, which enabled him to explore and express his religiosity to the outside world. Shaheda's father's expression of his religious identity demonstrates once again how the wearing of the *funjabi* is associated with a religious identity, attaching the wearer's heritage to the garment. Outsiders can locate him as a Bengali because of the *funjabi*, and how, within the UK, they would also attribute it to his dedication to his faith. The *lungi*, conversely, is a piece of clothing strictly associated with an ethnic/heritage identity expression with no explicit religious connotations. Shahed (interviewed in May 2014) conveyed his love for the *lungi* and that he wears it at home. However, he also expressed his frustration about how people associate wearing the *lungi* and the *shalwar kameez* with being 'backward':

> I still wear it [the *lungi*] at home. Sometimes I wear tracksuit bottoms all the time. But, when I'm like in Bangladesh, I give you an example, I don't wear tracksuit bottoms all the time, I enjoy wearing the *lungi*. Do you get what I mean? It's a sense of being part of a community, the culture, there's nothing wrong with it. It's not like you'd become less of a modern person. I think that's the ideology people have – that if I wear a *lungi*, or if I wear a *shalwar kameez*, I become backward. Or I'm not modernised enough. No, completely wrong. I could be worth a person [*sic*]. If I don't wear Rolex to show my wealth, it doesn't mean that I'm not rich.

Shahed's points are intriguing, as the perceptions around class positioning and 'being modern' reveal a great deal about the hierarchy of the *lungi*, particularly as my research did not focus much on the wearing of the *shalwar kameez* for men. Moreover, the *shalwar kameez* for men is generally associated with Pakistan. Shahed, therefore, becomes aware of how the *lungi* is positioned in Bangladesh, where it carries class undertones. What Shahed implies is that as a *bideshi Londoni fua* (UK boy), he should be cognisant of how to carry his class because he has 'made it'. Ann Bridgwood argues that 'men's bodies and dress convey different messages' because 'a man's presence is dependent on the promise of power, whether moral, physical, temperamental, economic, social or sexual, which he embodies'.[77] The perception of the *lungi* as representing 'backwardness' is eloquently illustrated in the poem 'Ode on the lungi' by Kaiser Haq, who writes:

> Hegemony invades private space
> as well: my cousin in America
> would get home from work
> and lounge in a lungi –
> till his son grew ashamed
> of dad and started hiding
> the 'ridiculous ethnic attire'.[78]

This reiterates the point made by Shahed whereby some men who use terms such as 'anti-modern' and 'backwardness' make it difficult for those who would like to wear the *lungi* in public but also hold back for fear of reprisal. Shofiul Alom Pathan and Munmun Jha have presented how the wearing of the *lungi* in the Indian context forms a visual aesthetic of the backward and religiously orthodox Muslim male. They further contend how 'this popular stereotype is usually associated with male bodies as they are more visible in public spaces compared to their female counterparts'.[79] Furthermore, Tarlo shows how the issue of modern versus backwards can be traced to Kolkata, the 'heart of British administration and home of many British residents, [which] became the centre for these composite fashions' during the British Raj.[80] In Kolkata, Bengali men adopted European clothing whilst retaining some aspects of Indian dress, indicating a form of 'hybridity' that nevertheless was enforced in their lives through social coercion. Ania Loomba adds that the 'problem of how to look modern without appearing western and look Indian without appearing "traditional" was a concern to be taken very seriously'.[81]

Interestingly, the discussion vis-à-vis the *funjabi* did not include the role of stigma, since research participants found the attire more acceptable in the public domain. Although the *lungi* was explicitly confined to the home, the *funjabi* had more flexibility in that regard, even though it was still restricted to *jummah* and special occasions, such as Eid. An intriguing point during my research is the mention of a politician from Bangladesh known for wearing the *lungi* everywhere he went. Alom (interviewed in January 2014) and Shamim (interviewed in November 2013) spoke of Maulana Abdul Hamid Khan Bhashani, a religious scholar and political leader in British India and later in East Pakistan.[82] As mentioned in the previous chapter, he was responsible for changing the name of Awami Muslim League to Awami League. Alom shares how Maulana Bhashani wore a *lungi* wherever he went, while Shamim goes into much more detail, relating the story of the peasant leader's influence on his dad's political life:

> My dad used to do something really funny. He used to be very well dressed at home, he would still wear a shirt and a jumper at home, and then he'd wear

a *lungi*. I found it really interesting. My dad, on purpose, he's a very educated man, very well known, and when he saw people wearing *lungi*s much in Brick Lane, he used to walk out in a *lungi*, he didn't care 'cause he never didn't care [didn't ever care]. He used to have this political leader that he was following in Bangladesh – his name was Abdul Hamid Bhashani – my dad was like quite high up in his political party and that guy came to the UK in a *lungi*, boarded the plane, came to the UK in a *lungi* – very similar to what Gandhi did in his *dhoti*, so there was a demonstration, which is 'I am here but I am me and if I am from somewhere else this is a part of it.'

I briefly explored Shamim's relationship with clothes, informed by his dad's political leanings in the introduction. However, in this section, I want to explore the comparison drawn with Gandhi's *dhoti*. Gandhi was famously known for wearing the *dhoti* as a 'sign of India's dire poverty and of the need to improve its wealth through *swadeshi*[83] and a wholesale rejection of European civilisation'.[84] In 1931, Gandhi, wearing his loincloth, arrived in London, 'where he had been invited to participate in the Round Table Conference[;] he argued that it was his duty to the poor that he refused to wear more clothes'.[85] He wore the loincloth 'throughout his stay in Britain, refusing to compromise his dress, even in front of King George V at Buckingham Palace', and it functioned as a symbol, asserting his anti-colonial identity.[86] Much has been written about the political career of Maulana Abdul Hamid Khan Bhashani. However, there is no mention of his *lungi*, which he wore at political rallies and events, as can be seen in the images used by Peter Custers.[87] I would argue that Bhashani was making a statement about bourgeois politics by wearing the *lungi*. As I previously mentioned, to date no male head of state or other senior male politician has been seen wearing the attire for formal state functions.

There are similarities one can draw between Gandhi and Bhashani. For example, Bhashani, in his *lungi* – a distinctive garment worn at the time in East Pakistan that marked one aesthetic difference between East and West Pakistan – fought for self-rule (*swayatshashan*) and to 'be granted to the province', as did Gandhi for India against the British in his *dhoti*.[88] Both men – Gandhi, a lawyer, and Bhashani, a religious scholar – were frequently perceived as saints.[89] Retreating to the *lungi*, Alom raised an insightful point about the everyday clothes he would see men wearing in the 1980s. In fact, when he moved to East London during that decade, he argues, the *lungi* and *funjabi* were not clothes visible on the streets of East London. An extract from the interview below illustrates his points:

Me: When you moved to East London in the eighties, was it visible, women wearing *sari*s in your generation?

Alom: There weren't women there when I came to East London in the eighties. It was all single men and all the men wore clothes that other, I guess white, people were wearing in East London at the time. So they were into flares, bell bottoms, platform shoes. And later on, many of our young men were into fashion, so they would wear Italian clothes, Italian shirts, socks, Farah trousers. Whatever was in fashion, polo shirts and stuff. Yeah, there were no women, really. The only few women that were here would wear the *sari*. There were a few of our parents' generation and they were wearing the *sari*s, yes.

It is interesting to note how flexibility and heterogeneity with clothes are extended to the male body but less so to the female body. Alom suggests that the weather may be a factor informing people's (read: men's) dress choices, causing them to refrain from wearing the *lungi*:

even then I think most Bengali women still wear the *sari*, regardless of how cold it may be. The men don't really wear *funjabi* or the *lungi*, but older women, our parents' generation, our mothers' generation, they still wear the *sari*. They don't wear trousers or shirts or tops and stuff. But I think they wear it because that's what they're used to.

This points to how there were fewer dress options for the Bangladeshi women who were arriving in the 1970s and 1980s. Culture was specifically marked through the woman's body. These women may not have had the ability to 'pick and mix' their self-expressions; however, I would argue that the shift towards a more explicitly religious identification through wearing the *hijab* and *jilbab* was made through this very 'pick and mix' process.[90] In the upcoming chapter, I explore clothing carrying religious connotations in more detail. When discussing the role of the various cultural attires, Jahedur (interviewed in February 2014) maintains that such clothes are acceptable to wear at functions or on special occasions, but that wearing them daily will hinder the community from integrating into society. Jahedur arrived in the UK as a young child, and he explains:

On a daily basis if I see someone wearing a *sari* or a *lungi* I will say this person is fully fresh, he/she is a freshie, because why would you do that?[91] Why would you wear that, putting yourself in the spotlight with people looking at you differently? Back in the eighties it was understandable they were just adjusting, but now you are a part and parcel of the society; if you can't wear trousers and a shirt, there is something not fully on.

As noted in the cited interviews, wearing the *lungi* and *funjabi* carries different meanings and symbolism. For many, the problem of what to wear remains personal. The varying thoughts and opinions reveal the multifaceted approach to clothes. In this instance, circumstances dictate what can be worn in the public sphere to avoid mockery from others, or wearing the *funjabi* to *jummah*, regarded as more acceptable for men while embodying no stigma. Respectability and acceptance from others are essential for many and function as measures for determining choice of clothing, and thus cultural identification.

Interestingly, the *funjabi* was regarded as more of a religious garment than the *lungi*. The interviews I have cited showcase how many attributed religiosity to the *funjabi* because they grew up observing their uncles, fathers, and other male members of their families wearing it to the mosque. However, others located the *funjabi* as a marker of one's ethnicity here in the UK, marking out one's Bengali heritage and having no relation to one's relationship to Islam. Despite some relegating the *funjabi* to the category of non-religious garment, they would still wear it for *jummah*. Navigating the *funjabi* and the *lungi* vis-à-vis religion and culture appears to be much more flexible than the discussions we have seen regarding the *sari* and the *shalwar kameez*. The former, perceived as ethnic clothing, was not once associated with Islam. In contrast, the latter enjoyed more of an association based on the research participants' understanding of how much the body should be covered. As emphasised by Avtah Brah, identification with culture and expressing represent a 'dynamic, and potentially oppositional, force which stands in a complex relationship with the material conditions of society'.[92]

Conclusion

This chapter has outlined how British Bangladeshi Muslim men and women negotiate their sense of identity vis-à-vis dress. It details the aesthetic decisions the research participants took, which depended on their experiences of work and familial environments, as well as environments created by different generations. In so doing, it has pointed to their various attempts to find a 'grounded way' to solve the differences between the different generations and the ways these negotiations are often unstable and a continuous journey. Furthermore, the participants who spent most, if not all, of their lives growing up in the UK negotiated dress through the discourse of appearing 'less' or 'more' Muslim. I argue that such conscious decisions made *qua* religion cannot be divorced from the constraints of hegemonic debates, i.e. the dominant discourse on national identity, integration and the Muslim as the 'other'.

Additionally, Tarlo and Annelies Moors argue that what to wear is 'influenced by popular culture and political contexts, which may be more or less conducive to developments in Islamic fashion'.[93] Clothes have, over time, come to entail different meanings for each research participant I interviewed. Some of the participants formed what could be described as a diasporic identity. This particular expression of identity is realised through the merging of elements, including different forms of dress – sometimes garments that are also hybridised – from both their British and their Bengali heritage. In doing so, the participants can navigate their way through multiple spaces, depending on the social contexts in which they find themselves. In particular, the various approaches taken by many of the research participants illustrate a heterogeneity of intersecting discourses with which they aim to fashion themselves as the constantly 'negotiating generation' for whom Islamic traditions function as the framework for what is deemed as (un)acceptable clothing. According to Christine Jacobsen, this intersection of two contrasting models of the self results in the 'willing submission' of young Muslims to Islamic traditions, which brings about a subjectivity that is 'appropriate to ethical self-determination and aesthetic self-invention … into the field of religious identity and practice'.[94] How the research participants dressed in specific contexts helped solidify the sentiments and feelings of belonging and inclusion, which formed, and continue to form, a crucial part of identity-making.

By interviewing research participants of various age groups and discussing their relationship with clothing, I have sought to emphasise the diverse forms of negotiations employed by British Bangladeshi Muslims. I focused on the private and public spheres and how those particular spaces affect clothing choices. However, I also showcased how East London enables the possibility of producing a counter-culture because the Bangladeshis are a visibly othered community. Particularly poignant was observing how the generation of men who moved to the UK hoping to return 'back home' carried confidence in (re)presenting their bodies informed through an explicit expression of a Bengali Islam. Those participants drew from their migration history, received through oral traditions, which Hamid Dabashi argues affords the Muslim 'the historical agency' needed to access their rich, cosmopolitan history.[95] In contrast to the female participants, they located the *sari* explicitly within the ethnic category, while the *shalwar kameez* was upheld as more in line with religiously sanctioned ideas around modesty.

Notes

1 C. R. Radice, 'Tremendous literary rebel: The life and works of Madhusudan Datta (1824–73)' (PhD dissertation, University of Oxford, 1986), p. 203.
2 See Introduction, n. 5, for a detailed explanation of the different garments.
3 E. Tarlo, *Clothing Matters: Dress and Identity in India* (London: Hurst, 1996), p. 16.
4 Ibid.

5 E. Wilson, *Adorned in Dreams: Fashion and Modernity* (London: Virago, 1987), pp. 2–3.
6 M. Roach-Higgins and J. B. Eicher, 'Dress and identity', *Clothing and Textiles Research Journal* 10 (1992), 1–8 (p. 1).
7 J. B. Eicher and B. Sumberg, 'World fashion, ethnic, and national dress', in J. B. Eicher (ed.), *Dress and Ethnicity: Change across Space and Time* (Oxford: Berg, 1995), pp. 295–306 (p. 300).
8 J. Strübel, 'Get your Gele: Nigerian dress, diasporic identity, and translocalism', *The Journal of Pan African Studies* 4:9 (2012), 24–41 (p. 30).
9 Eicher and Sumberg, 'World fashion, ethnic, and national dress', p. 301.
10 G. D. Berreman, *Hindus of the Himalayas: Ethnography and Change* (Berkeley: University of California Press, 1972), p. 85.
11 Princess Diana and Jemima Goldsmith-Khan wore the *shalwar kameez* in the 1990s and were seen as 'important fashion icons who catalysed the mainstreaming functions', even though the 'actual groundwork of keeping salwar-kameezes vibrant in Britain had been done by migrant women and their daughters'. P. Bhachu, *Dangerous Designs: Asian Women Fashion the Diaspora Economies* (London and New York: Routledge, 2004), p. 29.
12 Ibid. Ibid.Ib, p. 11.
13 Ibid.
14 Ibid.
15 Ibid., p. 54.
16 Ibid.
17 See I. Sheikh, ' "Dress over pants": Rest of the world finally catches on to Shalwar kameez trend', *Tribune*, 27 May 2015.
18 K. Kaur and A. Agrawal, 'Indian saree: A paradigm of global fashion influence', *International Journal of Home Science* 5:2 (2019), 299–306 (p. 300).
19 R. K. Chishti, *Saris: Tradition and Beyond* (Delhi: Roli Books, 2010).
20 A. Sandhu, 'When sarees speak: Saree pacts and social media narratives', *Feminist Theory* 23:3 (2022), 386–406 (p. 393).
21 Ibid.
22 An upper-caste Hindu.
23 Tarlo, *Clothing Matters*, p. 196.
24 N. Hussein, 'Bangladeshi new women's "smart" dressing: Negotiating class, culture, and religion', in N. Hussein (ed.), *Rethinking New Womanhood* (Cham: Palgrave Macmillan, 2018), pp. 97–121.
25 Roach-Higgins and Eicher, 'Dress and identity', p. 5.
26 E. Goffman, *Stigma: Notes on a Spoiled Identity* (Englewood Cliffs, NJ: Prentice Hall, 1963).
27 Tarlo, *Clothing Matters*, pp. 185–186.
28 Ibid., p. 110.
29 Ibid., p. 117.
30 V. Redclift, *Statelessness and Citizenship: Camps and the Creation of Political Space* (London: Routledge, 2013), p. 149.

31 S. Hall, 'Introduction: Who needs "identity"?', in S. Hall and P. Du Gay (eds), *Questions of Cultural Identity* (London: Sage Publications, 1996), pp. 1–17 (p. 4).
32 G. Baumann, *Contesting Culture: Discourses of Identity in Multi-Ethnic London* (Cambridge: Cambridge University Press, 1996), p. 157.
33 S. Hall, ' Cultural identity and diaspora', in J. Rutherford (ed.), *Identity: Community, Culture, Difference* (London: Lawrence and Wishart, 1990), pp. 222–237 (p. 225).
34 R. Brubaker and F. Cooper, 'Beyond "identity"', *Theory and Society* 29:1 (2000), 1–47 (p. 17).
35 R. Dwyer, 'The erotics of the wet sari in Hindi films', *South Asia: Journal of South Asian Studies* 23:2 (2000), 143–160 (p. 150).
36 B. S. Cohn, *Colonialism and Its Forms of Knowledge: The British in India* (Princeton: Princeton University Press, 1996), p. 137.
37 F. Sheth, 'The hijab and the sari: The strange and the sexy between colonialism and global capitalism', *Contemporary Aesthetics* 2 (2009), 1–20.
38 Ibid., p. 11.
39 Tarlo, *Clothing Matters*, p. 46.
40 J. Devika, 'The aesthetic woman: Re-forming female bodies and minds in early twentieth-century Keralam', *Modern Asian Studies* 3:2 (2005), 461–487 (p. 479).
41 Sheth, 'The hijab and the sari', p. 15.
42 Dwyer, 'The erotics of the wet sari in Hindi films', p. 144.
43 Ibid., p. 146.
44 A. Hoque, 'Generation terrorised: Muslim youth, being British and not so British' (PhD dissertation, SOAS, University of London, 2011), p. 48.
45 Dwyer, 'The erotics of the wet sari in Hindi films', p. 148.
46 R. Boswell, 'Say what you like: Dress, identity and heritage in Zanzibar', *International Journal of Heritage Studies* 12:5 (2006), 440–457 (p. 444).
47 E. Tarlo, *Visibly Muslim: Fashion, Politics, Faith* (Oxford and New York: Berg, 2010), p. 35.
48 Cf. S. Hirsch, *In the Shadow of Enoch Powell: Race, Locality and Resistance* (Manchester: Manchester University Press, 2018), to look at cases involving Sikh men who suffered dismissal from work for refusing to cut their beards or remove their turbans.
49 Tarlo, *Visibly Muslim*, p. 104.
50 House of Lords, 'Opinions of the Lords of Appeal for judgment in the cause: R (on the application of Begum (by her litigation friend, Rahman)) (Respondent) *v*. Headteacher and Governors of Denbigh High School (Appellants). Appellate Committee', Session 2005–06 [2006] UKHL 15, www.publications.parliament.uk/pa/ld200506/ldjudgmt/jd060322/begum.pdf (accessed 20 May 2023), p. 3.
51 Tarlo, *Visibly Muslim*, p. 104.
52 House of Lords, 'Opinions of the Lords of Appeal', p. 31.
53 Ibid., p. 2.
54 Tarlo, *Visibly Muslim*, p. 104.
55 Ibid.

56 Ibid., p. 122.
57 *Chador*, on the Indian subcontinent, refers to a large piece of scarf that covers the bulk of the upper body.
58 Brubaker and Cooper, 'Beyond "identity"', p. 7.
59 Hall, ' Cultural identity and diaspora', p. 225.
60 V. Redclift, F. Rajina and N. Rashid, 'The burden of conviviality: British Bangladeshi Muslims navigating diversity in London, Luton and Birmingham', *Sociology* 56:6 (2022), 1159–1175.
61 Dwyer, 'The erotics of the wet sari in Hindi films', p. 147.
62 Ibid.
63 J. Entwistle, *The Fashioned Body: Fashion, Dress and Social Theory* (Cambridge: Polity Press, 2015), p. 56.
64 Hussein, 'Bangladeshi new women's "smart" dressing'.
65 R. Dwyer and D. Patel, *Cinema India: The Visual Culture of Hindi Film* (New Brunswick: Rutgers University Press, 2002), p. 87.
66 Tarlo, *Visibly Muslim*, p. 52.
67 Ibid.
68 S. Ullah, '*Ode on the Lungi*: Kaiser Haq's portrayal of "the subaltern speaking"', *Erothanatos: A Peer-Reviewed Quarterly Journal on Literature* 2:4 (2018), 77–87, www.erothanatos.com/_files/ugd/3e169b_92e7b90f9bd14517836a5ad26012f0bb.pdf?index=true (accessed 3 April 2024).
69 Cohn, *Colonialism and Its Forms of Knowledge*, pp. 129–130.
70 Goffman, *Stigma*.
71 S. Begum, *From Sylhet to Spitalfields: Bengali Squatters in 1970s East London* (London: Lawrence and Wishart, 2023), p. 17.
72 M. R. Khan and K. Sharma, 'Purchase preferences and buying influences on religious occasions', *FIIB Business Review* 9:3 (2020), 216–227 (p. 224).
73 J. Entwistle, 'Fashion and the fleshy body: Dress as embodied practice', *Fashion Theory: The Journal of Dress, Body & Culture* 4:3 (2000), 323–347 (p. 339).
74 Goffman, *Stigma*.
75 C. Turbin, 'Refashioning the concept of public/private: Lessons from dress studies', *Journal of Women's History* 15:1 (2003), 43–51 (p. 45).
76 Goffman, *Stigma*.
77 A. Bridgwood, 'Dancing the jar: Girls' dress at Turkish Cypriot weddings', in Eicher, *Dress and Ethnicity*, pp. 29–52 (p. 43).
78 K. Haq, 'Ode on the lungi', *Asiatic: IIUM Journal of English Language and Literature* 2:2 (2008), 139–144 (p. 141).
79 S. A. Pathan and M. Jha, 'Miya Muslims of Assam: Identity, visuality and the construction of "doubtful citizens"', *Journal of Muslim Minority Affairs* 42:1 (2022), 150–159 (p. 154).
80 Tarlo, *Clothing Matters*, pp. 49–50.
81 A. Loomba, 'The long and saggy sari', *Women: A Cultural Review* 8:3 (1997), 278–292 (p. 279).
82 See P. Custers, 'Maulana Bhashani and the transition to secular politics in East Bengal', *The Indian Economic and Social History Review* 47:2 (2010), 231–259.

83 The Swadeshi (Indian-made) Movement became a significant movement against the British in order to restore the decline of the Indian economy. Furthermore, in Bengal, 'the call to *swadeshi* was most vigorously propounded from 1905 to 1910, following Lord Curzon's announcement of his intended partition of Bengal; there it was not merely an economic revival but a political protest and national ideal'. The Swadeshi Movement surfaced in the Bengal because 'some of the earliest attempts to redefine Indian dress emerged in Calcutta' (Tarlo, *Clothing Matters*, pp. 11, 58).
84 Ibid., p. 75.
85 Ibid.
86 Ibid., p. 76.
87 Custers, 'Maulana Bhashani and the transition to secular politics in East Bengal'.
88 Ibid., p. 241.
89 For Gandhi, see Tarlo, *Clothing Matters*, p. 78; and for Bhashani, see Custers, 'Maulana Bhashani and the transition to secular politics in East Bengal', p. 253. See also S. Basu, *Intimation of Revolution: Global Sixties and the Making of Bangladesh* (Cambridge: Cambridge University Press, 2023); and L. Uddin, 'In the land of eternal Eid: Maulana Bhashani and the political mobilisation of peasants and lower-class urban workers in East Pakistan, c. 1930s–1971' (PhD dissertation, Royal Holloway, University of London, 2016).
90 See Stuart Hall, 'Cultural identity and diaspora', in P. Williams and L. Chrisman (eds), *Colonial Discourse and Post Colonial Theory: A Reader* (New York and London: Harvester Wheatsheaf, 1993).
91 'Freshie' is a term used by South Asians to refer to an immigrant to the UK from the Indian subcontinent. This person tends to have a 'funny' accent or does not speak English very well.
92 A. Brah, 'Women of South Asian origin in Britain: Issues and concerns', *South Asia Research* 7:1 (1987), 39–54 (p. 44).
93 E. Tarlo and A. Moors, *Islamic Fashion and Anti-Fashion: New Perspectives from Europe and North America* (London: Bloomsbury, 2013), p. 2.
94 C. Jacobsen, *Islamic Traditions and Muslim Youth in Norway* (Leiden: Brill, 2011), p. 359.
95 H. Dabashi, *Being a Muslim in the World* (Basingstoke: Palgrave Macmillan, 2013), p. 5.

3

Visibly Muslim: The aesthetic choices

As more and more Bengalis have settled in the Whitechapel area of East London, markers of Jewishness once common in the area have virtually disappeared to be replaced by clothing repertoires associated with Bangladesh and Islam: *sari*s, *shalwar kamiz*es, *hijab*s, *jilbab*s, shawls and *niqab*s for women; beards and *kurta*s, particularly for older-generation Bengali men.[1]

In recent years, much of the focus on Muslims and clothing has been primarily on Muslim women and their clothing, particularly questions related to the *hijab* (the headscarf) in various European countries, most notoriously/prominently in France, where it has been banned in public institutions.[2] Many discussions pertaining to Muslims in Europe have thus far involved the role of the geopolitics of West Asia, the revival of Islam, and the need to preserve secularism and whiteness, since a lot of discourse, especially from the far right, positions the Muslim as changing the demographic makeup of Europe. Thus, excluding religious symbols from the public sphere in countries such as France furthers this anxiety that Muslims are challenging secularism and whiteness. My research delves into and draws from the participants' views, interpretations and experiences of religious clothes. This section of the chapter will not look into the theological point of view, since the study uses ethnographic methods to discuss religious clothing. Thus, I will be relying on the discursive experiences of the research participants to gauge their identification with the different pieces of clothing. This will enable access to various frameworks and perspectives, engaging with the individual's relationship with religious clothes and considering how broader socio-political discourses and their influence on communities shape such decisions. The discussion in this chapter will consider the ways in which Bangladeshi Muslim men and women frame the boundaries around religious clothing, looking at the *hijab*, *jilbab*, *thobe*, *niqab* and the growing of the beard. A critical intervention will include elaboration upon the distinctions created to juxtapose culture and religion by engaging with how the *hijab* is conceptualised via the *dupatta/uruna* (the scarf that accompanies the *shalwar kameez*).

One of the focal points will consist of the narrative surrounding (what are perceived to be) male religious clothes, shifting the focus away from the already existing gaze on the woman's body. I interviewed thirteen women, three of whom did not wear the *hijab*, while one wore the *niqab*. Three of the women I interviewed were in their homes, so did not wear the *hijab* in my presence but wore it for their day-to-day activities outside the home. I outlined in the introduction why I struggled to recruit more female participants. Out of the thirty men I interviewed, most had a beard, but the length varied, and most wore trousers with shirts or T-shirts, not one of them wearing the *funjabi*, *lungi* or *thobe*. Before commencing the fieldwork, I avoided paying too much attention to the *hijab* for female participants only. I left the question regarding it as open as possible for the research participants to provide their understandings and conceptualisations. As a result of the attacks on the World Trade Centre in 2001 and the attacks in London in 2005, there has been a growing interest in the Muslim woman and her body, with a specific focus on the *hijab*. As a consequence, there have been numerous studies on the *hijab* and how it functions as a marker of a woman's religiosity or her oppression.[3] The latter argument, along with the perception that the *hijab* defies the premise of secularism, has been used to justify the banning of it.

The debates pertaining to secularism and the *hijab* resulted in the first ban in Europe, implemented in France. The French government banned wearing the *hijab* in state schools in 2004[4] and, in 2010, prohibited the public wearing of the face veil, known as the *niqab*,[5] the ban coming into effect in April 2011. In the summer of 2023, the French government also banned wearing the *abaya* for Muslim girls in school.[6] Consequently, other European governments were inspired 'to follow suit in what is fast becoming a consolidation of sides in a clash between "Islam" and "the West" '.[7] The other countries that banned the *niqab* entirely are: Latvia (2016),[8] Bulgaria (2016),[9] Austria (2017),[10] Denmark (2018)[11] and Switzerland (2021).[12] The conflation of the *hijab* with women's oppression and lack of freedom, argues Emma Tarlo, is 'informed by a long legacy of Orientalist images and texts, integrated within the canons of Western art history, literature and colonial writings'.[13] In such depictions, women were portrayed as 'passive, exotic, oppressed and sensually alluring figures in need of protection and liberation – discourses which justified imperialist interventions and contributed to the building of long-lasting stereotypes'.[14]

The case of France's banning of the *hijab* and, a few years later, the *niqab*, is a situation that one can trace back to France's presence in and colonisation of Algeria. Frantz Fanon, in his essay 'Algeria unveiled', discusses how the female body represented and became a privileged signifier of culture:

> [F]or the tourist and the foreigner, the veil demarcates both Algerian society and its feminine component … The masculine garb allows a certain margin of

choice, a modicum of heterogeneity. The woman seen in her white veil unifies the perception that one has of Algerian feminine society. Obviously what we have here is a uniform which tolerates no modification, no variant ... The Algerian woman, in the eyes of the observer, is unmistakably 'she who hides behind a veil'.[15]

Fanon elaborates how 'this veil, one of the elements of the traditional Algerian garb, was to become the bone of contention in a grandiose battle, on account of which the occupation forces were to mobilise their most powerful and most varied resources, and in the course of which the colonised were to display a surprising force of inertia'.[16] The female body functioned as a domain for the negotiation and battle to drive the colonisers out of Algeria. For the colonisers, the veil justified their presence in order to civilise the Algerians. This pushes the woman to the periphery and silences her, while she is required to fulfil the roles set by the coloniser or those fighting the colonisers. However, this highlights that, to discuss clothes, we need to steer away from relegating the wearing of religious dress to 'the maintenance of religious boundaries and the reproduction of tradition'.[17] This particular reading is essential because it helps expose the messiness, and that religious boundaries are constantly reorienting to the demands of contemporary fissures. An example of this is how the *dupatta*, associated with Muslims and other non-Muslim South Asian communities, operates as a marker of respectability. However, this is not translated in the same way by Bangladeshi Muslims in the diaspora. Instead, it is useful to consider the representational aspect of wearing particular clothing items while recognising its limited framework and how the participants conceptualise the clothes that they should wear vis-à-vis the performance of their religious identities. Daniel Miller reminds us that clothing is not simply 'a form of representation, a semiotic sign or symbol of the person [but] plays a considerable and active part in constituting the particular experience of the self'.[18] In other words, while there is an oscillation between representation and attempting to create religious boundaries and traditions, at its core is how participants *relay* how they work through those elements.

Hijab, culture and religion

I met with Sohaib (interviewed in January 2014) in the Pie Factory opposite East London Mosque one afternoon, and when I asked him what *hijab* means to him, this is what he expressed:

> The *hijab* simply means a division between, sort of, if I'm standing here and someone's standing there and there's a barrier between us, that barrier's called a *hijab*, and what that barrier represents is, really, a level of decency in society,

as opposed to, it's, it's more of a state of mind first – though I don't mean to say that you can only have *hijab* in your mind and not in the outward sense. I think both, both are part of religion, but I think the emphasis happens to be on *hijab* in the outward sense, so a person could be fully covered legally but in their behaviour and what they do, they may not be practising *hijab* because they may be acting inappropriately towards the opposite sex and I've even seen girls covered, sitting on a guy's lap, you know, very bizarre, a bizarre scene, and so, you know, it may be possible for a person who's not wearing the *hijab* attire to actually be practising more *hijab* than a person who is. It's possible, I'm not saying that *hijab* as a dress is not important, that's not what I'm saying, what I'm saying is, I'm saying that I'm not saying that *hijab* is only in your heart, 'cause a lot of people say, *hijab* is in my heart, doesn't matter what I wear, so I can wear what I want, no that's also not true, but both need to be in conformity with, with Islam, Islamic principles, and it's important to understand *hijab* in a holistic sense.

Sohaib's emphasis on the *hijab* and its framing as both an external and an internal practice is a theme I encountered during the fieldwork. The centrality of the *hijab* within both the public and private spheres suggests that a specific framework is employed. It acts in ways such that, in public, the Muslim woman becomes a visible representative of the faith, at times requiring interventions in countering assumptions and preconceived ideas about Islam and Muslims.[19] Meanwhile, in the private sphere, it is linked to respectability tied to the broader Muslim community.

The importance of the religious narrative in situating oneself in the current, specific relational setting transpires from Sohaib's analysis of the *hijab*. Therefore, religious narratives lay the foundation for situating oneself and how a Muslim ought to act within the social sphere. This religious narrative is divided between, on the one hand, what is perceived to be essential in preserving one's religious identity and, on the other hand, what is considered an option. According to Sohaib, Muslims' identification with their faith is constituted through this duality. However, as argued by Rogers Brubaker and Frederick Cooper, 'social life is indeed pervasively "storied": but it is not clear why this "storiedness" should be axiomatically linked to identity'.[20] In the identifying constructions for Bangladeshi Muslims, this chapter argues that the need to revisit one's religious history and reify it into praxis allows individuals to assert their present identity. However, the dangers appear when the interpretations of religious history and narratives are projected as homogeneous, thus ruling out the possibility of re-engaging one's past to make discoveries. Such tensions arise when observed through the binary of culture versus religion, using the latter to create a 'pure' religious framework. To situate Sohaib's considerations, he emphasises his personal boundaries and sense of religious self by reflecting upon his religious teachings but also recognising the importance of culture. He notes that the cultural element is dictated by religion; thus, juxtaposing them as entirely separate entities would be flawed and limit the scope of understanding of people's ever-changing relationship with clothing items.

On the other hand, Shaju (interviewed in December 2014) specifically discussed clothes in the context of prayer rather than as garments to be worn daily to project a religious identity. He stated:

> I wouldn't wear something which would compromise my prayers, for example. If it's a summer's day I would make sure my knees are covered because when you pray of course you have to cover certain areas of your body. It's different, of course, for men and women, so I need to fulfil these prerequisites. But Muslims are encouraged to be moderate in the way they dress.

When asked about the role of religious clothing for women, he offered his sympathy for women who may be reluctant to wear the *hijab*. He recognises the current political climate and the fear women carry when considering becoming 'visible Muslims'. Shaju's sympathy and cultural consciousness for Muslim women is undeniably linked to the heightened focus on the British Muslim community. This consciousness is predicated on political questions about Muslims and their place in society, particularly after a terrorist attack. That is not to negate the role of the media with its constant, daily focus on the Muslim community; however, after an attack, the community faces an additional layer of questioning. Indeed, British Muslim women are reported as the primary victims of Islamophobic attacks following a terror-related incident.[21] Chris Allen argues that the 'ideological component' of Islamophobia is informed by the media, 'reinforced through messages and meanings from the social, political and cultural spaces ... [which] all have the potential to contribute to the process of stigmatisation, marginalisation and intolerance'.[22] This heightened awareness of one's religious identifications is stressed via the dominant political discourse, and its emphasis upon 'Islamic fundamentalism' has contributed to the formation of a Muslim consciousness.[23] This consciousness is tied to Muslim women, who are more easily identified as Muslim in public than Muslim men. In that sense, the hegemonic discourses dictate the relational power Muslims build and contend with because it is within this domain that they can access power and place demands for the Muslim community.

A trend Shaju has noticed in the Bengali community is the requirement for women to wear the *hijab* after getting married: 'definitely in the Bengali community, some new brides come into the family and they're now sort of expected to wear it because now you're a wife. And if you don't cover the full thing you should at least cover. To an extent they don't cover it in that scenario because of religious reasons.' Shaju did not elaborate on why he thought this form of covering was required after marriage but noted that it was not for religious reasons. This new change and shift following marriage significantly differs from what was discussed in the previous chapter, where the newly-wed woman was required to wear the s*ari* to indicate her married status. The married woman was also expected to wear the *anchal/asol*, the end of the *sari*, over her head, adding another layer to mark her married status and thereby establishing respectability. It could be argued that wearing the *hijab* after marriage, as suggested by Shaju, could be related to this old cultural tradition but is now expressed differently. Shaju acknowledges that religious preferences have permeated discussions around marriage suitability and acceptability. This 'interruption' in demarcating a woman's status stems from 'the dislocating rupture of the look from the place of the Other'.[24] In this context, this 'other' is the gaze held by fellow Bangladeshis who enforce a religious consciousness by defining one's religiosity through the woman's body, thus gaining social acceptance. Farhana (interviewed in August 2014), whom I interviewed for the second time at her house, is an atheist and does not wear the *hijab*. She pointed out that the *hijab* is 'not just about communicating religiosity to non-Muslims but also to other Muslims', and that it is also a sign of 'availability – signalling to those within their own community'. She argues that this is done to indicate women's readiness for marriage. The *hijab*, it seems, is treated not only as a religious garment for women but also as a form of embodiment that seeks to project spatial boundaries. The boundaries signal that:

> a woman's body and hair are off-limits to men and that she expects to be treated with a certain degree of distance and respect. In other words, through visibly indicating that she is to some degree concerned with issues of modesty, privacy and piety, a woman hopes to control or modify the way others interact with her as well as imposing constraints on her own behaviour.[25]

Dr Fahima, on the other hand, provided a lengthy response when asked about the role of clothes in order to express a religious identity:

> I think it's not just about wearing *hijab* or whatever, and it applies to men just as much as it applies to women, which a lot of people forget. But saying that, how you dress is your outer manifestation of your religion but it doesn't say anything about your religious beliefs, how strong your faith is ... so to me that's between the person and Allah, it's not for somebody to judge externally, so obviously I think girls are more comfortable wearing *hijab*, *jilbab* claiming their religious identity, but you can wear *hijab*, or any kind of *jilbab* and still not have any kind of faith ... I started to wear *hijab* when I moved to university, but that's because I thought it was the right time for me. It's not something my parents put me into, or you know, said that we should ... whereas my youngest sister, she started wearing *hijab* when she went to secondary school; none of my sisters did, but she felt she wanted to ... so it really has to come from you, for you to feel comfortable when doing it, when the right time is to you to change ... we're all dressed in a very western way.

In the above statement, the context for Dr Fahima's choosing the *hijab* at a later stage in her life compared to her sister is significant. This further demonstrates the emergence of an Islamic identity and how many Bangladeshis align themselves with it. Interestingly, many of Justin Gest's interviewees described their embrace of Islam as a reaction against their rejected Britishness.[26] However, the research participants for this book do not speak about embracing an Islamic identity as a rejection of another identification. Instead, they see it as an addition to their already multiple identities; however, the Islamic one is prioritised and becomes the dominant identity that dictates the others. Islam's presence in the dominant discourse, i.e. in the media and government policies, has influenced how it is consumed and prioritised within the locality of East London, thus creating what Gerd Baumann refers to as the 'dual discursive competence'.[27] Baumann further notes that embracing the dominant narrative and engaging with it 'emphasises the conservation of existing communities', while on the ground at a micro level the discourse allows a community to 're-conceive community boundaries and contest the meaning of culture'.[28] This new collective identity marginalises the heritage of being Bengali and proceeds to construct new cultural commonalities that override ethnic distinctions – something, I would argue, that is a more common occurrence in the diaspora. Dr Fahima's last point, that her family dress 'in a very western way', is relevant. All the women I interviewed, apart from one research participant in the *niqab*, with her long black *jilbab* and black *hijab*, wore trousers or jeans with long tops or dresses during the interviews.

Shefali (interviewed in May 2014) and I sat in a café just outside Aldgate East station after work. She sat down and took off her work lanyard. She wore a cream *hijab*, and she greeted the owner of the café, as he was a family friend. When we started the interview and reached the questions on religious clothes, Shefali thought carefully and started her response with a focus on the *hijab*:

> Well, I think *hijab*, as a concept, it's, you know, it refers to the idea of modesty, and I think, again, it's very, it's very blasé I guess, to some degree, to say this, but, you know, I think it is a matter of how it translates, individual to individual, in terms of what modesty is. I'm just like this; it's … I feel that it's considered quite modest … in some circles or in some environments where the majority of the people in that area are covered head to toe and are wearing a different kind of clothing, it could be deemed immodest. Like if I wore this in Saudi Arabia, in the actual Makkah area, you know, I don't, I think it's completely *halal*, but I could see where I could see that it might be perceived as something else. I think there, it's not a question of, you know, that's not religious – I think it's a question of respecting cultures, you know, situations, that kind of stuff.

Shefali was born and brought up in Tower Hamlets – something she raised early in the interview. It is significant to note here that being in the borough with a sizeable Muslim demographic facilitates ease for Muslims. The room to practise one's faith whilst feeling safe was prioritised. Shabna Begum, who traces the history of the Bengali squatters in 1970s East London, argues that for 'Bengali migrants, home extended to zones outside of the physical space, which in Sylhet is known as *para*'.[29] This particular spatialising of Tower Hamlets helps avoid outsiders' judgement while still contesting religious boundaries. Shefali spoke earnestly about clothing and whether it informed her relationship with God. She answered with a surprised tone and mentioned that she used to wear the *burqa* (which in the Indian subcontinent refers to the *jilbab*, a long gown/dress that excludes the *niqab* – the face covering) and elaborated:

> I used to feel that that was a religious ... not, not the *burqa* itself but the idea of wearing something that's long and flowy and whatever and I used to feel: ah, d'you know, this used to do the job and it's quite convenient. And when I used to go to – predominantly in Muslim circles, that was the expectation, so generally you do feel a slight inclination to it being more religious, just because the practice, where you, you know ... your religion in mosques, for example, you see it a lot, you make that assumption that, yeah, there is a relation there, when you're going to the mosque, when I go to the mosque, I see everybody in *burqa*s, when I go to school or when I go to a social function everyone's dressed differently or whatever, so there is that.

Shefali elaborates on how she felt socially obliged to wear *burqa*s in order to fit in. In this instance, her identification with her faith applies to Brubaker and Cooper's notion of 'groupness', which captures the degree to which individuals identify with a group and their collective expression.[30] The social imperative to dress as the majority is not unusual. Shefali felt that other group members shared the same meanings of how to identify with one's faith, and she adopted this without contesting it. However, as illustrated in the quote below, she does contest the varying weight given to particular attires:

> But, and even – yeah, like even the other day I wore a complete *abaya* ... I went to this house and everybody was, like, you know, and I felt like I had wear it, or, just to kind of like, they were all very, very, sort of, religious, kind of, and I wore a long *abaya*, and I remember saying, oh, I feel so religious! And it was a funny comment because it's exactly what you say. And I think I say that it is just because of how I've seen it, kind of thing. But I don't think it is. I don't think that you wearing certain clothing makes you feel more religious; I think ... I've constructed it in my head. ... I feel equally religious when I'm sat with a group of friends and we're talking about Allah and you get that spiritual energy, and I did that wearing my coat, so ... you know, we do create these

constructs before ourselves because of what we see and what we experience and what we've envisaged, but I think it's helpful to take a perspective on it that these are the reasons for that, that's it not directly related, as you probably sort of subconsciously lead yourself to believe. But no, I don't think there is.

Shefali here explored the different meanings and resonance of religious dress, exposing its articulation very differently in different spaces and suggesting how one needs to pay attention to context. However, despite the emphasis on context, Shefali expressed how it is not the 'religious dress' that helps foster a relationship with God. Instead, in this schema, there is a focus on centralising and conceiving faith through the self. Although any form of dress indeed carries a construct around what it symbolises, the *burqa*, while continuously negotiating its place vis-à-vis political structures, carries a religious meaning for Muslims via its historical attachment to the Gulf. Much like the *thobe*, the *burqa* is similar in that it is projected as a garment to represent a unified Islamic identity. Additionally, although not about the *burqa*, Nilüfer Göle argues, drawing on the work of Erving Goffman, that young Muslim women in Europe and the West adopt the *hijab* to claim the stigma identity, shifting its meaning to that of sacredness and desire.[31] This can plausibly be extracted and applied to the *burqa*, functioning as a way to subvert. Still, in the context of wearing it among other Muslims, it can also operate as a way of experiencing double-surveillance. First, the panopticon surveillance of the state conceives the Muslim woman as both dangerous and in need of saving simultaneously.[32] In contrast to that of the state, the second form of surveillance binds the Muslim woman to the unruly and contested norms of what constitutes a good Muslim woman, according to the Muslim community. Asserting the duality of this surveillance means not equating both forms as equal but rather emphasising how they simultaneously play a role in shifting the Muslim woman's daily encounters. As such, this double surveillance sheds light on the utopian approaches to ground the Muslim woman. Using Shefali as an example, even while seeking to defy both logics in some capacity – the state and fellow Muslims' surveillance – understanding her faith through her own negotiations is vital.

Fashion and modesty: Negotiating the *hijab* and *dupatta/uruna*

Modesty was a running theme while discussing religious clothing practices. Much like the earlier discussion on the *shalwar kameez* and its (re) configurations using modesty as the parameter, a similar discussion ensued concerning religious garments, or, put differently, the garments that participants perceived as meeting the religiously sanctioned requirements around modesty. One particular individual I interviewed argued that modesty could be practised in other ways and does not require one to wear the *hijab*, the headscarf. Nafisah (interviewed in May 2014) states:

> I don't wear a scarf [referring to the headscarf] because I believe you can be modest without wearing a scarf. And it actually makes me more upset because, when you are in Tower Hamlets, I've seen a lot of girls wearing their *hijab*s, like with hot pants, and I've seen it with boob tubes, regularly. This is not Islam, it makes us look worse, to recognise Muslims.

Two substantial issues arise from the quote. First, interestingly, even though Nafisah does not wear the *hijab*, there was still an expectation of women/ girls who do not wear the *hijab* to follow a dress code that will represent Muslims better and not 'make us look worse'. Second, the Muslim must always reinscribe their religion in public because of a need for immediate recognition. Consequently, this places the burden of representation on Muslim women, who, despite being the primary victims of Islamophobic hate-crime following an attack, are also tasked with ensuring Muslimness is projected accurately. During the conversation, Nafisah mentioned that she works in East London in mental health, and that most of her patients are local Bangladeshis. This is a notable point, as the fixation on representation is regurgitated for the Muslim gaze, producing a code through which women are surveilled. Nafisah's point regarding how the *hijab* is worn, not always fulfilling religious boundaries around modesty, was also articulated by Nasima. Nasima arrived as a young girl in Tower Hamlets and grew up in the borough until she recently left the area and moved closer to Ilford. She explained to me how, in Tower Hamlets:

> [The] *hijab* is not a religious thing anymore, it's just more of a fashion statement ... whereas I see girls wearing like, I don't know, another head on themselves, they have got humps on, and I'm thinking just 'why?'. I can justify myself, but I don't know how to explain to somebody who is a non-Muslim. It's within myself I suppose ... Islam is everybody's *jihad* within themselves, Islam is about finding oneself and fighting for your own 'cause I feel that everybody has to justify their own actions, not somebody else's.

Whilst recognising the struggles that people, especially young(er) women, may have with wearing the *hijab*, there is also an awareness that it is necessary to consider others, in this instance non-Muslims. The burden of conviviality thus falls on the Muslim woman, reinstating what I have described as double surveillance.[33] Nasima further expresses how her relationship with Islam differed vastly from her mother's, wherein she adopted the *hijab* while her mother did not. She expands:

> Hence why I do find girls wear the *hijab* whereas they've got short dresses on with very short, tight leggings, or no sleeves on, some of them have got their

belly button showing, they got their back showing ... Yet they feel as long as they've got *hijab* on, and it covers their hair, to them that's Islamic ... whereas to me that's confusion. That doesn't mean anything – that means you're following a trend and you need to be accepted because you've got your *hijab* on.

Nasima and Nafisah's approach to understanding the *hijab* and what it should be worn with is something Tarlo notes in her article 'Hijab in London: Metamorphosis, resonance and effects': 'young women do in fact police each other's dress to a considerable degree, exploring the boundaries of what is or is not acceptable in *hijab*. Those who expose their necks or leave hair visible often become targets of censure.'[34] Also, in Nasima's case, the cumulative impact of not having learned or been taught about the *hijab* in the 'correct manner' by her mother activated a conscientious attempt and effort to redefine her religious identity towards a personally reconfigured Islam, away from her parents' understanding. Another notable comparison is how Nasima, Shefali and Nafisah seek to affirm their religious identity above others. Central here is the understanding of how a Muslim consciousness is deployed as a way to frame their experience of the world.[35] The self-ascribed categorisation and identification, as well as the various influences at play, are crucial to point out here. As rightfully argued by Brubaker and Cooper, using 'identity' as an analytical category is not sufficient.[36] Rather, 'identity' needs to be explored as a verb, since, otherwise, it can imply everything or nothing at all, providing only a superfluous demonstration of sameness or difference.

Moreover, Nasima showcases how, while her mother failed to address religion appropriately with her, Nasima is keen to rectify this with her own daughter. She states how she is attempting to 'instill it in my daughter, but then, Tasneem is trying to find herself at the moment'. She elaborates on how she would like her daughter to wear the *hijab* one day. However, in the meantime, Nasima alludes to religious boundaries around modesty that she expects her daughter to abide by daily. Furthermore, with the proliferation of religious material available online in English, accessing religious knowledge is no longer confined to children learning from their parents.

Another factor to consider when discussing the *hijab* is its overlap with the *dupatta* (the scarf that comes with the *shalwar kameez*) and/or the *anchal* (the end part of the *sari*). Pnina Werbner explains that 'the *dupatta* is embedded in and embodies the female code of honour in subtle and nuanced ways'.[37] But can this be applied to the *hijab*? While writing about dress among South Asians in Britain, Claire Dwyer stated that the *dupatta* is 'a powerful and overdetermined marker of difference, an essentialised symbol of a "traditional" identity associated with being South Asian or Muslim'.[38] While the *dupatta* is aligned with social mores and contingencies not too dissimilar to the *hijab*, as showcased in the above discussion, the *dupatta* does not hold the exact same religious weighting as a scarf wrapped around the head and carefully pinned. The *dupatta* on the head, without any assistance from pins or clips, tends to expose a partial amount of hair. Alom (interviewed in January 2014) moved to the UK as a young child, stated how his mother 'wore *sari* all her life, never wore anything else, and prayed five times a day and was very religious. Our mums don't change their clothes when they pray. If anything, they cover their head with the end of the *sari*. But they didn't change their clothing when it came to praying *namaz*.[39] So is *sari* Islamic clothing or a Bengali clothing?'.

Alom invests in the idea that definitions of modesty vary and ought to be decided by the individual. He further notes that the *hijab* is a very '*British* [my emphasis] thing, and therefore it's [more] to do with our young people here than with our parents' generation. So you'll find the difference between what the young people are wearing and what our parents' generations wear. *Hijab* is, in fact, alien to Bengali, the whole [of] South Asia in fact, for that matter.' However, Alom recognises and acknowledges that the Bangladeshis born and raised in the UK have adopted a (re)configuration of their faith and what constitutes 'Islamic dress'. Herein, he further expands how around Brick Lane, parents from his generation continue to wear the *shalwar kameez* and have the *dupatta* on their heads. In contrast, the daughters are wearing the *hijab*, perfectly pinned. When I probe him further about how he thinks South Asian Muslims understand and conceptualise modesty, he discloses:

> When it comes to praying or religious practices, when you hear the *adhan* you quickly pull the *anchal*, the end of the *sari*, to cover your head. If you're wearing one of the *dupatta*, you use that to cover your head. And for men, when we used to go to mosque, we would wear our *toki*, our inner hat. That's it, really. Other times we don't wear them.[40]

Although Alom conceptualises modesty in heterogeneous ways, including the *dupatta* and the *anchal/asol*, this is not necessarily translated into the wider Muslim community. Despite the *dupatta*'s 'association with tradition', the *hijab* in Britain, just as in the rest of the Muslim world, expresses a 'new' identity, part of a deterritorialised global movement. Dwyer argues that identity is not necessarily, however, '"fundamentalist", "Islamist" or radical, since its meaning and the politics of embodiment it represents may differ widely in different contexts and even from individual to individual'.[41] Nevertheless, Dwyer makes the argument that the *dupatta* can also function as a marker of a South Asian's Muslimness,[42] though this is refuted by Nasima, who perceives the wearing of the *dupatta* not as a religious act but as an act that embodies respect towards one's elders and nothing more:

> When I was growing up, there was a handful of people, maybe, who would wear a *dupatta* on their head. It wasn't a full *hijab* like it is now. We didn't even know it was called *hijab* then, it was just a scarf you put on your head. You put it on, and that was it. Especially if you saw an elderly man or someone who was older than you, that's how you show that respect … it wasn't because [of] a God fearing thing that we do now.

The emphasis on the performative power of dress is striking because the *dupatta*, if placed on the head, is not seen as sufficiently 'Islamic'. The reference to the 'full *hijab* like it is now' implies that the actual covering of the head provides the ability to fear God, as covering 'works as a technique of the self, as a bodily act that serves not only as a marker of piety but also as "the *ineluctable means* by which one trains oneself to be pious"'.[43] Here one can note Nasima's Muslim subjectivity as she tries to construct the performance and role of what constitutes *hijab* through her reality and history. She uses her past experience of wearing the *dupatta*, which is still not exclusively attributed to Muslim women in the subcontinent itself. However, because of her reality here in Britain, she centres her current socio-political context on defining her subjectivity. Concerning the relationship between clothes and subjectivity, Miller argues that clothing is not simply 'a form of representation, a semiotic sign or symbol of the person [but] plays a considerable and active part in constituting the particular experience of the self'.[44] Thus, the self is not constructed solely on the basis of aesthetics, but also aggregates other variables that shape the individual's understanding of their surroundings.

Symbolism and representation: The *niqab* and its boundaries

The wearing of the *niqab*, on the other hand, is on the rise amongst British Bangladeshi women, as shown by Tarlo:

> In Whitechapel, in particular, where there is a high density of British Bengali Muslims, face covering has over the past decade acquired some sort of normative status amongst married Muslim women. It signals that they are present for purposive action (the purchase of vegetables) but not for further degrees of unnecessary interaction (casual chat, flirtation, being seen). Here the *niqab* has become integrated into patterns of looking, enabling rather than preventing displays of civil inattention, allowing women to go about their daily chores without hassle.[45]

For this project, I only interviewed one woman in the *niqab* who reached out to me to participate following the circulation of the research project. Sultana was born in Tower Hamlets and has lived in the borough her whole life. Her familiarity with the area was evident while we were walking around the area, trying to find a quiet café to conduct the interview. I first met and interacted with Sultana during my fieldwork at the Maryam Centre, East London Mosque. We started talking about Tower Hamlets and how things have changed rapidly for the Bangladeshi community. On the day of the interview, we met not too far from East London Mosque and went to a local café. We went upstairs, where there were no other customers, allowing Sultana (interviewed in April 2014) to lift her *niqab* whilst talking to me, although halfway through the interview other customers started coming up to the second floor, so she completed the remainder of the interview with her *niqab* on. When we started speaking about the *hijab* and *niqab* and what they meant to her as a young twenty-year-old, she said:

> Personally, to me, it's part of my identity. Obviously I wear *hijab* and *niqab* – I feel it's helping me to become a better Muslim, but it hasn't made me. I don't know how to explain; it's really hard. Okay, I wear *niqab* because say if I go outside I know that people ... Firstly, I don't think *niqab* is compulsory, I think it's a recommended act because we know that the Prophet (PBUH)'s wives, they wore it, so it's something that they did which was commended.[46] But, at the same time, I wear it because I think I will go outside and it will remind me of who I am and I know that people are seeing me as a Muslim first, so it's like monitoring my behaviour and helping you to become a better person when I am interacting with people because I know that they will see me as a Muslim first so it is important to me.

Sultana's reflections consolidate what others have explored about the socio-religious efforts many Muslims make to coordinate their religious expression with that of the Prophet Muhammad (PBUH). It is, however, also essential to consider how she positions herself publicly considering the curiosity of non-Muslims who may have questions about Islam. Moreover, this particular domain of foregrounding one's cognitive and embodied religious identity is indicative of the prevailing notion that Muslims should always be ready to dismantle false ideas about the faith. Sultana further shared the story of her first day of wearing the *niqab* and encountering racism:

> The first day I wore *niqab* we went to Goodmayes in Essex to volunteer for this Eid event that this charitable organisation was putting on. It was a majority-white area, so we had the whole racism thing going on. It was odd, obviously, seeing in the majority-English area two ladies walking down in *niqab* or just in black in the summer as well. So we had middle fingers flipped at us and shouting from the cars. I never let it affect me, though, because I think, whenever we ... You can try and help people to understand you, but because your way of life and your outlook on life is so different they might not always understand you, and you just accept that and you work towards building that link with

them and you are talking to them and helping for them to educate you about them and for me to educate them about me. But if it doesn't work then it doesn't work and don't let it get you down because you will always meet good people at the end of the day even you meet a bad one.

Karen Tranberg Hansen, drawing on the work of Sophie Woodward, argues that 'our lived experience with clothes, how we feel about them, hinges on how others evaluate our crafted appearances, and this experience in turn is influenced by the situation and the structure of the wider context'.[47] This illustrates the interweaving of clothing, performance and body together with clothes as embodied practice. The circumstance Sultana was confronted with illustrates how 'the covered woman is both hyper-conspicuous and hyper-concealed, creating an impression of being simultaneously present and absent, public and private'.[48] Nilu Ahmed contends that Bangladeshi Muslim women, in East London in particular, try to make sense of Islam and how to 'live' it in their everyday lives inside and outside their homes.[49] Further, Sahar Ghumkhor argues that 'the veiled and unveiled became an imperial tool of navigating the encounter with the Muslim and continues to influence and shape western and Muslim notions of self'.[50] The way the self is referenced is a notable point because the participants acknowledged many political moments that have shaped their decisions regarding dress, while those moments have also inadvertently shaped the desire to wear clothing that is sanctified within the Muslim community but simultaneously offers moments of subversion where, within the dominant discourse, these outfits have been stigmatised and associated with terrorism.

Shaheda (interviewed in May 2014), whom I met in a café in Bethnal Green, spoke fondly of her parents' religiosity and how they express their identities with great confidence and pride. When I asked her how her parents had influenced her identity and if she has adopted different ways of practising Islam than her parents, she responded:

> Yes, I guess ... my mum wears the *niqab* and I know that you don't have to wear it, but she has chosen to wear it; and I've never really asked her why she chose to wear it or when she decided to wear it. But I don't think that I would do that. And it's down to interpretation because yes, it's down to how modestly you want to dress and your covering to that extent of your body and that's absolutely fine, but I don't think you need to cover your face to show that.

Shaheda here problematises the *niqab* and its relation to her own religious articulations. It indicates her awareness of the diverse interpretations and that such configurations and understandings come from varying historical trajectories. The sudden emergence of the *niqab* amongst British Bangladeshis, Tarlo argues, is a recent phenomenon:

> At the same time, research in Tower Hamlets suggests that British Bengali women today are more pre-occupied with issues of religious piety and practice than in the past, partly as a result of having more time to devote to such matters but also having more access to religious instruction and texts. What is clear is that both in London and in major cities in Bangladesh the use of face veils and *burqa*s is a relatively recent innovation that was not commonly practised by previous generations of women. In Bangladesh it is the reformist party, Jama'at-i-Islami, and the Islamic organisation, Tabliqi Jama'at, which actively encourage such practices, particularly amongst urban educated women.[51]

Though Shaheda acknowledges the individual choice and interpretation of wearing the *niqab*, Nasima takes a similar approach. She argues for freedom of choice but provides her argument for why she disagrees with the *niqab*:

> *Niqab* is ... I don't really agree with wearing the *niqab* ... My justification of it is if [and] when you go to *Kaaba*, and you're doing your *Tawaaf*, you're told not to wear a *niqab*.[52] Then if Allah says to me I can't wear it in the spiritual and the holiest place on earth, then why would I need to wear it? But then, everybody has freedom of choice. Everybody has the freedom of choosing what pathway they need to choose. If somebody chooses to wear the *niqab* then that's up to them but ... I feel it doesn't make you more Muslim or more knowledgeable by wearing *hijab* or *niqab*. It's individual choice.

Nasima affirms the theological argument that covering the face is unacceptable when Muslims circumambulate the *Kaaba*, Islam's holiest site, in Mecca, Saudi Arabia, during pilgrimage. So, then, why would it be permissible to wear the *niqab*? Within these parameters, she accepts the wearing of the *niqab* as a religious choice rather than obligation. Dr Kadir, however, holds an alternative view on the issue and feels, though with reservation, that some women may be wearing the *niqab* to provoke a reaction:

> Most scholars say *niqab* is not an essential thing but some people express themselves and this has become a big debate. Personally, no one in my family does that, but I wouldn't dare to say someone [it's] wrong if someone wears that, and because those who wear [it], they expose themselves to security and other reasons and I think this has become a political issue unfortunately. And some young girls do this deliberately to provoke probably, I don't know.

While Nasima adopts a theological argument and disagrees with the *niqab*, Dr Kadir uses the contemporary political context to situate the wearing of the garment. The discussions around the *niqab* provoked various opinions among the participants. What transpires in Saba Mahmood's work is worth mentioning, whereby the Muslim woman's sartorial choice is made legible through a language of agency as resistance.⁵³ As much as the women who wear the *niqab*, and other garments, emphasised choice as a site of negotiation, few considered the political dimension of such choices. There was no engagement with why and how the *need* for meaning is projected and informed by broader events shaping the specific encounters of racism via clothing to the general unfolding of political moments. In this sense, 'identification and belonging are produced and subsequently articulated into structures of individuality'.⁵⁴ The absence of the political domain in conceptualising why clothing items elicit the reactions and responses they do renders the mode of power absent and provides an incomplete picture.

Referring back to Sultana's interview, the most striking part of our conversation regarding her relationship with the *niqab* was her reference to other religious symbols and how they also serve as a reminder to her of her Muslimness:

> I know it's weird, but I always get really happy when I see an orthodox Jew, and they have their hat on, and I think it's nice to see someone else that's committed in that way to their religion. If I see a nun I get really happy [laughs], I don't know why [laughs]. You always feel like, with us, it's always like 'oh the weird one who covers and this and that' and you don't really hear that [about] Christians or Jewish people that much. We have a synagogue just there, you see – it's not really used as much, but you will see the odd Jewish person walking past. Always when I am at Royal London Hospital, I see an orthodox Jewish man; I just smile under my *niqab*, like, 'ooh'. It's nice. It symbolises their beliefs and in some ways their commitment to their faith which you see externally. You don't know the internal state again, but, you know.

The café where we conducted the interview was close to one of the oldest synagogues in East London – the carved signage of the synagogue is still up, though the building is now used as office space. Mahmood contends that it is through the repeated performance of outward religious practices, including dress, that a virtuous self is produced.⁵⁵ In this regard, clothing plays a special part in Sultana's case, as the 'complex communicative staging' with which humans usually present themselves though the way they dress in social interactions. Woodward points out that clothing is not used just to 'straightforwardly communicate' our inner selves to others, and that wearing 'the particular item of clothing enacts an internal and behavioural change in the woman'.⁵⁶ Sanja Bilic continues to argue that, on a social level, this typically results in locating ourselves symbolically,⁵⁷ in what Fred Davis calls 'some structured universe of status claims and life-style attachments'.⁵⁸ This lifestyle attachment, which Sultana sees in other outwardly religious individuals, fills her with happiness, knowing that others are on a similar journey.

Religion and fashion: Locating the beard

People's references to the wearing of the beard for men appeared to be more nuanced and allowed room for flexibility, as expressed by Nasima (interviewed in June 2014), whom I interviewed in her living room close to Ilford:

> My husband's got a beard, but he has chosen to wear it short. Again, he feels it is okay for him to have that short beard. Whereas in Islamic ruling and *hadith*, it says you have to have a fistful, but he hasn't got that, but that's his choice.[59] Maybe he will eventually wear that but then a beard doesn't make you more pious than a non-bearded person. Just because you have a beard doesn't make you more Muslim than me or anybody else. Again, it's just the freedom of choice.

Khalid (interviewed in January 2014) reiterated a similar point that it is an individual's choice, but also addressed the issue of how the beard now functions as a fashion statement and has less to do with religion. Husna (interviewed in October 2014) is a professional lawyer and runs her own law firm in East London. I interviewed her in her office one morning just before her appointments with her clients. She also believes the beard has become fashionable over time and has more to do with following current trends than religious expression and conviction. These were their responses when they were asked about the role of the beard:

> **Khalid:** The beard? I have no idea. I don't think it's important. Although it's *Sunnah*, I believe, because you follow the way of the Prophet. It's up to you as an individual.[60] The thing about Islam, the beauty of Islam is you can dress the way you want, you can do whatever you want, it's your relationship with Allah, with your God, and only He can accept your prayers and actions; only He can, alone. No one else on this earth, no human being can judge you by what you are doing and what you are carrying on a day-to-day basis. So having the beard, and again I've seen so many people having the beard for the sake of having the beard because it's fashion, it's cool. Some people naturally assume: 'he must be religious, he's got a beard'. It's far from it. He's only got it because he wants to have a fashion statement. 'Cause he looks cool. It's what's in at the moment. I've seen other brothers who don't have a beard who pray five times a day and are a lot more [*sic*] better than some people I know. I think [the] beard's become a bit more of a fashion statement, as opposed to having it for religious purposes.
>
> **Husna:** I mean at the moment, it seems to be really fashionable because all the Englishmen have a beard and Americans have beards, so it's no distinction between, you know, a Muslim man with a beard and white person with a beard actually. But it's increasingly more and more young Muslim boys have got beards I can see.

The emphasis that the beard is a part of expressing one's faith, yet articulating it as a choice, is intriguing. It discloses a relationship with the beard that, to some extent, conforms to broader societal regulation and discipline. The beard, then, is not simply regulated in its own right via a religious reading, but also exists as a site of merging with contemporary trends. The oppositional juxtaposition of 'a Muslim man with a beard and white person' requires further analysis. The 'white person' is projected as non-Muslim, while the 'Muslim man' is de-raced. While Muslimness has come to be strictly associated with the South Asian Muslim communities in Britain, even though there are Muslims of various ethnic backgrounds, it has also extended to non-Muslim South Asians. This particular framing of the Muslim dispenses with religious differences from non-Muslim South Asians, leading to blanket attacks on all South Asians with a beard. For example, a Sikh man was attacked in a Tesco in 2015 because the attacker assumed he was Muslim.[61] Similarly, four days after 9/11, a Sikh man, Balbir Singh Sodhi, was murdered because his killer assumed that he was a Muslim on account of his beard and turban.[62] Thus, unlike the white man with a beard (even if Muslim), the racialised Muslim man with a beard is bound by preconceived ideas of the dangerous Muslim.[63]

This is illustrated by my interview with Jahangir (interviewed in December 2014), an undergraduate student studying Arabic. Jahangir summarised the importance of wearing *hijab*, *niqab*, and the role of the beard for men with a very concise response, relating it to Islamic Law:

> These are like *fiqh-ey* differences. Sadly, in the Bengali community our *fiqh* or our understanding has been influenced by Tabligh and Deoband. By the way, Deoband[is] think it's *wajib* (compulsory) to have a *niqab* on and absolutely *fard* to have *hijab* on. With regard to *hijab*, I do think it's important, but the ideals of *hijab* are much more than just a headscarf, like modest interaction and all of the things like that, that's a bit more conservative. I guess that's the way I see it, that it is more than a headscarf. And I have come across sisters or figures that have much more manners than those with *hijab* on.[64]

This disposition is congruent with what Sohaib shared earlier, crucially pointing out that *hijab* encompasses the interior and exterior. Younger Bangladeshi Muslims are more inclined to appeal to the original canon, i.e. the Qur'an and *Sunnah*, to identify what is truly 'authentic' and acceptable within religious rulings. Ahmed's work entitled 'Tower Hamlets: Insulation in isolation' also invokes this particular shift towards accessing religious literature. Ahmed found that even the first generation of women were keen to (re)discover more about their religion, especially those who are now in their forties and fifties, whose parents had migrated to Britain. Ahmed found that the women interviewed for the project stated that: 'faith provided a familiar source of comfort and solace in their isolation. The growing availability and accessibility of Islamic literature cultivated their knowledge about Islam, making them no longer reliant on others for their understanding of the faith.'[65]

However, Hassan (interviewed in December 2014), who does not have a beard or wear any 'outward symbols of Islam', told me how people still assume he is a Muslim simply because he is brown. Though he does not have a beard himself, he considers the beard to be an obligation: 'I do consider it an obligation; I don't think it makes you more religious necessarily, but it's certainly a fulfilment of your religious obligations.' Hassan is the only research participant who believes the beard is an obligation, though interestingly, he did not have one at the time of the interview. Also, when I asked him about the *hijab* and the *niqab* he refused to answer, as he felt it is 'patronising' and 'surely it is for women to answer that question, not for me as a guy'. Hassan was the only participant who felt unease when I posed the questions related to *hijab* and *niqab*, whereas other male participants did not hesitate when answering those questions. In his study on young Bangladeshis in East London and their civic engagement, Justin Gest argues that the maligning of the Muslim part of the younger generation's public identity has, in fact, opened up and activated the need for young Bengali Muslims to reclaim 'the stigmatised identity' and invert it into 'a positive civic attribute'.[66] In that sense, Bangladeshi Muslim men having a beard as a fashion trend also disrupts the notion that Muslims are motivated by their faith at all times and illustrates that the men are claiming 'the geographic and social space where their British, Bangladeshi and Muslim identities overlap'.[67] The hybridisation of what men wear to express how they identify with their religion problematises the relationship between religion, ethnicity and identity further because it is evident that the expression of religion vis-à-vis clothes is intertwined with 'various factors contributing to "new patterns and forms" of transplanted religion'.[68]

Islamic dress for men: The *thobe* and its articulation

Dr Fahima (interviewed in September 2014), while speaking about the importance of dress to expressing one's religious identity, shared that 'even if you go to any kind of Middle Eastern countries, the way they dress is a cultural thing; it sometimes has nothing to do with how religious they are … whereas here you'd probably be confident that if somebody is dressing in a certain way, then they probably are more religious'. There is an underlying recognition that clothes from the 'Middle East' are creating a space for new classifications and understandings of what constitutes male Muslim dress in the UK. Meanwhile, the very same outfits would carry different meanings elsewhere. The region's proximity to the birth of Islam definitely adds to the exalting of the *thobe*. In that regard, the younger generation of Bangladeshis who were born, or at least raised from a very young age, in the East End are likely to adopt the *thobe* as a marker of religious identity, whereas those with closer ties to Bangladesh, as observed in the previous chapter, adopted the *funjabi*, associating it with religious identity expressions manifested through one's ethnic identity in the UK. This identification shift within the British Bangladeshi Muslim community in East London allows the possibility of providing insights into the complexities of, and multifaceted approaches that people take towards, clothes. Creating an 'imagined Islamic dress' is significant. It shows that more acculturated Bangladeshi Muslims desire to belong to the *ummah*, constructed by using the *thobe* as the unifying Islamic dress.

Sohaib establishes a link between the discourse of imposing a standardised dress code and the perception and requirements that an institution creates for the public to consume whilst discussing a local *madrasah* (Islamic school). He advised the East London Mosque *madrasah* to avoid making the *thobe* their religious uniform. He explains:

> I was speaking to some of the people who were setting it up, and I said 'For God's sake, please don't make the *thobe* your religious uniform – your school uniform.' And they did exactly that, which is a very bad mistake. Because I said to them 'Look, every child hates the uniform. They see it as an imposition.' So when you go to school, all the children are trying to distinguish themselves, differentiate themselves, to get a blazer, or sort of … Men are like peacocks, they want to sort of stand out, you know, be different from the crowd. People don't want to be like everyone else, and the uniform puts you into a straitjacket, and people hate the uniform. So I said, 'Do you want your children to leave school hating the *thobe*?'.

This draws attention to the significance of locality for the purposes of institutionalisation. Notably, Kim Knott's *Hinduism in Leeds* describes the fusion and compromise occurring in the diaspora and how this is shaped in a multitude of ways. Such negotiations occur because that space is then shared with ethnic 'others' who are also from the same broad tradition.[69] Within this logic, observing how Sohaib contends with this new paradigm for the school is revealing, as he attempts to advance a negotiation of the uniform for the school, recognising the role of dialogic and intercultural dynamics at play for younger Bangladeshi Muslims. He continued to reiterate the importance of allowing younger Bangladeshi Muslims to negotiate their religious identity and expression via clothes, and that imposing the *thobe* as the standardised religious attire creates a distance, perhaps even rejection, of the garment. What is clear, notes Tarlo, despite very little literature on Muslim men's dress, is that 'since 9/11, increasing numbers of young Muslim men in Britain have adopted beards and, to a lesser extent, caps and *thobe*s (robes), and that some attempts are being made to develop new visibly Muslim men's fashions adapted to a Western environment'.[70] The adoption of the *thobe* as a school uniform could be an 'explicit attempt to replicate the actions, example and appearance of the Prophet'.[71] Although the *thobe* is a specific garment hailing from the Arabian peninsula, it has come to signify Muslimness. It emerged as the de facto dress for Muslim men with the heightened experience of Islamophobia since the commencement of the War on Terror. Not only that, but this particular form of Arabisation – i.e. the hegemony of Arab culture – determines the boundaries of what constitutes being a visible Muslim.

When the conversation continued, and we started to discuss the beard and the *thobe* and their importance, Sohaib shared 'My legal opinion is that the beard is not an obligation, it's not the most important thing that a Muslim needs to do; contrary to what many people think, it's a, it's a recommended *Sunnah*, it's highly recommended … the *thobe* is, is not a religious requirement, of course.' He added a further nuance pertaining to trousers and expressed how the Prophet Muhammad (PBUH):

> once wore Roman trousers and he liked it, it was easier to ride a horse on it; and so, if you wear a pair of trousers nowadays knowing that, and out of love for what [the] Prophet (PBUH) loved, for me that would also be a practice of Islam, so as I wear these suit trousers, there's no difference, in a theological sense, between this and a *thobe* – see what I mean?

Sohaib justifies this by referring to the embrace of one's cultural identity and not dismissing its role. He states that many people attempt to 'dismiss culture and say we should have religion without, or bereft of, culture' when, in many instances, 'religion has survived through permeating cultures, [and] where the religion, where the principles were lost, the culture survived, and through the culture, the principles came back … so the *thobe* carries a cultural significance that is embedded in religion'.

The point raised by Sohaib is significant, in that it does not present culture and religion as two mutually exclusive categories. On the contrary, their collaboration and intertwined history are essential to understanding the possibilities of having a more holistic Islamic identity. The adoption of dress in its varying iterations, illustrated in the example provided by Sohaib of the Prophet Muhammad (PBUH) wearing what were deemed foreign, 'Roman trousers', showcases the multiple ways individuals connect, receive and embody religious dress through their everyday social practices. Within that vision, however, it remains an empirical question as to when and why the *thobe*, at times, functions as a more dominant marker of religious identity over other garments. The central roles of position and power relay how the dialogic nature of religious identity-processing shapes and determines which identities predominate. In that sense, religion is captured through a paradigm of power, with imageries of the *thobe* cementing it as the all-encompassing ummatic garb.

Sohaib's challenge to reconceive 'community boundaries and contest the meaning of culture' links to the desire that the *thobe*, in its institutionalised sense, dilute its valour.[72] Sohaib's observation implicitly suggests that, since the *thobe* is intrinsically tied to one's religious identification – although he did complicate this earlier – it places an additional layer of pressure on young Bangladeshis in East London to struggle publicly with their religious boundaries. As a result, such a struggle will make their sensitivity to social judgement (by all parties) particularly acute.[73] This process of culture-making and attempting to create a religious identity that young Bangladeshis can identify with concerning the *thobe* is significant, as Sohaib's 'dislike' of the *thobe* as a school uniform may serve as a marker of Bangladeshis distancing themselves from their religious expressions. Another reading of the *thobe* designated as the school uniform is that East London Mosque is making room to assert a more reified, stable representation of an Islamic identity. The *thobe* as uniform reasserts the dominant political discourse of Muslims being treated as a homogeneous entity, displaying the power of the ways in which this discourse inserts itself into the microcosms of the everyday in Tower Hamlets. In this respect, Baumann points out that 'a community, however new or old, that cannot point to a culture which it stands for, serves or owns, risks losing that part of its legitimacy that is orientated on the past'.[74] This dominant Islamic discourse surrounding the *thobe* illustrates the presence of a hegemonic past with a perceived linear outline of what constitutes appropriate religious dress for Muslim men, which Sohaib himself alludes to in his previous quotes. However, in this instance, he further recognises the need to adopt creative processes in changing how young Bangladeshis form their religious identity while recognising the spatial concatenations.

Dr Kadir (interviewed in November 2013) responded passionately when I asked him whether how you dress as a Muslim is important. He holds the belief that there is no such thing as 'Islamic dress', but that there are a variety of dresses representing the land to which the Muslim belongs:

> I haven't thought on that. There is no religious dress, in my opinion. It's all cultural dress. So people wear *punjabi* or *sherwani* in South Asia, [and there are] people who wear the *thobe* in Arab countries, so personally I don't consider them as religious dress. Religiousness is something that you wear modest

dress to beautify yourself, and you don't reveal your body. That's religious dress, especially [as] Islam says that. Because Arab and South Asian Muslims have been historically Muslims [since] long ago, that's why they dress [according to] certain types. Apparently, it looks like Islamic dress, but I wouldn't call them Islamic dress. They are the Muslim dress of that land. That's what I can say. Otherwise, there isn't one single Islamic dress, then Muslims are closer to wearing the same dress. In Indonesia, Malaysia people wear *lungi* as their Islamic dress. Personally, because I come from South Asia, I personally prefer *punjabi* compared to *thobe*, but people in this area don't do this.

Dr Kadir's assertion starkly sits with Sohaib's view that religion and culture coexist; however, Dr Kadir explicitly posits that different forms of dress express an Islamic identity according to that country. This further articulates a growing shift in the conceptualisation of religious clothes for different generations of Bangladeshis.

Ismail, whom I interviewed in his office in Central London, addresses the debate around male religious dress. He speaks of how his conception of religious clothes vastly differs from that of his father, who believes that the *funjabi* functions as the garment to identify with one's religion. Ismail, though, contends: '[T]hat's not to say he is wrong, because the Prophet (PBUH) used to wear long shirts that is along that line, but it's not Islamic dress – that's what the Prophet (PBUH) used to wear.' The discussion surrounding the Muslim dress code for men pertains to the wearing of the *thobe* mostly, as Tarlo remarks how styles, 'especially those regionally associated with the Middle East and North Africa', are 'being accorded the status of authentically "Islamic"'.[75] Interestingly, though the *thobe* is perceived as a religious garment, this may not necessarily be the case in the Gulf countries, where the wearing of the *thobe* may hold little, or no, religious significance. In that sense, Dr Kadir does not invalidate how the broader political discourse shapes and has power over how Bangladeshis associate themselves with their faith. In all probability, he is aware of how young Bangladeshis align themselves more closely with Gulf-styled clothing and seeks to contest their ethnically influenced religious identifications. Gest observed that many young Bangladeshis in the East End reject their Bangladeshi heritage and want to 'operate according to a pan-Islamic moral paradigm in all aspects of their lives, in full'.[76] However, Fadwa El Guindi argues that, contrary to what is often assumed by outsiders, these textual sources contain more references to men's dress than to women's.[77] Shiraj (interviewed March 2014) referred to the Saudi *thobe* as a religious dress that he wears for Eid celebrations, 'But sometimes I do wear other religious dresses on different occasions – like the Saudi *thobe* and all that, we would wear during Eid time.'

Both Dr Kadir and Ismail have closer ties to Bangladesh that inform their religious conceptualisations. Nonetheless, they assume very different approaches to what religious clothing means to them. On the one hand, Dr Kadir identifies the need to consider overall modesty, which is not contingent upon a specific cultural garment. Dr Kadir believes modesty is an expression not bound by geography. On the other hand, Ismail does feel the need to manifest one's religious affiliations through geographically specified cultural clothing to ascertain some 'authenticity' or religious 'legitimacy'. Stuart Hall refers to this discursive identification as a 'construction, a process never completed – always "in process" '.[78] In this respect, I would argue that this religious identity articulation is constructed, and set through a narrow historical trajectory. Furthermore, it helps to create a religious expression by reifying a cultural understanding to enculturate the younger Bangladeshis' conceptualisations of faith through the dominant discourse of expressing an Islamic identity uniformly: The notion that one's Muslimness is constructed from the place of the 'other' – it does not necessarily facilitate the 'always in "process" ' as suggested by Hall.[79] Once the boundaries have been clearly defined, the process itself is halted to reify a religious articulation to assert a unified Islamic identity.

Conclusion

In this chapter, I illustrate how clothing choices pertaining to the observation of religious boundaries and injunctions involve multiple layers. First, one of the practices entailed managing the gaze of fellow Muslims via the local micropolitics of the East End. While preoccupied with local socio-religious dimensions, people were also concerned with how they could utilise the very embodied Islam as a way to proselytise non-Muslims and rectify misconceptions. In this sense, there was a conscious interpellation of two streams informing their sartorial choices, which I term double surveillance. On the one hand, Muslims must manage the state's surveillance and its positioning of Muslims as dangerous and of aspects of Islam as outdated, while, on the other, they negotiate the surveillance they receive from fellow Muslims. Consequently, the shuffling of the two dimensions shapes racialised Muslim bodies' embodiment of clothing and their attachments.

Second, another concern, mainly raised in relation to the *thobe*, is how it has come to be the modus operandi outfit to express an Islamic identity in a way not possible for other garments. This local micropolitical discourse permeated the Bengali community through institutions such as East London Mosque. It appears to have created a 'clear-cut' religious articulation that, as evident from the research participants' responses, remains contested as people attempt to see their religious identifications in more multifaceted terms. The meanings they attribute to the different dresses and clothes are defined in relative rather than in absolute and objective terms. For example, in Sultana's case, the notion of self–other relations is articulated through religiosity, something she extends to non-Muslim religious individuals, thus complicating the simple binary of 'us and them'. Interestingly, discussions around the beard relegated it to a fashion trend, even while recognising the religious articulations of growing a beard. Consideration of the beard, and which racialised body wears it, is a notable point in understanding who accesses fashion trends without facing possible life-threatening danger.

Another layer to factor in is how the self-consciousness of Muslims is subjective. However, it is crucial to point out that the identity assigned to us by others can be a powerful force in shaping all of the research participants' self-concepts. They may argue otherwise – that they are doing it on their own terms – but the very parameters of those terms are being informed via the discursive placing of the Muslim. For example, Talal Asad writes that *deen* (often translated as 'religion') 'relates more to how one lives than to what one believes ... For Muslims ... it is virtues – mastery of the body, the ability to be patient, and the capacity to judge soundly – that matter, not states of mind.'[80] While some of the participants articulated Asad's formulation, there was an explicit reference to their parents' lack of sufficient 'proper' knowledge. This resulted in what Sarah Glynn calls 'the new Islam', which claims its authenticity and legitimacy from the religious texts, and extends to the topic of clothes and religious identity.[81] Efforts to reconcile these schisms and expressions of identity will remain in flux, and we can expect new(er) changes that will (re)shape how British Bangladeshi Muslims manage these shifts in the years to come.

Notes

1 E. Tarlo, *Visibly Muslim: Fashion, Politics, Faith* (Oxford and New York: Berg, 2010), p. 45.
2 See S. Tissot, 'Excluding Muslim women: From hijab to niqab, from school to public space', *Public Culture* 23:1 (2011), 39–46.
3 See H. Afshar, 'Can I see your hair? Choice, agency and attitudes: The dilemma of faith and feminism for Muslim women who cover', *Ethnic and Racial Studies* 31:2 (2008), 411–427; T. F. Ruby, 'Listening to the voices of hijab', *Women's Studies International Forum* 29:1 (2006), 54–66; N. Meer, C. Dwyer and T. Modood, 'Embodying nationhood? Conceptions of British national identity, citizenship, and gender in the "veil affair"', *The Sociological Review* 58:1 (2010), 84–111.
4 A. Smith, 'France divided as headscarf ban is set to become law', *Guardian*, 1 February 2004.

5 S. Erlanger, 'France enforces ban on full-face veils in public', *New York Times*, 11 April 2011.
6 H. Schofield, K. Cisse and K. Pieri, 'French shrug off Muslim upset at abaya ban in schools', BBC News (8 September 2023), www.bbc.co.uk/news/world-europe-66753665 (accessed 6 April 2024). An *abaya* is a loose-fitting, full-length robe worn by some Muslim women.
7 J. W. Scott, *The Politics of the Veil* (Princeton: Princeton University Press, 2009), p. 19.
8 R. Pells, 'Islamic face veil to be banned in Latvia despite being worn by just three women in entire country', *Independent*, 21 April 2016.
9 A. Krasimirov, 'Bulgaria bans full-face veils in public places', Reuters (30 September 2016), www.reuters.com/article/idUSKCN1201L4/ (accessed 6 April 2024).
10 BBC, 'Austrian ban on full-face veil in public places comes into force', BBC News (1 October 2017), www.bbc.co.uk/news/world-europe-41457427 (accessed 6 April 2024).
11 *Guardian*, 'Denmark passes law banning burqa and niqab', *Guardian*, 31 May 2018.
12 Al Jazeera, 'Swiss vote to outlaw facial coverings in "burqa ban" poll', Al Jazeera (7 March 2021), www.aljazeera.com/news/2021/3/7/swiss-look-set-to-approve-ban-on-facial-coverings (accessed 6 April 2024).
13 Tarlo, *Visibly Muslim*, p. 3.
14 Ibid.
15 F. Fanon, 'Algeria unveiled', in F. Fanon, *A Dying Colonialism* (New York: Grove Press, 1965), pp. 35–67 (pp. 35–36).
16 Ibid., pp. 36–37.
17 E. Tarlo and A. Moors, *Islamic Fashion and Anti-Fashion: New Perspectives from Europe and North America* (London: Bloomsbury, 2013), p. 4.
18 D. Miller, *Stuff* (Cambridge: Polity Press, 2010), p. 40.
19 V. Redclift, F. Rajina and N. Rashid, 'The burden of conviviality: British Bangladeshi Muslims navigating diversity in London, Luton and Birmingham', *Sociology* 56:6 (2022), 1159–1175.
20 R. Brubaker and F. Cooper, 'Beyond "identity"', *Theory and Society* 29:1 (2000), 1–47 (p. 12).
21 B. Ganesh and I. Abou-Atta, *Forgotten Women: The Impact of Islamophobia on Muslim Women in the United Kingdom*, European Network against Racism (ENAR) (2016).
22 C. Allen, 'Islamophobia in the media: Evidence to the APPG on Islamophobia' (16 October 2013), Issuu, https://issuu.com/drchrisallen/docs/media_vers2_-_chrisallen-evidence-o (accessed 30 May 2023), p. 7.
23 N. Meer, *Citizenship, Identity and the Politics of Multiculturalism: The Rise of Muslim Consciousness* (Basingstoke: Palgrave, 2010).
24 S. Hall, 'Introduction: Who needs "identity"?', in S. Hall and P. Du Gay (eds), *Questions of Cultural Identity* (London: Sage Publications, 1996), pp. 1–17 (p. 9).

25 Tarlo, *Visibly Muslim*, pp. 10–11.
26 J. Gest, *Apart: Alienated and Engaged Muslims in the West* (London: Hurst, 2010), p. 107.
27 G. Baumann, *Contesting Culture: Discourses of Identity in Multi-Ethnic London* (Cambridge: Cambridge University Press, 1996), p. 195.
28 Ibid.
29 S. Begum, *From Sylhet to Spitalfields: Bengali Squatters in 1970s East London* (London: Lawrence and Wishart, 2023), p. 17.
30 Brubaker and Cooper, 'Beyond "identity"'.
31 N. Göle, 'The voluntary adoption of Islamic stigma symbols', *Social Research* 70:3 (2003), 809–828.
32 S. Hussein, *From Victims to Suspects: Muslim Women since 9/11* (Sydney: NewSouth, 2016).
33 Redclift et al., 'The burden of conviviality'.
34 E. Tarlo, 'Hijab in London: Metamorphosis, resonance and effects', *Journal of Material Culture* 12:2 (2007), 131–156 (p. 152).
35 Meer, *Citizenship, Identity and the Politics of Multiculturalism*.
36 Brubaker and Cooper, 'Beyond "identity"'.
37 P. Werbner, 'Honor, shame and the politics of sexual embodiment among South Asian Muslims in Britain and beyond: An analysis of debates in the public sphere', *International Social Science Review* 6:1 (2005), 25–47.
38 C. Dwyer, 'Veiled meanings: Young British Muslim women and the negotiation of differences', *Gender, Place and Culture: A Journal of Feminist Geography* 6:1 (1999), 5–26.
39 *Namaz* is the Bengali word for prayer. Muslims also use the Arabic word, *salah*, to refer to the five daily prayers.
40 The *adhan* is the call to prayer.
41 Dwyer, 'Veiled meanings', p. 5.
42 Ibid., p. 22.
43 S. Mahmood, *Politics of Piety: The Islamic Revival and the Feminist Subject* (Princeton: Princeton University Press, 2005), p. 158. Emphasis Mahmood's.
44 Miller, *Stuff*, p. 40.
45 Tarlo, *Visibly Muslim*, p. 134.
46 'Peace be upon him' (PBUH) is used as an honorific by Muslims after referring to the Prophet Muhammad.
47 K. T. Hansen, 'The world in dress: Anthropological perspectives on clothing, fashion, and culture', *Annual Review of Anthropology* 33 (2004), 369–392 (p. 373).
48 Tarlo, *Visibly Muslim*, p. 132.
49 N. Ahmed, 'Tower Hamlets: Insulation in isolation', in T. Abbas (ed.), *Muslim Britain: Communities under Pressure* (London: Zed Books, 2005), pp. 194–207.
50 S. Ghumkhor, *The Political Psychology of the Veil: The Impossible Body* (Cham: Palgrave Macmillan, 2020), p. 260.

51 Tarlo, *Visibly Muslim*, p. 143.
52 *Tawaaf* is when Muslims circle the Holy *Kaaba* seven times in an anti-clockwise direction as part of the *Umrah* and *Hajj* pilgrimages.
53 Mahmood, *Politics of Piety*.
54 L. Grossberg, 'Identity and cultural studies: Is that all there is?', in Hall and Du Gay, *Questions of Cultural Identity*, pp. 87–107 (p. 98).
55 Mahmood, *Politics of Piety*.
56 S. Woodward, *Why Women Wear What They Wear* (Oxford: Berg, 2007), p. 21.
57 S. Bilic, 'Muslim women in the UK and Bosnia: Religious identities in contrasting contexts' (PhD dissertation, University of York, 2013).
58 F. Davis, *Fashion, Culture and Identity* (Chicago: University of Chicago Press, 1992), p. 4.
59 *Hadith* refers to what most Muslims believe to be a record of the words and actions of the Prophet Muhammad as transmitted through chains of narration.
60 *Sunnah* refers to the traditions and practices of the Prophet Muhammad and all the Muslims in his time who witnessed these and pass them on to future generations. These practices are considered the model for Muslims to follow.
61 M. Piggott, 'Savage machete attack on Sikh in Tesco was "revenge for Lee Rigby"', *International Business Time*, 22 June 2015.
62 G. Elizondo, 'No bitterness 10 years after Sikh killing over 9/11', Al Jazeera (6 September 2011), www.aljazeera.com/features/2011/9/6/no-bitterness-10-years-after-sikh-killing-over-9 (accessed 6 April 2024).
63 S. Valluvan, *The Clamour of Nationalism: Race and Nation in Twenty-First-Century Britain* (Manchester: Manchester University Press, 2019).
64 *Fiqh* refers to the jurisprudence/theory of Islamic law, based on the teachings of the Qur'an and Sunnah; *wajib* means compulsory and is a synonym of *fard*.
65 Ahmed, 'Tower Hamlets', p. 197.
66 Gest, *Apart*, p. 193.
67 Ibid., p. 195.
68 K. Knott, *Hinduism in Leeds: A Study of Religious Practice in the Indian Hindu Community and Hindu-Related Groups* (Leeds: Community Religions Project, University of Leeds, 1986), p. 10.
69 Ibid.
70 Tarlo, *Visibly Muslim*, p. 7.
71 Ibid., p. 10.
72 Baumann, *Contesting Culture*, p. 195.
73 Gest, *Apart*, p. 100.
74 Baumann, *Contesting Culture*, p. 197.
75 Tarlo, *Visibly Muslim*, p. 7.
76 Gest, p. 116.
77 F. El Guindi, 'Veiling resistance', *Fashion Theory* 3:1 (1999), 51–80.
78 Hall, 'Introduction', p. 2.
79 Ibid.

80 T. Asad, *Genealogies of Religion: Discipline and Reasons of Power in Christianity and Islam* (Baltimore: Johns Hopkins University Press, 1993), p. 219.
81 S. Glynn, 'Bengali Muslims: The new East End radicals?', *Ethnic and Racial Studies* 25:6 (2002), 969–988.

4

Being Bengali: More than just the language

Amaar bhaasha tumaar bhaasha, Bangla bhaasha, Bangla bhaasha

(My language, your language, is the Bengali language, the Bengali language)
Rabindranath Tagore

Introduction

Scholars have long observed how language is a core element of one's identity expression. Harald Haarmann argues that, with regard to ethnicity, language 'is not a necessary criterion of ethnicity and therefore does not play a fundamental role in all processes of ethnic fusion and fission'.[1] While Haarmann's analysis may apply to some examples, this would not apply so neatly to Bangladesh. In the struggle for independence in Bangladesh, the Bengali language was one of the critical factors functioning as a boundary for self-identification and categorisation that differentiated Bangladeshis from Pakistanis.[2] John Edwards states that 'nationalism from its modern inception was inextricably bound up with language; language was seen as an outward sign of a group's peculiar identity and a significant means of ensuring its continuation'.[3] Another facet to consider is that, while Bangladesh used Bengali to mark itself as different from Pakistan, it is vital to note that nation-states use one language to cement a usually homogeneous project. Such a confined boundary does not recognise linguistic diversity. In that sense, Haarmann's point that language 'is not a necessary criterion' for ethnicity is crucial, because ethnicity is often marked and coded through the way the nation-state sets itself up, collapsing ethnicity with national identity when they are two separate entities. While such conversations regarding language and national identity will continue, the characterising of ethnicity via the nation-state's use of language cannot be repurposed to discuss the Bengali diaspora in the UK. Instead, this research focuses on language maintenance and its link to the continuation of an ethnic identity in the diaspora.

For example, Rusi Jaspal and Adrian Coyle argue that there has been 'a substantial amount of empirical and theoretical work on the relationship between language and ethnic identity'.[4] However, social psychologists have undertaken little work on language and ethnic identity specifically among British South Asians, the largest ethnic minority group in the UK. However, they contend that some attention has been paid to the question of ethnic identity in general. In that sense, although more from a sociological standpoint, focusing on the Bengalis who settled in the East End will bring forth new analyses. The Bengalis who settled in the East End and eventually brought over their families from Bangladesh were keen to retain their families' link to their language. The parents would send their children to *fora*,[5] where they received lessons in Bengali, reading, writing and comprehension skills as well as Qur'an recitation. Nurul Hoque and Anwara Begum set up a Bengali language supplementary school. This school was named East End Community School (Figures 4.1–4.3).

Hoque discusses the importance of preserving heritage culture via language in the British Film Institute documentary *Defending a Way of Life*. He notes 'for the children who go to state school during daytime, they attend our school only in the evening. In the state school, they do not teach Bengali language, Bengali history, Bengali culture or Bengali religion. These things we teach

Figure 4.1 The front of the East End Community School. Image by the author.

Figure 4.2 Anwara Begum reading from a Bengali book to a group of children sitting across the floor (British Film Institute, *Defending a Way of Life*).

Figure 4.3 Nurul Hoque teaching children Bengali (British Film Institute, *Defending a Way of Life*).

here; that is why parents send their children to our school.'⁶ The documentary also shares how the Bangladeshi community in the 1970s organised cultural events to mark the Language Movement of Bangladesh. While *fora* no longer encompasses the Bengali language, it has shifted to a site where Bangladeshi Muslims in the East End learn Arabic, explicitly focusing on learning how to recite the Qur'an. *Fora* evoked many memories for the research participants. For some, these included memories of banter and seeing friends whom they saw only at *fora*. In contrast, other participants discussed the Bengali element of *fora* as useless and providing no meaningful skill, which at the very least they would derive from learning Arabic.

The research participants I interviewed for this project expressed their affinity for or discontinued interest in the language in multiple ways. Some used it to communicate with their parents at home only as this became a site where they could practise their language skills. Thus, the home became a space with an emphasis on the Bengali identity and its development. In his PhD dissertation entitled 'Growing up glocal in London and Sylhet', Benjamin Zeitlyn observes that many young Bangladeshis use the language at home and with extended family; however, at times, children have attempted to resist such impositions.⁷ This chapter will explore how and why some resisted speaking Bengali at home, what this meant and the meanings that speaking the language conjured.

One focus group held at the beginning of the fieldwork brought up insightful commentary on language and what it meant to the participants. The focus group was with young undergraduate and postgraduate students at a Russell Group University. All five students spoke about how the language allowed them to tap into their 'funny' and 'jokey' side when speaking Bengali because the same 'banter' could not be expressed in English. Two of the group's young men, one non-Sylheti and the other also non-Sylheti but an Italian-Bengali who had moved to London as a teenager with his family, spoke about Bengali and its role in their lives. Both of them admitted to finding Sylheti 'strange-sounding', because they were exposed to *shuddho Bangla* (Standard Bengali) at home.⁸ However, growing up in London with their Sylheti friends helped them learn and understand the language. I spoke to the group in Sylheti, and the two non-Sylhetis responded with a blend of Sylheti and *shuddho Bangla*.

In 'Language shift in Banglatown? Evaluating ethnolinguistic vitality in East London', Sebastian M. Rasinger notes that young Bangladeshi children introduce English into the home, thereby rupturing the tradition of speaking Bengali only.⁹ Another critical aspect is how the high concentration of Bangladeshis in Tower Hamlets gives Sylheti a strong 'language vitality', as the language can be heard, listened to and spoken within the borough.

There are interpreters available at various GP centres, hospitals and post offices, and many signs in public buildings and on the roads are in Bengali as well as English. One could argue that the visibility of the language provides a sense of belonging and pride, which could boost the community's use of the language. For example, East London Mosque delivers Friday sermons in Bengali, Arabic and English. During the fieldwork, I spoke to a community worker who explained that the centre where she worked provided workshops on domestic violence and money management, as well as other life-skills courses in Bengali, enabling women to use this resource.

Jaspal and Coyle interviewed participants who spoke Mirpuri, Punjabi and Gujarati, and found that these languages continue to be used among second-generation Asians.[10] This is presumed to be because South Asian communities in Britain tend to have dense (intragroup) social networks, and regular visits to their respective countries of origin are common.[11] Additionally, Jaspal and Coyle remark that a possible psychosocial explanation for the maintenance of South Asian heritage languages is that language plays a critical role in determining ethnicity.[12] In the case of the Bangladeshi community, Mahera Ruby showcases the importance of the grandmother's presence in a Bengali household.[13] The grandmother, Ruby discovered, acts as an essential figure who facilitates the continuation of Bengali/Sylheti to the third generation growing up in Britain. While observing three families and the impact of the grandmothers on their grandchildren, Ruby reports that 'through using Bangla, Piara [the grandmother] feels she is able to pass on cultural and faith values as well as manners that are drawn from both the cultural and faith practices'.[14] Further recent research conducted by QMUL Language Acquisition Lab, Mile End Community Project, Human Stories Films and Blooming Parenting found that the grandparents continue to shape the linguistic outcome of grandchildren's ability to express themselves in Bengali.[15]

The first chapter provided a more detailed outline of the history of the Bengali language before and after 1947. For this chapter, in particular, I will distinguish, wherever possible, between Standard Bengali (*shuddho Bangla*) and the Sylheti language. The majority of the research participants spoke Sylheti. Those whose families did not originate from Sylhet came from Chittagong, Noakhali and Dhaka. They spoke their respective regional dialects – some considered them entirely separate languages – with their relatives. Many of the non-Sylhetis I interviewed also spoke Sylheti in addition to their dialects/languages. They spoke Sylheti because of the hegemony of the language in the Bengali diaspora, their exposure to the language from a young age, hearing it across East London, and also because most of them had married Sylheti men and women.

Sylheti: A language or a dialect?

Before analysing the data on the role of language and deciphering the relationship with one's ethnic and/or religious identity vis-à-vis language, it is necessary to provide a brief overview of the Sylheti language and its history – a different historical trajectory from standard Bengali. Sylheti is spoken in the Sylhet region of north-east Bangladesh. It is estimated that 95 per cent of Bangladeshi people in the UK speak Sylheti.[16] Rod Chalmers states that although Sylheti shares 80 per cent of its vocabulary with Standard Bengali, it gains its distinction in terms of phonology and morphology.[17] Sylheti is perceived to be so different from Standard Bengali that other Bengali speakers mistake it as 'Pakistani' because of the heavy influence of Urdu on Sylheti and the many words shared by both languages.[18]

Shahela Hamid argues that there have been historical contradictions in attributing a language-related identity to Sylhetis and the area.[19] On the one hand, there are arguments suggesting that Sylhetis do not, and did not historically in an undivided India, consider themselves the same as other Bengalis.[20] However, on the other hand, there are arguments proposing that Sylhetis resisted joining Assam in modern-day India, wishing to be a part of the Bengal, as they could not identify with the Assamese language and felt that the Bengali language would be neglected.[21] In the first chapter, I discussed the political and cultural repression of the Bengali language and how it became synonymous with, and a marker of, a Bengali ethnic identity. In fact, Hamid argues that the demand for Bangla as the state language was 'first raised in the journals and periodicals published from Sylhet' while 'the first meeting resisting the adoption of Urdu as state language was held in Sylhet on 9 November 1947'.[22]

Consequently, Bengali speakers can find Sylheti 'hardly intelligible',[23] which makes it a language in its own right. In this respect, as argued by Paul Baker et al., while Sylheti is currently not officially recognised as such in Bangladesh, it is, nevertheless, viewed as 'a separate language by many government agencies in the UK that deal with large number of Sylheti speakers, e.g. the health and social services departments in Tower Hamlets, London'.[24] Helen Grady points out that the high number of Bengali speakers coming to Britain under the student visa scheme will challenge the Sylheti language's hegemony amongst Bengalis.[25] Baker et al. make the following arguments regarding the status of Sylheti and its role as a written language before and after Partition:

> Sylheti has been under pressure for many years; it has not been officially recognized as a language in Bangladesh since 1947. Up to that point, Sylheti was taught alongside Bengali in the Sylhet district of Bangladesh. However, in 1947 the teaching of Sylheti was dropped from the school curriculum and replaced

by Urdu. As well as being marginalized in Bangladesh, Sylheti also lacks basic linguistic resources. For example, although dictionaries of Bengali do occasionally make reference to certain words as being specific to Sylheti, there exists no comprehensive, modern dictionary of the language. As a consequence of the marginalization of Sylheti, the script used to write the language – Nagri – has few users. Word processing in Nagri is not available, and speakers of the language are obliged to use Bangla script if they wish to represent Sylheti. However, Sylhetis who have been brought up outside Bangladesh are unable to read and write Bengali unless they have attended classes where it has been taught. Consequently, in the UK it is often the case that Sylheti remains a purely oral language.[26]

As standard Bengali is employed in Bangladesh in its literature, education, film, media and official communication, Sarah Lawson and Itesh Sachdev contend that this makes standard Bengali of the 'high' variety, making Sylheti a 'diglossic low' variety.[27] Similarly, Zeitlyn acknowledges that 'Standard Bangla is regarded as the language of a tradition of literature and culture which Bengalis are proud of, while Sylheti is seen as a dialect or language with a relatively limited vocabulary and literary history.'[28] Furthermore, standard Bengali is associated with Rabindranath Tagore's writing and the Bengali dialect used in Kolkata.[29] In addition, many Bangladeshis see Sylhet as a conservative rural backwater compared to more sophisticated, liberal and dynamic urban centres such as Dhaka.[30] Zeitlyn's point above also reinforces that Sylheti is perceived as 'just a dialect' and does not hold the same status as standard Bangla.[31] This became evident during my fieldwork. Many participants would distinguish between standard Bangla and Sylheti, emphasising that they do not know the former and 'just about' speak the Sylheti 'dialect'.

Bangla and/or Sylheti: How they are used

During my fieldwork, all the research participants spoke to me in English, though some of them added some Bengali words into their responses to add emphasis or because they felt the English word/s did not quite capture what they were trying to express. At the beginning of each interview, I informed the interviewees that they could use Bengali words or even do the entire interview in Bengali. I made this clear in order to allow the interviews to run as organically as possible and enable the research participants to control how *they* wanted to express themselves. Nevertheless, the interviewees chose to speak in English, an active assertion of identity during the interviews, indicating that while the majority spoke Bengali at home, they remained far more proficient in English. It is the language they use most throughout the day. This argument was perfectly captured by Shamim (interviewed in November 2013), who shared his experience of growing up with both English and Bengali in his household, having agreed with his mother that he would speak only Bengali at home in order to practise it, whereas he would speak English whenever he was out (see pp. 3–4):

> And that was the way she got me to learn Bengali and that was really important, because lots of my friends despise the news, they despise everything that was going on in Bangladesh; it was not because they actually understood what was going on, but they could not understand the language used on television, or in the *natoks*,[32] in the dramas. I got an appreciation for all this from this [experience with my mum].

Shamim's response illustrates his multilingual upbringing and how each language became restricted and designated to a specific, allocated space and time. Nevertheless, his mother not allowing him to speak English at home enabled him to maintain and foster his proficiency in Bengali while developing a strong English foundation outside the home. An essential point to consider here is that the 'language used on television, or in the *natoks*' means Standard Bengali, not Sylheti. Linguistic specificity is crucial in understanding the relationship between meeting the demands of speaking the language at home, which is Sylheti, while simultaneously feeling disconnected from one's heritage, situated through Standard Bengali. As we saw in an earlier chapter (pp. 3–4), in our conversation after the interview, Shamim spoke fondly of his dad's politics and activities, and how he had greatly admired the Bangladeshi figure Maulana Bhashani. Shamim's parents' investment and persistence enabled Shamim to speak Sylheti fluently.

Khalid (interviewed in January 2014) had a different experience with the Bengali language from Shamim, and distinguished between the use of Standard Bengali and Sylheti. Throughout the interview, Khalid used a lot of Bengali words with ease and without hesitation. Interestingly, when asked how attached he felt to the Bengali language, he said he did not feel too attached to it, and he shared:

> It's not very important because … It's becoming easier to communicate [in] other ways. For example, we communicate through WhatsApp a lot more than I communicate by talking on the phone. A hell of a lot more. I remember I spent hours on the phone with other people, hours on end, because … I don't know why. But now it's more phased out, I'm always talking English. You always do when you write your texts – it's always easier to write in English. You always write in English. You never actually have the need to write anything else in Bengali, because English covers it and it's become such a normal way to communicate, because even though Bengali was the first thing I was

taught, English is my language. I might not be able to speak as fluently as other people are, like academically expressing myself. There are certain things [where] I haven't been able to express myself properly, but I know that when I talk in English, it just seems I express myself a lot better than when I say it in Bengali. Sometimes I have to express myself in English, because I can't get it out. *Bangali* word *fayna* [i.e. I can't find the Bengali word]. I tried so hard – *ami chesta khormu* [I try hard] – just trying to – only recently, only a few years, only more and more recently I've become accustomed to certain words like, erm ... trying to talk nice Bengali, I suppose. I don't know what nice Bengali is!

The striking feature of our interview was that despite conducting the entire interview in English with some Bengali words sprinkled around, Khalid still expressed frustration about expressing himself fluently in English. One of the contestations here is that the power dynamics present during the interview, within the presence of a researcher, initiated a fear of not articulating ideas thoroughly. I attempted to mitigate this by offering Khalid the option to use Bengali; however, maintaining and preserving a heritage language is difficult for diaspora communities for many reasons,[33] so Khalid's admission that he lacks the vocabulary to speak fluently is complementary to the literature exploring diaspora and its relations with language maintenance.[34] By contrast, English allows him to engage with others more fluidly and to share his thoughts. I enquired further into his knowledge of Standard Bengali and Sylheti:

Me: Do you mean standard Bangla like *shuddho Bangla*?
Khalid: *Shuddho nay* [not Standard]. More Sylheti, where my *bari* [village] is from.[35] My friend is from Beanibazar [a district in Sylhet] and I've picked up his words. When I repeated back my words when I got to my dad or my mum, 'What does that mean?'. Like, for example, we call it *razai* [duvet]; some people call it *lef*. Or *lembu* [lemon]; we call it *lebu*. Some people call it *lobon* [salt] or *noon*. Or ... It's those little differences where – that's why the Bengali language for us here, it's not much of an issue, because we can always talk in English. All of my friends talk in English. They always talk.

The exposure to different linguistic expressions from the varying districts of Sylhet is a common theme in the data. Exposure to Sylhetis from other districts further helps expand one's cultural knowledge within the community. Furthermore, it enables one to manifest a sense of Bengali identity vis-à-vis the language, which is inextricably linked to expressing one's 'Bengaliness'. This is consonant with Jean Mills's suggestion that 'biculturalism, in the sense of two distinct cultures co-existing or combining, in some way, in one individual, is related to that individual's sense of identity'.³⁶ For example, when I engaged with Khalid's Sylheti roots, he provided a detailed outline of when and where he uses Bengali:

> Me: But what about your family? Do you speak Bangla with your family?
> Khalid: I speak Bengali with my family, with my mum, with my dad.
> Me: Why not English with your family?
> Khalid: Because I was raised like that. Because I was the first one in my family to – I'm the eldest in my family. So, I've always had to talk Bengali with them because there's never been an opportunity for me to communicate with my family in English. *Tara buzta nay* [they won't understand], whereas *ekhon* [now], now, we're a family of six in total. My youngest [siblings] – they talk in English to mum, with each other, very rarely a word of Bengali comes out from their mouths. If I was to ask my brother to talk in Bengali, I'd guarantee that the third word he'd probably say –
> Me: Switch to English?
> Khalid: That's it. He wouldn't even know. He wouldn't even understand what I'm saying. Sometimes he *buzena amra kitha khoyram* [does not understand what we are saying]. Me and my mum have conversations *fura* [fully], full on *Bangaliye*, or when *desho* [back home], when I call home, full on Bengali, full on Bengali to my *khalus* [uncles], and he hasn't got a clue what they're saying. It's amazing how much – that's why I'd say the language is not as important as it was before, because there are other ways of communicating, of expressing myself. That says because English is becoming more – it's not my first language, definitely not. But English is a lot easier to use than Bengali sometimes. Sometimes.

Khalid's role as the language broker in the family is an intriguing observation. The eldest child holds the social responsibility of being the arbiter for the communication between younger siblings and parents.³⁷ However, along with this role, Khalid also oscillates between using Sylheti and Bengali as the one and the same thing. This articulation is not isolated to Khalid only, as it will become apparent throughout this chapter that many of the participants used both terms interchangeably. The times they explicitly wanted to refer to standard Bengali, they added the adjective *shuddho*. *Shuddho* means 'correct' or 'pure'; however, it is translated into English as 'Standard' when it operates as an adjective before *Bangla*/Bengali. The use of *shuddho* further implies a hierarchy, placing it as the normative. Likewise, Stephen May points out that maintaining a minority language does not in any way 'preclude ongoing cultural and linguistic change, adaptation and interaction'.³⁸ On the contrary, he asserts that 'those who wish to maintain their historically associated language, usually alongside that of another more dominant language, actually exhibit a greater ability to manage multiple cultural and linguistic identities'.[39] May's argument further adds and entrenches a complexity already present, whereby Sylhetis are trying to maintain their language whilst negotiating their identity with the dominant Standard Bengali. This is because they are exposed to hearing *shuddho* Bengali on TV, most probably watched by parents and grandparents. At the same time, Sylheti functions as the dominant language in their everyday life.

Of further interest here is how Khalid was one of the few participants who used code-switching as a way to explore elements of language maintenance and its use. Another noteworthy point is how the other participants spoke in Bengali before or after the recording of the interview. Stuart Hall notes that young people in the diaspora tend to rely on code-switching as a way to practise an unwritten covenant to express their cultural identifications. Specifically, he argues that young people

> learn the system and conventions of representation, the codes of their language and culture, which equip them with cultural 'know-how', enabling them to function as culturally competent subjects. Not because such knowledge is imprinted in their genes, but because they learn its conventions and so gradually *become* 'cultured persons' – i.e. members of their culture. They unconsciously internalize the codes which allow them to express certain concepts and ideas through their systems of representation – writing, speech, gesture, visualization, and so on – and to interpret ideas which are communicated to them using the same systems.[40]

In May 2014, Shefali spoke about the importance of the Bengali language, and about feeling upset that she was unable to speak it well. She said she was eager to pass on the language to her children and hoped that perhaps, one day, they could teach *her* the language. She made a clear distinction between her use of Sylheti and *shuddho* Bengali, and felt that she was fluent in the former and struggled with the latter:

Me: Do you speak Bangla?
Shefali: I do. I speak Bengali at home. It's not the greatest. I did Bengali GCSE at my school, [at] Mulberry School we used to learn – I think most schools in Tower Hamlets, just generally in these areas, we do get the opportunity to study our native language. Generally, it's okay. It's not the best, but I can speak Sylheti quite fluently. *Shuddho basha* [standard language] – it's a work but I can read Bengali.
Me: For you, how important is the Bengali language as part of your Bengali identity?
Shefali: I really want to say it's very, very important, because I know how much people have fought for this ... but I think it's just my lack of use; I don't consider it as much as I actually wish I did. Upon reflection, I think it is important. It's fundamental just in how I communicated

>
> with the generation of Bengali and the elderly folks in our communities. It's a huge part of how I communicate with Bangladeshi people.
>
> **Me:** Would you consider passing on Bengali to your children?
>
> **Shefali:** Absolutely. I will, absolutely. I think it will be hard, because I don't use it myself a lot, but I would definitely make a point of it, because I think it's important to know heritage despite wherever you are. This is your lineage. I think it's something I'd definitely get my children to ensure they do know much better than me. Maybe perhaps they could teach me.

Like Khalid and Shamim, Shefali also speaks Bengali at home to maintain basic competency levels, and locates it as a fundamental way to communicate with her elders and other Bangladeshis. In their study on Bengali pupils in London studying for GCSE Bengali, Lawson and Sachdev also note that 'English was reported as being used most in all domains except family/home with all interlocutors except older relatives. Bengali was used most in the home, talking about family and household matters, and with older relatives.'[41] Interestingly, Shefali shared that she could read in Bengali, whereas many interviewees could neither read nor write in it. At the time of the interview, Shefali worked in a secondary school that provided the option to study GCSE Bengali. It is essential to mention here the local council's defunding of community language services.[42] While the same council, led by the former mayor, John Biggs, cut funds for language learning and access to Bengali language classes, it also added a sign to Whitechapel Station in Bangla.[43] The political disposition is to treat the local Bangladeshi community as infantile, requiring a mere vinyl placard to dissuade them from holding local politicians accountable. The irony of placing a sign in Bangla at a central station in Tower Hamlets when younger Bangladeshis can no longer access their heritage language did not go unnoticed by local residents.[44] Following the election of the current administration under the Aspire Party, led by former mayor Lutfur Rahman, community language services have been reinstated.[45]

Notably, Rasinger's study of Sylheti and Bengali usage in Tower Hamlets found that adults are likelier to use Sylheti in the home.[46] Observing that English was increasingly used more at home, as in conversations with children, he speculates that this trend might be due to 'the desire to teach children English or due to children's refusal or inability to talk Sylheti'.[47] Further to this, he notes that there is less interethnic interaction between Bangladeshis and others, creating room to maintain and retain the language. While no longer the case today, during Rasinger's study it was concluded that institutions' support of Bengali in schools across Tower Hamlets added to the 'vitality' of the language and its continued use, highlighting the power of local discourse in asserting a localised identity.[48] By contrast, deriving his conclusions from the results of his fieldwork in Islington, Zeitlyn notes that

Bangladeshis are more likely to interact with other communities because there are fewer Bangladeshis in the borough, which obviously affects the vitality of the language and identification with it.⁴⁹ Adding to this, Zeitlyn remarks upon the use of language and its prolific presence in the home to communicate with parents or relatives, and contends that 'at home, children speak more Bangla than anywhere else, apart from on visits to Bangladesh'.⁵⁰

Shiraj (interviewed in March 2014) was interviewed in an office inside East London Mosque. When the discussion around language came up, he started explaining how grateful he was that his children's local secondary school in Tower Hamlets offered Bengali; however, he noted that it allowed them access only to very basic Bengali. '[T]hey did learn something in the mainstream education in the British school. You get an option to learn Bengali, especially in Tower Hamlets. They did do their basic GCSE but that's very, very basic. I don't think they can write a couple of sentences properly.' Anchoring the language inside the home and in schools across Tower Hamlets is vital to elaborate on here. The borough and its large demographic of Bangladeshis have made the area a fertile source for the continued maintenance of their heritage via language. As a result, Bangladeshis have been able to create a space for those in their community to identify with their heritage and to foster it institutionally and within their homes. Bangladeshis, then, can draw on their history and observe the contestations between different mosques and organisations, forming a space to negotiate the perceived homogeneity of the community vis-à-vis the dominant discourse: one that views Bangladeshis as a homogeneous group. The local space – i.e. the making of the *para* that extends beyond the house, thus constituting home – opens up the potential to challenge and undermine the dominant figuring of Bangladeshis; however, this does not mean this prevailing discourse loses its salience. Accordingly, as argued by Baumann, the 'very existence of a demotic discourse which separates *culture* and *community* and reconsiders its meanings, is a reaction, arising in a plethora of different contexts, to the dominant one'.⁵¹

Nafisah (interviewed in May 2014), a psychologist for the NHS, shared her experiences working in Tower Hamlets and how she had had to use her Bengali language skills whilst working with Bengali women suffering from depression and anxiety. She found that to be able to help these women efficiently, she had to practise more of her Bengali at home with her relatives:

Me: Do you speak *shuddho basha* [standard language]? Do you read and write Bangla?

Nafisah: [Laughs] I can understand a bit of *shuddho Bangla* [Standard Bengali]. I'm really bad, as my husband's family told me repeatedly often! And I can't really write at all. Basically, when I was younger I learnt like 'O', 'A' [referring to the Bengali vowels], but I'm terrible, it's really hard – like when I started working in Tower Hamlets, they were like real Bengali, you have to run these groups, I have to run like Jagonari Centre and there I have to run depression groups and anxiety management [groups] in Sylheti, in Bengali.[52] I have no clue … it's only … It's the practice at home with my mum, and my aunt, what I say. Eventually I grew confident and it became a bit better, but what helped me was a lot of like the woman who was telling me 'Oh no worries', including my patients as well: '… you sound just like my daughter'. So I understood, so … I was like, I speak Benglish [laughs].

We see Nafisah's expansive boundaries of belonging and defining her Bengali identity by incorporating the language into her work life to gauge the women's mental health issues. In Nafisah's case, unlike those of the other research participants quoted, the Bengali language is not secluded within her home. Instead, the language travels with her into her work life, thus adding a layered experience of her Bengali identity in the public sphere. Her work at the Jagonari Centre is also highly symbolic for her as a Bengali woman, as it was a women's centre opened by a Bangladeshi woman for other Bangladeshi women. It was set up so that women could have access to resources related to domestic violence and mental health services, as well as many other classes and lessons. After the interview finished in the little café close to Altab Ali Park, Nafisah excitedly shared how her current work with the women allowed her to expand her Sylheti language skills beyond the everyday conversational sets.

While most Bangladeshis in Tower Hamlets hail from Sylhet, interestingly they are still very conscious of how their language is not the 'proper Bengali' and juxtapose it with Standard Bengali. Of relevance, Hamid points out that 'Sylheti has vitality in terms of its numerical strength in the UK and is the lingua franca of the majority of the Bangladeshis in the UK.'[53] Since the Bengali GCSE is based on Standard Bengali, young Bangladeshis are exposed to the national language of Bangladesh in their youth and become aware of the multiple linguistic statuses attributed to each language. Bangladeshis were thus exposed to Sylheti within the local discourse and construction of British Bengaliness, which was challenged in a classroom or through Bengali channels using Standard Bengali. Simultaneous use of Bengali and English demonstrates the need to choose the language that will inform the identity expressed at that time. When visiting London, politicians from the Bangladeshi Parliament meet with prominent figures from the British Bangladeshi community. In this respect, Justin Gest reports that since the mid-1980s, financial involvement in Bangladesh, through remittances and family properties, has been institutionalised by the 'work of many "development groups" controlled by lineage leaders closely linked with the activities of Bangladeshi political parties in London, in particular the Awami League'.[54] Other transnational collaborations are particularly evident during A Season of Bangla Drama, organised by local Bengalis in collaboration with Tower Hamlets Council, inviting Bengalis from Bangladesh and West Bengal to travel to the UK, and perform and collaborate with British Bengalis.

Jahangir (interviewed in December 2014) voiced his concerns about the future of the language in the UK. Specifically, he said: 'I mean, there is something I fear that is our generation is the last generation I think that are going to speak Bangla – that's something that I fear. It's like we ... we are talking about our kids. I don't think they are going to be speaking Bangla, at all, to be honest, and I fear that. I think it's quite sad.' Jahangir shared the increasingly undeniable reality of his teenage children losing the ability to speak Bengali, very much characterised by the way English functions as the main language of communication. Jahangir noted that the language is one crucial element of asserting Bengaliness: 'If I am Bengali, then I have to speak Bangla I think – that's my view anyway.' Douglas H. Brown provides the following description of the relationship between culture and language: 'A language is a part of a culture and a culture is a part of a language; the two are intricately interwoven so that one cannot separate the two without losing the significance of either language or culture.'[55] This suggests that language and culture are inseparable and that the former 'is also the symbolic representation of a people, since it comprises their historical and cultural backgrounds, as well as their approach to life and their ways of living and thinking'.[56] Elaborating on the relationship between language and cultures, Hall argues that we cannot speak about 'one experience, one identity' with any exactness unless we acknowledge 'the ruptures and discontinuities' in the history of 'a people', whether that people result from a 'voluntary' diaspora or from dispersal and enslavement enforced by an imperial power.[57] As long as a language is part of a culture, it will experience changes. This has been illustrated seamlessly by many interviewees who used Bengali words while mixing it with English. Hall refers to this 'creolisation' of language as a syncretic dynamic process where aspects from the dominant culture are appropriated and subsequently 'creolised', thereby unsettling, decentring or disrupting identification with the language and its use.[58]

The debates around Standard Bengali and Sylheti and whether the latter is intelligible vis-à-vis standard Bengali have been ongoing. Alom (interviewed in January 2014) was interviewed in his office room at his workplace and had a long think while we started our conversation regarding Sylheti and how he felt about contemporary framings of the languages. He exclaimed that he did not differentiate between Standard Bengali and Sylheti. Regarding the former, he argued that 'nobody speaks in that language any more, that's just for radio and TV and books'. When further probed about the importance of passing on the language to his daughter, he responded:

> I myself have struggled with that question for many years – is it really important for our young people to learn Bengali – and I still don't know, to be honest, but I do think identities are important ... because one could find [out] about Bengali culture or could be exposed to Bengali culture without knowing the language. He could study that in English and find out about the history.

However, would the community at large accept the individual as a member of the community? What would the process of validation to 'fit in' constitute? There is also the argument that language is a crucial element in accessing a 'culture'; however, Alom did not define what he meant by culture. In a similar way, Hamid puts forward the following argument: '[T]here is no denying, of course, that Sylheti and Bangla are closely related as they share a large percentage of core vocabulary which may help towards understanding ... despite common root words, Sylheti's simpler sound system and phonological variations make many words sound different from their Bangla counterparts.'[59] Therefore, Alom's emphasis that Sylheti and Bangla are not two separate languages could also be a projection of the multilocational identities of being a British Bangladeshi. This can be explained by Hall's argument that the positionality of 'difference' within identity encompasses shifting its boundaries at different times in relation to different questions.[60]

Another theme that became prevalent during my fieldwork was the discussion surrounding Sylheti's status and that it was not prioritised as 'proper' Bengali. Not only is Sylheti perceived to be just a dialect, but Standard Bengali and Sylheti can never be similar. This emerged in the interview with Shiraj, an active attendee of the East London Mosque, who provided insights into the interchangeable use of Sylheti/Standard Bengali in different contexts:

> **Me:** So going back to Bengaliness and growing up here in Tower Hamlets, do you think that also helped you to preserve the speaking of Bangla? Do you speak Standard Bangla or Sylheti?
>
> **Shiraj:** I do speak both, Standard and Sylheti. Yeah, it did help. I have interaction with a lot of non-Sylheti people as well. And that helped me to improve my Bengali. Otherwise, I think my Bengali would've been really just Sylheti dialect. But because of my interaction – for example, I also attend in the mosque – we have Bengali *tafseer*, the explanation of the Qur'an, every Saturday. And I've been attending that for a long time. So the *imam* speaks in the proper Bengali.

Me: *Shuddho Bangla?*
Shiraj: *Shuddho Bangla.* Yes, that's proper Bengali. So a lot of people will actually improve their Bengali as well.

In her study focusing on both Hindus and Muslims from West Bengal and Bangladesh, Nayanika Mookherjee reports witnessing a similar attitude during her fieldwork, noting that 'non-Sylheti Bangladeshis, who discuss and engage in various artefacts of Bengali identity, namely Bengali literature and other Bengali cultural forms, express their ambivalence about Sylhetis and the authenticity of their Bengali identity'.[61] She continues to argue that Sylhetiness, seen by other non-Sylheti Bangladeshis as *moulobadi* (fundamentalist), was emphasised by the events of 1993, when Jamaat-e-Islami, an Islamic political party, 'issued a *fatwa* against the writer Tasleema Nasreen ... for her alleged newspaper interview where she proposed that changes should be made to the Koran'.[62] The perception of Sylhetis as being different from other Bengalis is underpinned by two reasons: first, the difference in language; second, its emphasis through discursive encounters with Sylhetiness in Bangladesh and the transposition thereof to the UK. The general perception of Sylhet is that it is a backward and religiously conservative place.

Standard Bangla/Sylheti in the East End's mosques and homes

As the conversation continued with Shiraj, he shared his thoughts about the East London Mosque attendees and asserted that 60–70 per cent of the congregants were Bangladeshis. He noted that the mosque attempted to accommodate all and held its *khutbahs* in Bengali, along with Arabic and English:[63]

> We try to accommodate everyone because our *khutbah* is in three languages. If you look at it, first [it] is in Arabic, about four, five minutes in Arabic. Then it's Bengali, and then it's English. So, we accommodate for most of the *musollis*, the worshippers here. Still, we have a big number of first generation Bangladeshi. So we have people like my father's age and then our age group – most of them understand Bengali; they may not be able to speak proficiently in Bengali. And then, we had, in the last twenty years, we had a big influx of first-generation Bangladeshis who came here through marriage. So there's a big [population of] first-generation Muslim Bangladeshis still there, and they're coming to our mosque as well.

Shiraj believed that, in the next twenty to thirty years, the Friday prayer sermons would cease to include Bengali, as this was merely adhered to as a way to cater to the first generation; in the future they would be given only in English and Arabic. However, the inclusion of Bengali at the mosque – although Shiraj did not clarify whether Standard Bengali or Sylheti was used for the Friday sermons – implies that the worshippers and those working at the mosque are symbiotically having to inhabit multiple identities constantly, and speak multiple languages to enable all congregants to understand the sermon. As such, the oscillating between these identities emerges as a result of the needs of the congregation, especially those attending Friday prayers. Pnina Werbner suggests that those in power 'must reify ethnic segments as perpetual communities in order to control conflict or allocate resources in an "equitable" manner'.[64] While Shiraj addressed the importance of multilingual Friday sermons, he continued to emphasise the importance of preserving the Bengali language in Britain:

> I think learning any language is an asset – it's not a liability, especially [as] Bengali is a very prominent language. I think more than 300 million people speak Bengali in this world. I think it's about in the top twenty, if not more. It's a very nice language and, as our mother tongue, it is important to preserve, but not at the expense of maybe learning English, for example, because we have to live here. If learning Bengali is hampering my development in learning English language, then, probably, you will have to compromise. But if [in] some way people can do both, that's the best, actually. And this one is an asset. The more languages you know, the better it is for you, better career prospects. That is that people – we, Bengalis – are probably suffering from [an] inferiority complex.

This pragmatic formulation of balancing English and Bengali is a prevalent theme in the data. The resurfacing of this equation suggests that Shiraj supports the move away from 'an ideal construct' to 'a pragmatic acculturation',[65] and believes that the community members in East London 'must learn to inhabit two identities, to speak two cultural languages, to translate and negotiate between them'.[66] While Shiraj is not contesting the inhabiting of multiple locational identity expressions, nonetheless his perspective fails to consider the wider political discussions around ethnic minority communities and the 'lack' of English-speaking skills. For example, in 2016, then Prime Minister David Cameron linked Muslim mothers' non-proficiency in English to the proliferation of radicalism.[67] The conception that language operates as an arbiter, thus preventing radicalism, is used as a device to continue to 'other' Muslims – a demographic of whom a large proportion comprises Bangladeshis. In this set-up, Peter Mandaville argues that 'the construction of group identity is inherently a socio-political process, involving as it does dialogue, negotiation and debate as to "who we are" and, moreover, what it means to be "who we are"'.[68] In this regard, the question of 'who we are' is thus constructed by Shiraj concerning British society overall. He recognises the need for English to function as the primary language and, wherever possible, for the retention of one's attachment to the Bengali language.

The dominant public discourse defines minority communities as homogeneous and assumes that they are easily identifiable through a recognised, reified common identity, usually imposed by the state. Therefore, it is unsurprising that Shiraj internalises this view and emphasises the importance of learning English. He engages with the dominant public discourse, which demands ethnic minority communities' fluency in English, adding pressure on those communities to ensure that they learn the language. In return, the dominant discourse is challenged by defying the very stereotypes attributed to those communities. This is not to render the dominant discourse any less hegemonic; however, it is necessary to consider that Bangladeshis, in particular, use it 'whenever their judgements of context or purpose make it seem appropriate'.[69] The demotic, local discourse and framing, in return, allow for subversion by contesting the dominant discourse's projected cultural markers, thereby reifying cultures 'while at the same time making culture'.[70] In this way, Bangladeshis are commanding and making use of a dual discursive competence: that of the dominant discourse and that of the demotic discourse, where both are continuously shaping lived experiences.[71]

Additionally, Shiraj further uses his identification with the English language as a strategic and positional one. Hall provides the following analysis of such an identification:

> [T]his concept of identity does not signal that stable core of the self, unfolding from beginning to end through all the vicissitudes of history without change; the bit of the self which remains always-already 'the same', identical to itself across time … It accepts that identities are never unified and, in late modern times, increasingly fragmented and fractured; never singular but multiply constructed across different, often intersecting and antagonistic, discourses, practices and positions.[72]

This strategic purpose enables one to tell a particular narrative. In this instance, it is to subvert the idea that ethnic minority communities are unwilling to learn English and merge into the dominant society. The danger in such a narrative is that it may entrap itself in an essentialist means of expressing such identification. As Werbner puts it, 'in their performative rhetoric the people we study essentialize their imagined communities in order to mobilise for action' – hence the national hyper-vigilance of Tower Hamlets and its politics – mainly focusing on Lutfur Rahman.[73] Rahman was elected as executive mayor in 2010, and then again in 2014. It was in his second term that he was ousted following a court case around vote-rigging. In 2022, he returned after a five-year ban from political office.[74] Rahman's case study is a useful way to observe how Bangladeshis are putting forth an essentialised image of the community as a way to sanitise and manage stereotypes about themselves. This brief consideration helps contextualise how Bangladeshis organise their identities vis-à-vis the dominant framings. However, while considering local political context *qua* the national and how it shapes people's relations with the Bengali language, there are other factors to consider too. This is where Shiraj's framing of Bengalis as embodying an 'inferiority complex' requires further scrutiny. He feels that those in their twenties and younger had a dismissive attitude to their heritage roots and he expands that 'they think Bangladesh is a very poor country and people feel that there's nothing there to be proud of. Even actually with my own children. When we talk about Bangladesh, they always say "Ah, it's Bangladesh." It's like putting it down. Anything to do with Bangladesh and Bengali. They don't seem to appreciate the language.'

Central here is the proposition that because of their distant relationship with Bangladesh Shiraj identifies his children's lack of interest as a form of rejection. In such contexts, when references are made to identifications vis-à-vis group identity, Rogers Brubaker and Frederick Cooper suggest that, in order to capture such a collective identity, the use of 'groupness' or 'connectedness' would, analytically, provide richer nuance.[75] However, Shiraj's children's self-understanding and contestation of Bangladesh and the language are connected to their socialisation in Britain. Similarly, Gest also acknowledges having observed that, even though young Bangladeshis occasionally honoured their ethnic roots, the political system of Bangladesh was seen by them as 'irrelevant, and, if it is even known … typically perceived as backward or corrupt'.[76] In addition to this, even though Shiraj's children did GCSE Bengali, which covered Standard Bengali, his children struggle to understand Standard Bengali:

> They speak Sylheti dialect. They don't understand. There's another thing I've noticed. When I watch the Bengali news, my children, I asked them 'Do you understand?'. They don't understand 95 per cent of it, because it's a completely different language to [ours]. They understand Sylheti if you speak to them in Sylheti, but when the newsreader is reading in pure Bengali, they don't understand anything.

This reiterates Mandaville's point about the role of dialogue and negotiation, most evident not only between Shiraj and his children, who rely on their father to 'translate' the news into Sylheti for them, but also in his children's reliance on their elders to help enforce their spoken Bengali.[77] Generational priorities influence the construction and reconstruction of identities, as those acculturated and socialised in Britain prioritise English over standard Bengali and/or Sylheti. Another participant who also invoked the 'inferiority complex' mode was Sohaib (interviewed in January 2014).

He addressed the issue and claimed 'I noticed this across many people, and so because of that, I think Bangladeshis sort of feel that they need to give more attention to, say, an Arab issue, or even the Kashmir issue. If you look at the Kashmir issue, it's a very live issue.' Sohaib's explanation of the notion of an 'inferiority complex' is similar to Shiraj's perspective. Still, the core difference is that Sohaib places this complex concerning other ethnic minority communities in Britain. He continued to expand that Bangladeshis within organisations will 'be very good at doing a lot of the work, but they wouldn't have the confidence, perhaps to give leadership [a go] or to stand on a podium and speak'; consequently, others would take credit for their work instead. Furthermore, to assert themselves, they had to prioritise other global events unrelated to their own Bangladeshi identity. In a similar vein, Gest notes that his interviewees adopted a post-Bangladeshi identity: a specific 'identity construction where their roots in Bangladesh informed their ideas and social habits, but did not dictate them'.[78]

While speaking to Ismail (interviewed in March 2014) about preserving Bengali with his children, he took a long breath and exclaimed that it was a tough question for him, as his stance on teaching his children Bengali had changed over the years. This is how he elaborated on the issue in the context of his family's changing priorities:

> It's a tough question. My daughter, when she was growing up, I did send her to learn Bengali and stuff like that. My second son is seventeen. I did send him for a year and then stopped. The youngest one I didn't send at all. I mean, for myself, the importance is going. I think we're dealing with competing priorities, that's what it is. An identity is something you have to really be focusing [on]. I don't think I identify myself as Bengali as much as I used to. I still am Bengali, but what I mean is I don't prioritise that identity over being Muslim, over being British or anything else. Whereas me being me when I was growing up, it used to be the other way round. I think amongst young people, from my work with young people, what I see is the same thing. They see themselves as British. And then the other identities come in. So, that priority dictates how much they feel the language is important.

Interestingly, Ismail also noted the role of the supplementary schools referenced at the beginning of the chapter. He reflected and shared his thoughts on how they 'used to be everywhere', but now one had to look for them: now, he continued, 'it's actually bonded onto the *madrasah*. Whereas it was different, it's separate because it had that importance. It needed to be different. But now it's one day a week, there's Bengali being taught. So you can see it's losing its – but it depends, how your outlook is.' His observation of the reduced number of supplementary schools offering Bengali is intriguing, as it suggests that Bengali is neither a priority for, nor a demand made by, many Bengali families across East London. Also, as noted earlier, the community language services went through funding cuts, preventing people from accessing Bengali. However, Ismail argued that fifteen years previously he would push Bengali channels to broadcast their programmes and shows in English, but many had refused, claiming that they were a 'Bengali channel'. Nevertheless, he had noticed a difference in how the programmes are recorded because they have acknowledged that the younger generations need to be engaged in English rather than Bengali. He stated:

> Now every Bengali channel does programmes in English. Because they know young Bengalis – it's not going to come to them unless they speak English ... So now they're talking about language movement in English, the Bengali language movement in English. Because it's a historical thing that is being taught. So it's for historical purposes, it's not for anything practical. Bengali newspapers are still there but they are [a] dying breed. Who reads Bengali? [It's] only because you've had a big influx of Bengali students in the last five years that it's still surviving. But most Bengalis that were born here, thirty years ago onwards, most of them would not read Bengali newspapers. It's the elder generation or the new people.

Similarly, Grady argues that Bengalis arriving on the student visa scheme will challenge the hegemony of the Sylheti language;[79] however, as it appears from Ismail's comments, they will also be the new 'group' who will revive the Bengali language and keep it afloat in the market. They will challenge the hegemony of Sylheti but simultaneously provide a steady continuation of written Standard Bangla. It is through the arrival of the new Bengali migrants from mainland European countries that one can notice Bengali's presence in the public sphere, where it would otherwise have started to disappear. Moreover, Shiraj continued, with regret in his voice, that he encouraged his wife to speak Bengali with the children because she was from Bangladesh. However, he acknowledged that it was also his fault for not trying to speak more Bengali with the children. He solemnly stated that they tried very hard, but it was no longer a possible task. He found it much easier to communicate with his children in English and saw that everyone was doing the same with theirs. Consistent with Shiraj's experience, Hall asserts:

> So-called 'ethnic minorities' have indeed formed strongly marked, cultural communities, and maintain [them] in everyday life, especially in familial and domestic contexts, distinctive social customs and practices. There are continuing links with their places of origin. This is especially the case in densely settled areas ... As in most diasporas, traditions are variable from person to person, and even within person, and are constantly being revised and transformed in response to the migration experience.[80]

As Hall mentioned, this transformation is occurring in the linguistic realms amongst British Bangladeshi Muslims with the new wave of migrants from Bangladesh and other mainland European countries,[81] but not exclusively those who come as students. Mohammed (interviewed in March 2014) spoke about the role of Bengali amongst Bangladeshis in East London and how they could learn from the Chinese community, which, as he emphasised, is one of the oldest communities in the East End. He continued, explaining that it would be a loss if Bangladeshis stopped passing on the Bengali language to the next generation:

> I think it's a big shame, and it's a big loss. But the use of the Bangla language is not going to be as much as it was with our parents' generation. We're bilingual, so we can speak Bangla, English, Arabic, whatever, Urdu ... and a lot of people are doing that. And I think, as the generations move on – in Tower Hamlets we've got the Chinese community as well, they've been here for hundreds of years, but they still preserve their language, it's passed down, yeah ... and, through the language is a way of life – where, for us, you know, language is important but it's not something that is [a] way of life, in the Muslim psyche, anyway, yeah? You got the added pressure – remember I said we used to go the *madrasas* for, how many days, three days? And Bangla for ...? Two days, so more – always emphasis was given on the Arabic, and more and more families are choosing Arabic.

Like Ismail and others, Mohammed states that the priority was always given to Arabic, but that it would not be impossible to pass on Bengali if Bangladeshis made an effort like the Chinese, who have been able to preserve their language. However, there is no evidence to suggest that the Chinese community in the East End did preserve their language in the way Mohammed claims. François Grosjean suggests that 'in the end, language attitude is always one of the major factors in accounting for which languages are learned, which are used, and which are preferred by bilinguals'.[82] Mohammed's argument that a language enables a way of life is interesting, as it suggests that one cannot access that 'world' without access to the language. He further reflects on how it is not a part of the 'Muslim psyche' to regard language as a way of life, but then states that Arabic was given more priority in his childhood. This prioritisation implies that Arabic is linked to what Mohammed refers to as the 'Muslim psyche', while other languages are placed on a lower pedestal. The next chapter will elaborate on the Arabic language and how Muslim consciousness is intricately tied to it. Mohammed's historical link and comparison with the Chinese community regarding the upholding of the Bengali language in East London is an intriguing one, as other research participants spoke about how being brought up in East London had, in fact, helped them to perpetuate, preserve and develop a Bengali identity through the language thanks to its high visibility and presence.

Faruk (interviewed in April 2014) shared his thoughts on East London and how being in and around the area helped his wife to reconnect with her roots. He noted that after spending her childhood in the East End, she had moved to North London for fifteen years, where she had had little opportunity to speak Bengali:

> I'll give you an example. My wife, she's from North London, and when she was out there [i.e. North London] she said she forgot her roots, because she was in a white Jewish dominated area, where you know, you were not able to speak your language apart from coming home and speaking with your parents and other people. And you didn't get that kind of feeling of community, you couldn't just walk down the street and see ladies in *sari*s and *sasa*s in *tupi*s [uncles in hats] and stuff like that, the markets selling stuff like vegetables and things like that, so it was very difficult, and then when we got married, and she moved to Tower Hamlets, she saw a different side to it 'cause she said 'I have not seen this for fifteen odd years, because I have been stuck in North London and now I am exposed to all of this.' She loves it!

Within this context laid out by Faruk, we recognise the potent ways that East London as a space and location provides the basis for maintaining one's language practice. Relatedly, Hall reminds us that 'identity emerges as a kind of unsettled space … between a number of intersecting discourses'.[83] This reflection is crucial in recognising the argument I have advanced in previous chapters about the role of the *para*: how the notion of neighbourhood is marked as an extension of the home. It becomes, in short, a schema for people to speak Bengali openly without feeling a sense of shame, or consciousness of having to prove their ability to speak English in order to put the public at ease.[84] In this sense, East London makes provisions for the Bengali identity via language to persist, reaffirming and defining the sense of self, but only with other Bengalis.

Transnational marriages and language

The theme of transnational marriage and its potential role in shaping language provisions was present. The British Bangladeshi experience of marrying someone from Bangladesh, and how that influences the dynamics of the diaspora community, is a dimension that requires further enquiry, as this book will not do justice to this area. However, for the data for this book, Ismail raised the subject of transnational marriage while giving the example of his wife, who is from Bangladesh, and whom he encouraged to speak Bengali with the children because he stated that she spoke it better than he did. Another participant who addressed this point was Nasima (interviewed in June 2014), who spoke very fondly of speaking Sylheti and *shuddho Bangla*. The former became prominent in her household and with her children, as her husband is from Bangladesh. She provided the following account:

> I can, yes [speak] Sylheti and *shuddho*. It depends *khaar loge matram* [who I'm speaking to]. If a *shuddho* person came, then *mattam farmu tan tanor loge* [I would be able to speak with them], and I can speak in a non-*shuddho* way, in a Sylheti dialect if I can … my children also speak Sylheti dialect, my husband, Sylheti dialect … so we have been forced to speak it, because my husband's from Bangladesh himself. He didn't grow up here; he came over and then we got married here.

Here, Sylheti became the lingua franca in the household because of Nasima's husband. In this regard, Hamid argues that when 'Bangla is not fostered in the family and is used in very limited contexts its retention becomes increasingly difficult.'[85] In Nasima's case, she continued to explain that her husband, who was born and raised in Bangladesh, placed importance on speaking Bengali at home. She felt that otherwise it would not have been there, as she speaks English with her daughters. In Ismail's case, he encouraged his wife to speak more Bengali with the children, whereas Nasima stated that her husband influenced her to speak more Bengali, which 'rubbed off' on their daughters, who speak Sylheti well. Furthermore, Nasima, like Ismail, remained more connected to her Bengali roots, thus enabling a fluid and flexible dissemination of the two cultures in their household. She pontificated on how her husband has influenced her and their family structuring: 'So in a way, I had to adopt certain things because I was married to a Bangladeshi who grew up in Bangladesh; the traditional values were more instilled because he was quite traditional. So we had a mixture of cultures.' These complex overlaps of transnational families, and the forging of familial structures that bring forth some discrepancies, are noted by Zhu Hua and Li Wei in the British Chinese family context.[86]

When I interviewed Nasima, although we converse primarily in English with many interventions expressed in Bengali, this alone requires further dissection. There was certainly a comfort present, but the very complex dimensions the participants were addressing regarding language maintenance also surfaced during the interview. For example, in parts of the interview where participants felt they had to add a particular emphasis, they used Bengali to articulate these points. This very rapid switch and complementary attention given by using the two languages during the interview highlighted what Mills refers to as the ability to 'have access to experiences in different communities and also acquire features of different cultures in various combinations'.⁸⁷ Witnessing this dynamic during my interviews reminded me of the different worlds one can tap into, encompass and divulge in with, and through, different languages. The interviewees unfolded the possibilities of embarking on a journey to understand a culture through a language and the nuances that comes with it.

It is also intriguing that many of the interviewees felt at ease using 'Benglish' with me, a Bengali speaker, as illustrated by Nasima and Khalid's interviews.⁸⁸ This, perhaps, added more comfort, as the research participants were able to perform their dual identities with no difficulty, thus actualising the 'twoness' of their identities during the interviews. This rapid switch from Bengali to English and vice versa, as suggested by Mills, is the ability to 'have access to experiences in different communities and also acquire features of different cultures in various combinations'.⁸⁹ In this regard, the interviewees unfolded the possibilities of embarking on a journey to understand a culture through a language and the nuances that come with it. Bakhtin further states that while in dialogue, 'a person not only shows himself outwardly, but he also becomes for the first time that which he is, not only for others but himself as well. To be means to communicate dialogically.'⁹⁰ Those who married someone from Bangladesh facilitated and enabled Bengali to remain a constant in their own lives and those of their children. This starkly contrasts with their young adult children, who use Bengali purely for functional communication. Some relegate the language and claim that it has no relevance whatsoever in their lives.

The desire of parents to pass Bengali on to their children is referred to as 'linguistic parenting',⁹¹ a tactic employed in trying to preserve the 'mother tongue' and to foster and 'pass on' a sense of cultural identity to their children. During my fieldwork, the parents expressed their concern with helping their children navigate all the different worlds they constituted. Still, when it came to their children's Bengali identity, parents were keen to 'push' it more, as they feared its relegation without their constant 'pushing'. Furthermore, East London allows the research participants to be around traditions, values and language fostered around them by generations of Bangladeshis, both as a space of belonging and as a space of familiarity that provides the stability of identity. In this sense, the transnational marriage site allows for the constant activation of a double consciousness because each parent will emphasise one specific aspect of that identity. This was most explicit in Nasima's example of her husband, who, having moved to the UK after marriage, 'visibilised' and 'verbalised' the language because of his exposure to it. If he had been British Bangladeshi or had adopted the same approach as Ismail's wife, who is also Bangladeshi but did not speak Bengali with her children, the experience of Bengali identity would have been less. Claire Kramsch states that 'members of a community or social group do not only express experience; they also create experience through language'.⁹² To summarise, language cements a grounding within transnational marriages, which is not always possible in non-transnational marriages. In other words, the preservation of language is continuously shifting and changing, and its latest iteration will be no different, whether via transnational marriage or other means.

Conclusion

This chapter considered the varying ways language is maintained and the processes involved in maintaining language. The primary focus was on Sylheti and a consideration of how this language is preserved within the home while, in some contexts, this domestic space expands beyond the bricks and mortar of the house itself. The first delineation considered how Sylheti is imagined and located as a language and how the participants discussed its use. The interviewees also used Sylheti interchangeably with Bengali, and clear distinctions were made when participants specifically referenced standard Bengali, *shuddho Bangla*. There was a belief that Sylheti is not given the status of a language and is continuously referenced as a dialect. Although Sylheti no longer has a written form, it historically had its own Nagri script. However, its current iteration in East London is oral alone. In recognising the limitations imposed on the language in the schema where standard Bengali is the lingua franca for accessing television dramas and the news, there is also an appreciation of the way the geography of East London still provides a residual attachment to Sylheti because of its prominence whilst completing mundane tasks. There was a commitment to set up *fora*, after-school supplementary schools to provide language skills to young Bengalis growing up in the East End. However, as referenced by some of the participants, these schools are non-existent, and would have to be sought out as a service. The supplementary schools available beyond compulsory education now cater primarily to religious needs, explicitly focusing on teaching the Arabic language in order to read the Qur'an and practise the Islamic faith.

Following the elaboration on Sylheti's status, there was a focus on how the local government shaped the borough's future relationship with the Bengali language. Another mode of language circulation is manifested in the communication of young adults with their elders – including parents – in Bengali, while their teenage siblings and cousins rely more on English. It should be emphasised here that grandparents, or the *murobbis*,⁹³ played a vital role in making Sylheti available as an everyday language.⁹⁴ However, the local environment has a role in enabling Sylheti to act as the central marker for self-identification, as explained by Faruk, who uses his wife as an example. Sylheti's homogeneity in (re)presenting Bangladeshis in the UK cannot be reiterated enough, as the majority of the British Bangladeshi community hails from the north-eastern region of Sylhet. The connection with the region has been retained further through transnational marriages, informing some of the respondents' perceptions of heritage and the meaningful ways it can be incorporated into the home via language. In this sense, East London facilitates a world that is not antagonistic to its racialised communities, especially the Bangladeshi community. With this, it opens up room to negotiate their identities away from the dominant gaze. It provides the possibility of refusal in a way that allows Bangladeshi Muslims to conjure new(er) readings of their identifications.

Notes

1 H. Haarmann, *Language in Ethnicity: A View of Basic Ecological Relations* (Berlin and New York: Mouton de Gruyter, 1986), p. 38.
2 A. Riaz, 'Being Bengali abroad: Identity politics among the Bengali community in Britain', in M. N. Chakraborty (ed.), *Being Bengali: At Home and in the World* (Abingdon: Routledge, 2014), pp. 159–180.
3 J. Edwards, *Language, Society and Identity* (Oxford: Basil Blackwell, 1985), p. 23.
4 R. Jaspal and A. Coyle, '"My language, my people": Language and ethnic identity among British-born South Asians', *South Asian Diaspora* 2:2 (2010), 201–218 (p. 201).
5 Literal meaning is 'reading'. The recitation of the Qur'an and, in some cases, the Bengali language were also incorporated into these lessons. They usually took place after school or at weekends.
6 British film Institute, *Defending a Way of Life*, 18 minutes, https://player.bfi.org.uk/free/film/watch-defending-a-way-of-life-1980-online (accessed 26 May 2023).
7 B. Zeitlyn, 'Growing up glocal in London and Sylhet' (PhD dissertation, University of Sussex, 2010), p. 229.
8 In the UK context Bengali is almost always used in reference to Sylhetis. In that regard, because of its flexibility, I will employ both terms interchangeably. However, when I need to highlight the distinction, I will refer to Standard Bengali as *shuddho Bangla*.
9 S. M. Rasinger, 'Language shift in Banglatown? Evaluating ethnolinguistic vitality in East London' (2004), University of Sussex, www.sussex.ac.uk/webteam/gateway/file.php?name=lxwp2.pdf&site=1 (accessed 26 May 2023).
10 Jaspal and Coyle, 'My language, my people'.
11 Y. Hussain and P. Bagguley, 'Flying the flag for England? Citizenship, religion and cultural identity among British Pakistani Muslims', in T. Abbas (ed), *Muslim Britain: Communities under Pressure* (London: Zed Books, 2005), pp. 208–234.

12 Jaspal and Coyle, 'My language, my people'. See also A. Rosowsky, 'Muslim, English, or Pakistani? Multilingual identities in minority ethnoreligious communities', in P. Martinez, D. Moore and V. Spaëth (eds), *Plurilinguismes et enseignement: Identités en construction* (Paris: Riveneuve, 2008), pp. 127–140.
13 M. Ruby, 'The role of a grandmother in maintaining Bangla with her granddaughter in East London', *Journal of Multilingual and Multicultural Development* 33:1 (2012), 67–83.
14 Ibid., p. 74.
15 QMUL Language Acquisition Lab, Mile End Community Project, Human Stories Films and Blooming Parenting, *Stories from Home* (2021), https://humanstories-films.com/sfhhome.html (accessed 30 May 2023).
16 K. Gardner, 'International migration and the rural context in Sylhet', *New Community* 18:4 (1992), 479–590 (p. 582).
17 R. Chalmers, 'Sylheti: A regional language of Bangladesh', ENBS/ES Research Paper 5/6–96 (Bath: European Network of Bangladesh Studies, 1996).
18 R. Chalmers, *Learning Sylheti* (London: Centre for Bangladeshi Studies, Roehampton Institute, 1996), p. 7.
19 S. Hamid, *Language Use and Identity: The Sylheti Bangladeshis in Leeds* (Bern: Peter Lang, 2011).
20 A. Imam, 'Ancient Sylhet, history and tradition', in S. U. Ahmed (ed.), *Sylhet: History and Heritage* (Dhaka: Bangladesh Itihas Samiti, 1999), pp. 173–202 (p. 186).
21 K. M. Mohsin and S. M. Haroon, 'Importance of Greater Sylhet in the local history of Bangladesh', in Ahmed, *Sylhet*, pp. 3–13.
22 Hamid, *Language Use and Identity*, p. 16.
23 Chalmers, *Learning Sylheti*, p. 7.
24 P. Baker, M. Lie, T. McEnery and M. Sebba, 'The construction of a corpus of spoken Sylheti', *Literary and Linguistic Computing* 15:4 (2000), 421–432 (p. 422).
25 H. Grady, 'Student visa numbers soar after new rules take effect', BBC News (22 November 2009), http://news.bbc.co.uk/1/hi/8368709.stm (accessed 8 April 2024).
26 Baker et al., 'The construction of a corpus of spoken Sylheti', p. 422.
27 S. Lawson and I. Sachdev, 'Identity, language use, and attitudes: Some Sylheti-Bangladeshi data from London, UK', *Journal of Language and Social Psychology* 23:1 (2004), 49–69 (p. 50).
28 Zeitlyn, 'Growing up glocal in London and Sylhet', p. 231.
29 Chalmers, 'Sylheti', p. 6.
30 N. Kabeer, *The Power to Choose: Bangladeshi Women and Labour Market Decisions in London and Dhaka* (London: Verso, 2000), p. 195.
31 Zeitlyn, 'Growing up glocal in London and Sylhet'.
32 Drama shows.
33 See K. Gharibi and S. H. Mirvahedi, ' "You are Iranian even if you were born on the moon": Family language policies of the Iranian diaspora in the UK', *Journal of Multilingual and Multicultural Development* (2021), 1–16.

34 See S. Wright and N. Kurtoglu-Hooton, 'Language maintenance: The case of a Turkish-speaking community in Birmingham', *International Journal of the Sociology of Language* 181 (2006), 43–56.
35 The word for village in Sylheti and Standard Bengali would be *gaon* or *gram*, while *bari* is equivalent to 'home back home', but in the diaspora *bari* is used as a synonym for *gram/gaon*.
36 J. Mills, 'Being bilingual: Perspectives of third generation Asian children on language, culture and identity', *International Journal of Bilingual Education and Bilingualism* 4:6 (2001), 383–402 (p. 389).
37 R. S. Weisskirch, 'Child language brokers in immigrant families: An overview of family dynamics', *MediAzioni* 10:1 (2010), 68–87.
38 S. May, *Language and Minority Rights: Ethnicity, Nationalism and the Politics of Language* (Abingdon: Routledge, 2012), p. 158.
39 Ibid.
40 S. Hall, 'The work of representation', in S. Hall (ed.), *Representation: Cultural Representations and Signifying Practices* (London: Sage Publications, 1997), pp. 13–74 (p. 34).
41 Lawson and Sachdev, 'Identity, language use, and attitudes', p. 55.
42 R. Huber, 'Protesters mount fight against cuts to vital language services in Tower Hamlets', *Eastlondonlines* (28 February 2020), www.eastlondonlines.co.uk/2020/02/protesters-mount-fight-against-cuts-to-vital-language-services-in-tower-hamlets/ (accessed 8 April 2024).
43 A. Oluwalana, 'Whitechapel London Underground station gets sign change so it's now written in Bangla and English', MyLondon (16 March 2022), www.mylondon.news/news/east-london-news/whitechapel-london-underground-station-gets-23403847 (accessed 8 April 2024).
44 Ibid.
45 L. Rahman, https://twitter.com/LutfurRahmanTH/status/1654519021088145409 (accessed 31 October 2023). See also the announcement in the manifesto: https://lutfurrahman.co.uk/wp-content/uploads/2022/04/Manifesto-1.pdf (accessed 31 October 2023).
46 Rasinger, 'Language shift in Banglatown?'.
47 Ibid., p. 6.
48 Ibid., p. 2.
49 Zeitlyn, 'Growing up glocal in London and Sylhet', p. 251.
50 Ibid., p. 239.
51 G. Baumann, *Contesting Culture: Discourses of Identity in Multi-Ethnic London* (Cambridge: Cambridge University Press, 1996), p. 195 (emphasis in original).
52 *Jagonari* can be translated as 'the awakened women' or 'wake up, women!'. The centre is now permanently closed.
53 Hamid, *Language Use and Identity*, p. 173.
54 J. Gest, *Apart: Alienated and Engaged Muslims in the West* (London: Hurst, 2010), p. 88.

55 D. H. Brown, *Principles of Language Learning and Teaching* (Englewood Cliffs, NJ: Prentice Hall Regents, 1994), p. 165.
56 W. Jiang, 'The relationship between culture and language', *ELT Journal* 54:4 (2000), 328–334.
57 S. Hall, 'Cultural identity and diaspora', in J. Rutherford (ed.), *Identity: Community, Culture, Difference* (London: Lawrence and Wishart, 1990), 222–237 (p. 225).
58 Ibid.
59 Hamid, *Language Use and Identity*, p. 150.
60 Hall, 'Cultural identity and diaspora'.
61 N. Mookherjee, 'In pursuit of the "authentic" Bengali: Impressions and observations of a contested diaspora', in Chakraborty, *Being Bengal*, p. 152.
62 Mookherjee, 'In pursuit of the 'authentic' Bengali', pp. 140–158 (p. 152). Tasleema Nasreen is a Bangladeshi author, an outspoken feminist and a human rights advocate. She has been critical of Islam, which has resulted in her being exiled from Bangladesh. She currently resides in the United States of America.
63 Sermons held after Friday prayers.
64 P. Werbner, 'Introduction: Black and ethnic leaderships in Britain, a theoretical overview', in P. Werbner and M. Anwar (eds), *Black and Ethnic Leaderships in Britain: The Cultural Dimensions of Political Action* (Abingdon: Routledge, 1991), pp. 12–27 (p. 21).
65 Riaz, 'Being Bengali abroad', p. 167.
66 S. Hall, 'The question of cultural identity', in S. Hall, D. Held and A. G. McGrew (eds), *Modernity and Its Futures* (Cambridge: Polity Press, 1992), pp. 274–316 (p. 310).
67 R. Mason and H. Sherwood, 'Cameron "stigmatising Muslim women" with Englsih language policy', *Guardian*, 18 January 2016, www.theguardian.com/politics/2016/jan/18/david-cameron-stigmatising-muslim-women-learn-english-language-policy (accessed 8 April 2024).
68 P. Mandaville, 'Reimagining Islam in diaspora', *Gazette* 63:2–3 (2001), 169–186 (p. 170).
69 Baumann, *Contesting Culture*, p. 30.
70 Ibid., p. 31.
71 Ibid., p. 34.
72 S. Hall, 'Introduction: Who needs "identity"?', in S. Hall and P. Du Gay (eds), *Questions of Cultural Identity* (London: Sage Publications, 1996), pp. 1–17 (p. 3).
73 P. Werbner, 'Essentialising essentialism, essentialising silence: Ambivalence and multiplicity in the constructions of racism and ethnicity', in P. Werbner and T. Modood (eds), *Debating Cultural Hybridity: Multicultural Identities and the Politics of Anti- Racism* (London: Zed Books, 1997), pp. 226–254 (p. 230).
74 See 'The rise and fall and rise again of Lutfur Rahman', *Prospect*, 27 March 2024, www.prospectmagazine.co.uk/politics/65477/lutfur-rahman-tower-hamlets-mayor-labour-gaza (accessed 29 April 2024).

75 R. Brubaker and F. Cooper, 'Beyond "identity"', *Theory and Society* 29:1 (2000), 1–47 (p. 20).
76 Gest, *Apart*, p. 182.
77 Mandaville, 'Reimagining Islam in diaspora'.
78 Gest, *Apart*, p. 193.
79 Grady, 'Student Visa numbers soar after new rules take effect'.
80 S. Hall, 'The multicultural question', in B. Hesse (ed.), *Unsettled Multiculturalisms: Diasporas, Entanglements* (London: Zed Books, 2000), pp. 209–241 (pp. 219–220).
81 H. Clarke, 'Italian Bengalis: Meet London's newest ethnic minority', *Independent*, 29 November 2015.
82 F. Grosjean, *Life with Two Languages: An Introduction to Bilingualism* (Cambridge, MA: Harvard University Press, 1982), p. 127.
83 S. Hall, 'Ethnicity: Identity and difference', *Radical America* 23:4 (1989), 9–22 (pp. 9–10).
84 V. Redclift, F. Rajina and N. Rashid, 'The burden of conviviality: British Bangladeshi Muslims navigating diversity in London, Luton and Birmingham', *Sociology* 56:6 (2022), 1159–1175.
85 Hamid, *Language Use and Identity*, p. 150.
86 Z. Hua and L. Wei, 'Transnational experience, aspiration and family language policy', *Journal of Multilingual and Multicultural Development* 37:7 (2016), 655–666.
87 Mills, 'Being bilingual', p. 389.
88 'Benglish' = a mixing of English and Bengali words.
89 Mills, 'Being bilingual', p. 389.
90 M. Bakhtin, 'Discourse in the novel', in M. Holquist (ed.), *The Dialogic Imagination* (Austin: University of Texas Press, 1981), pp. 259–422 (p. 287).
91 Mills, 'Being bilingual', p. 386.
92 C. Kramsch, *Language and Culture* (Oxford: Oxford University Press, 1998), p. 3.
93 Elders of the community.
94 Ruby, 'The role of a grandmother'.

5

Audibly Muslim: Arabic as the lingua franca?

Introduction

Much like clothing, language shapes how communities see themselves, especially in the diaspora. However, this is further complicated while practising a religion that requires the learning of a language in addition to that of one's heritage. In Britain, there are a growing number of organisations and institutions catering to the needs of British Muslims' desire to learn Arabic. Nonetheless, it is difficult to locate the exact data on the number of schools and institutes where Arabic language provisions are available. Rasha Soliman and Saussan Khalil have shown that 'the majority of the mainstream schools that teach Arabic as part of their curriculum are independent and faith-based schools', and that the provisions in these schools 'may not be the same every year and may vary depending on the number of students, availability of resources and the expertise of teaching staff'.[1] Although their research focused on Arab communities in the UK and their learning of Arabic as a heritage language, the context differed for British Bangladeshi Muslims. Their desire to learn Arabic stemmed from a growing awareness of and affinity with their religious identity. As Andrey Rosowsky notes, Muslims cannot pray without reading the opening chapter of the Qur'an, which is in Arabic, and the remainder of the prayer is itself performed in Arabic.[2] The Bengali Muslims interviewed for this project were no longer satisfied with 'just' learning the language to recite the Qur'an, but are investing additional time, at weekends or by attending evening classes, to learn the Arabic language (specifically classical Arabic) in its entirety, including the grammar, in order to be able to speak the language and understand the religious texts without relying on someone else or a mere translation. Out of the forty-three research participants, only two spoke fluent Arabic. In contrast, everyone else could recite the Qur'an, as they attended after-school *fora* where they received lessons in Qur'an recitation (*tajweed*).

In this chapter, the way religious identity is construed via language, with a particular focus on Arabic and Bengali words will be explored. As with the previous chapter, analysing how the participants conceptualise language and how they attribute meaning-making is vital in order to comprehend how Bengali Muslims create this constellation of languages, recognising that religion also has its linguistic demands, as language assists the making of identities.[3] The two languages will not only provide traces of how Muslimness is managed in the East End vis-à-vis the languages themselves, but will also consider how, historically, the role of these languages has shifted. For example, the Persian-origin terms in Bengali addressed in the chapter are crucial to understanding Persian influence in the construction of a particular South Asian Muslim and Islamic expression. This includes the ways people connote religious, forthright references to prayers and litanies, and how many of these terms are currently in use, though contextually variant. For example, Persian, prior to the focus on the Bengal during the colonial period, continued to enjoy 'prominence as the language of state and business, and predated the coming of the Mughals in Bengal', while the practical needs of administration 'made Bengali the language of power and authority'.[4]

However, Anindita Ghosh also notes the prevalence of Bengali. Bengali Muslims in the nineteenth century remained faithful to the Bengali language influenced by Perso-Arabic terms, which came to be known as 'Musalman-Bengali', defined by Ghosh as 'colloquial Bengali, intertwined with popular local myth and legend, ritual and superstition, and very different from the chaste Arabic and Persian in which Islamic religious texts were usually written'.[5] Ghosh adds that the intersection of these communal and linguistic agendas led to 'the distilling of a specific community identity for the strand, and partly explains the enormous popularity of these works among Muslims of the period'.[6] With the transformation of Musalmani-Bengali, Ghosh argues that elite Bengali Muslims 'had always identified with Persian, Arabic or Urdu, rather than Bengali, which was perceived as the language of the masses. The linguistic divide here was thus split along lines of class, rather than religion.'[7] Needless to say, this historical outline does not unfold in the same way in the East End. Rather, there are variations in the ways in which Arabic and Bengali intermingle while also asserting different positionings. The claims-making *qua* a religious identity is morphed through various political junctures, particularly while forging a religious identity along with other Muslims.

Persian versus Arabic

Considering the prevalence of Persian-origin terms in the Bengali language, the research participants described the use of varying terms in a multitude of ways. Exploring the shifts and varying positionalities of Bengali terms among the research participants is essential to gauge the overlap of Persian with Arabic and how the interviewees use the languages among different Muslims. The negotiation of boundaries and who will 'understand' these Bengali terms became a prominent feature in the interviews. The research participants created the Bengali Muslim vs. non-South Asian Muslim vs. non-Muslim paradigms to filter which language they should use, thus creating language boundaries to gain 'acceptance' at that moment in time. In this regard, Erving Goffman defines 'acceptance' as the respect and regard that the 'uncontaminated' receive.[8] This complicates matters further, as language use depends not only on whom one is speaking to but also requires the creation of boundaries around other Muslims who are likely to understand Arabic terms rather than Bengali ones as a result of receiving their Islamic education in Arabic. The prioritisation of Arabic suggests it befits a collective, ummatic Muslim identity instead of a specific regional Muslim identity from the Indian subcontinent. As Mushirul Hasan suggests, 'boundaries are multiple, and at no time is one boundary the sole definer of an identity. Yet at different times and for different reasons, there is a "relevant boundary" that gains prominence and defines the "us"/"them" divide.'[9]

Historically, South Asian Muslims' linguistic expressions were delivered with terms of Persian origin such as *Khuda Hafiz*, *namaz*, *jaynamaz* and *Khuda*.[10] Furthermore, Alia P. Ahmed, who cites Badar Alam – a veteran journalist and editor-in-chief of Pakistan's foremost investigative news magazine, the *Herald* – notes the role of sectarianism in having a 'preferential' language:

> As Muslim societies in the post-cold war era are increasingly viewing themselves in terms of very literal interpretations of Muslim history and theology, anything that offers a culturally different point of view is shunned and discarded. Language purification is part of a larger purification. Even in Bangladesh, where pride in the Bangla language is part of the national identity, *Allah Hafiz* is now a common way of saying goodbye. And Persian, after all, is the language of Shia Iran. In a contest between Shia and Sunni Islam, the Sunnis must prefer Arabic over Persian.[11]

This political (dis)regard for the Persian language emerges through contemporary geopolitical configurations, further informed by denominational politics. The preference is given to Arabic as a way to centralise a specific Sunni Muslim identity, relegating Persian to Shia Muslims. Although *Allah Hafiz* derives from *Khuda Hafiz*, substituting *Allah* for *Khuda* raises the question of not only the language use but also the removal of the need for Shia Muslims to learn Arabic in order to complete prayers. Whilst this is a separate discussion pertaining to South Asian studies more broadly, the data on British Bangladeshi Muslims in the East End and their relationship with the two languages provide a different grounding. The use of Arabic implies a connection with the formation of a religious identity, and perhaps even a conscious effort is made to embed Arabic in order to give the religious identity more authenticity. The dominance of Arabic in the constructions of difference, by placing Persian as the 'other', is intriguing, and suggests a process of sanctification of Arabic. The necessity of expressing one's religiosity or closeness to the *deen* (belief) was communicated profoundly through the use of Arabic terms, even during the interviews; such articulations construct a binary of Persian vs. Arabic. The outward expression of religiosity is attached not just to the clothing one but also to the language one employs, and this is where Arabic holds a more significant position than Persian.

Both John Eade and Katy Gardner and Abdus Shukur have argued that young British Bangladeshis began to prioritise religion in the wake of influential political and ideological developments in Britain, which opened a space where many of them began to identify themselves above all as Muslims, rather than as Bengali or Bangladeshi.[12] Therefore, religion provided a positive identity in which young British Bangladeshis found solidarity, and in this solidarity, Arabic arguably came to form a distinct identity marker away from the culture associated with their ethnicity. A similar point is put forward by Bhikhu Parekh:

> A community inherits a specific way of life … which sets limits to how and how much it can change itself. The change is lasting and deep if it is grafted on the community's suitably reinterpreted deepest tendencies and does not go against the grain. A community's political [and cultural] identity then is neither unalterable and fixed, nor a voluntarist project to be executed as it pleases, but a matter of slow self-recreation within the limits set by its past.[13]

The process of self-creation, as argued by Parekh, does not occur in a historical vacuum but is enabled through the cultural reproduction of a Bengali religious identity imported from Bangladesh, which may not be perceived as strong enough, thus warranting a more inclusive identity provided by the Arabic language in the diaspora. For immigrant communities, religion continues to play a significant and vital role in maintaining and upholding group identities.[14] One reason could be attributed to the desire and need to remain an in-member of a group in order not to feel isolated. The involvement in a consistent identity with a group perceived as similar to 'us' depends on eliminating differences, as acknowledging similarity allows a sense of belonging.[15] This 'consistency' is declaring not that identity is static but that people may opt to sustain their identities through their similarities. At the same time, they are still altering and negotiating new social identities and forging old identities into new salient ones that they may prioritise.

Shamim (interviewed in November 2013) captured this consistency in remaining part of a group but also considering, re-evaluating and building up a new religious-linguistic identity, which he attributes to generational difference and the second generation's more substantial exposure to Arabic than to Bengali:

> You mean the transition from *bhai* to *akhi*? [Laughs.] In Britain itself, in East London itself, you have lots of institutions, organisations and groups, and lots of people start having these as part of their identity; from there they pick up cultures or ways of being. A part of that is that you become an *akhi* or an *ukhti*. I don't think it's a bad thing; it shows a social connection, what you wish to adopt and that's what people do. And there is a lot of it as well with we're not taught to use the Persian or the Bengali words as much as our parents did; we grew up here, and this is what we see, and this is what we adopt, just like in Bangladesh, that's what they saw and they did that. And then for us, we've got, well ... we're spoilt for choice. Identity is a pick-and-mix, fluid sort of subject and we're spoilt for choice and we pick what we think is cool, or what we wish to do for whatever reason, and it's often socially, like with your friends.

Shamim contextualises the use of Arabic amongst young British Bangladeshi Muslims and how it is more of a recent phenomenon. He refers to the use of *akhi* as opposed to *bhai* (both words mean 'brother'; the former in Arabic and the latter in Bengali; *ukhti* is Arabic for 'sister') and implies that many of the institutions and organisations across East London are also adopting the new Arabic terms as a way to communicate with fellow Muslims. Shamim's awareness of the linguistic shift also indicates the stark difference in how religious terms are expressed between his and his parents' generations. For his parents' generation and earlier, it became an inevitable norm to make religious references in Bengali, as these particular Persian-origin terms were already embedded within the Bengali language for Muslims. However, though the younger generation was exposed to the same terms as their parents, the religious expressions are different because of their exposure to other influences, including Muslims of other backgrounds. The influences include exposure to the Arabic language and adopting Arabic words to articulate religious terms and expressions, thus connoting the fluidity available to the younger generations born and/or raised primarily in the UK, who are adopting and producing a religious-linguistic identity different from that of their predecessors.

Accordingly, Nasar Meer argues that 'a Muslim consciousness *for itself* has become ascendant more recently than racial and ethnic self-identifications'.[16] I would argue that the ascendance of a more religious identity has become prominent because of the dominant political discourse. This discourse focuses on Muslims and their interaction and engagement, or lack thereof, within the broader society. Identifying with one's religious identity was not a priority for the first generation, although, since 9/11, they have changed their self-understanding vis-à-vis their faith. On the other hand, most of the generation who were in their early teenage years when the Twin Towers were struck grew up witnessing the media's scrutiny of their religion. In attempting to understand global events, which dictated the dominant political discourse in the UK, many young Muslims reconfigured their faith and their relationship with it. In this respect, Anandi Ramamurthy suggests that:

> America's global strategy disseminated by the dominant media also began to feed into attitudes towards Muslims to create feelings of difference between groups that previously searched for similarities fuelling anti-Islamicism amongst not just whites but also Asian Hindus, Sikhs and Christians. Culture and religion became conflated and 'Muslim' became the new 'ethnicity'.[17]

However, this is not to assume that the first-generation Bangladeshis had a homogeneous and monolithic approach to religious expressions. I would argue that this is because of the proximity to and continuous relationship with Bangladesh, enabling that generation to retain similar religious expressions to their elders. In contrast, this dynamic is being reformulated by Bangladeshis born and/or raised primarily in the UK, who are far less attached to Bangladesh. Furthermore, as argued by Erik H. Erikson:

> The process of identity formation emerges as an evolving configuration – a configuration that gradually integrates constitutional givens ... favoured capacities, significant identifications, effective defenses ... and consistent roles. All these, however, can only emerge from a mutual adaptation of individual potentials, technological world views, and religious or political ideologies.[18]

The adaptation Erikson refers to could be applied to younger Bengali Muslims, who are more likely to interact with Muslims of other ethnic backgrounds in school and, consequently, have them as part of their circle of friends. As a result, Arabic then becomes the most appropriate language to verbalise religious expressions amongst other Muslims. This was articulated by Shaju (interviewed in December 2014), who differentiated between the public and the private spheres, consequently determining which language he used to express terms such as prayer mat, prayer and so on. For example, when asked about which language he used amongst Muslims when he wanted to reference prayer, he said, 'well, casually, I might say *namaz* or *salah* – it just depends ... If I'm speaking Bengali, I might use the term *namaz*. But if I'm speaking English, I'm more likely to use the word *salah*. If I'm speaking to someone who's a non-Muslim, I'd use the word prayer.' Shaju's response illustrates and encapsulates the fluidity of his religious identification and how it is differently manoeuvred depending on the context. He uses the Arabic terms specifically when communicating with other Muslims, most typically those of non-South Asian origin, ensuring that everyone understands his reference without feeling confused. The assumption made by Shaju is that Arabic would be more appropriate, as it is perceived to be the lingua franca of Muslims and, therefore, likely to be instantly understood without any additional explanations. With a non-Muslim, he opts for English, suggesting it is the 'safer' language in this instance, as the non-Muslim may not be familiar with 'Muslim lingo'; using 'prayer' neutralises the situation without the non-Muslim feeling 'left out'.

Shaju's precise articulation is consonant with Kath Woodward's assertion that 'we present ourselves to others through everyday interactions, through the way we speak and dress, marking ourselves as the same as those with whom we share an identity and different from those with whom we do not'.[19] It is the sameness with other Muslims that makes Shaju use the Arabic terms, as he believes other Muslims will have been exposed to these as well, and it is through difference that he communicates in English. Therefore, his choice of language is determined through the discourse he is engaging in that particular context. Additionally, he uses Bengali terms with other South Asian Muslims because of their sameness. Indeed, what Shaju exemplifies is how three very different spaces vis-à-vis three different languages shape his Muslimness. In this regard, instead of W. E. B. Du Bois's twoness, Shaju displays his active participation with his threeness.[20] The threeness appears through the lens of how he feels he ought to behave with non-South Asian Muslims, non-Muslims and other South Asian Muslims.

Similarly, Sultana (interviewed in April 2014) also created boundaries between her home and the outside world. Many participants adopted this particular reading of home and outside-the-home concerning clothing too, which helped them to establish clear demarcations as to where each language could be used. The home space allowed Sultana to articulate her religious identity in a more familiar way than, for example, her workplace. She highlights the significance of these spatial divisions and the use of *namaz* or *salah*:

> Sultana: If I am at home speaking to my mum, then I say it [*namaz*] ... I don't know, when I go to work, it's different, it just changes – you just say *in sha Allah, masha Allah* more than when you are at home. At home, I would say *namaz*. Oh, it's *namaz* time!
> Me: So, in different contexts, you use different terms?
> Sultana: I don't know why that happens. In the mosque, I would just say it is prayer time or something ... I would say it's *salah* time actually [laughs].

Me: And do you say *Khuda Hafiz*?
Sultana: No, no. We have never said it. I know *Allah Hafiz*, but we just always say *assalamu alaykum*.
Me: Even when you say goodbye?
Sultana: Yeah, sometimes my dad, when I am talking to him on the phone, he says *Allah Hafiz* at the end, but I don't know how to reply to it, so I just say *assalamu alaykum* again, and he has to say *wa alaykumu s-salaam*.[21]

While continuing the conversation, Sultana asked what would be the appropriate response to the use of *Allah Hafiz*, and I explained it was up to her if she wanted to reply using *Allah Hafiz* or *Khuda Hafiz*, but then she pointed out that the former was probably correct. Although she did not know a response, her nod to the former amounts to an understanding that the Muslim can only be located via Arabic. In this sense, the social relation with Islam, and the communicative response to fellow Muslims, has to involve Arabic to cement the 'right' legitimacy that binds the Muslim into place. Pnina Werbner explains and encapsulates culture as an 'organic hybridisation' that 'casts doubts on the viability of simplistic scholarly models of cultural holism'.[22] Arabic can create an internal homogeneity within the *ummah* because of the familiarity with Arabic-infused references. Meanwhile, the Bengali words within the home facilitate an intergenerational understanding, as their use is more prevalent in this specific space. In this respect, Sultana's use of Arabic outside her home also suggests an interplay of the dominant religious discourse that prioritises Arabic as a means to express one's religiosity. Furthermore, Shaju noted that Arabic functions as the lingua franca, as everyone will be familiar with the terms. Rusi Jaspal and Adrian Coyle report having observed a similar attitude among their research participants, one of whom highlighted the following: 'we [Muslims] all speak the same language ... You can go anywhere and Muslims in Morocco, Yemen, Palestine speak Arabic so it's just one language and there's unity with Muslims.'[23] Jaspal and Coyle continue to argue that language is 'often constructed as being cohesive and uniform'.[24] As exemplified by Shaju, Arabic binds Muslims together and enables the possible lived experience of engaging with an 'imagined community', i.e. the Muslim *ummah*.[25]

In Sultana's case, discourses of linguistic difference reveal the boundaries drawn internally amongst Muslims. This is intriguing, as her workplace is located in the heart of East London, and most of her clients are likely to be fellow Bangladeshi men and women, yet Sultana chooses to use Arabic. Her choice of Arabic implies that language is not necessarily exercised and encouraged by the demographic one engages with but is instead determined and defined in relation to an apparently coherent religious identity that brings Muslims of different backgrounds together under the umbrella of Arabic. In this sense, Muslims participate in a dominant religious discourse, creating a linear approach to the linguistic expression of one's identification with Islam. In this regard, ethnic identity is left unexamined, suggesting that one gains 'acceptability' by occupying this coherent religious identity and that it is central to the formation of group boundaries. Similarly, Tariq Rahman contends that 'language becomes a major determinant of identity after religion, and it is chosen as a symbol of group identity by leaders from a modernizing community who covet power'.[26] I would argue that language has become the determinant for creating a solid religious identity to make it authentic in the case of the British Bangladeshis I have interviewed. In sum, although Bengali is still prevalent both as an ethnic identity marker and as the functioning language, because of the prominent placement of religion as the primary identification focus, the Bengali terms are being actively replaced by Arabic.

One theme that materialised during my fieldwork is the lack of clarity that some interviewees had regarding the Bengali terms, as aptly illustrated by Sultana's confusion above. After my June 2014 interview with Nasima, we continued discussing the research. At one point, Nasima returned to the role of language and religion. She started to explain how she understood the word *Khuda* and that the word, to her, was the same as 'god' with a small 'g', which would go against her beliefs since Islam teaches *tawhid* (the absolute Oneness of God) and that nothing else can be associated with Him. Therefore, reference to God should be made with a capital 'G'. For that reason, she does not use *Khuda Hafiz* and uses the Arabic greeting instead, like Sultana. Nasima's commentary gives much food for thought on how a language can be an essential element of identity construction, defining commonality or difference and ultimately determining whether one is included or excluded. However, she appeared confused and startled when I explained that *Khuda* means 'Lord' or 'God' in Persian, referring to the singular, not the plural. Despite having grown up hearing the Bengali terms, Nasima was unaware of this difference. The language configuration suggests that relegating Bengali terms, wherever possible, is a precipitating factor in the cultivation of a linguistically homogeneous Muslim identity.

Pervez Hoodbhoy puts forward the argument that, while such linguistic changes occurred in Pakistan, they were not happening socially but rather were slowly enforced by the state:

> As a part of General Zia's cultural offensive, Hindi words were expunged from daily use and replaced with heavy-sounding Arabic ones. Persian, the language of Moghul India, had once been taught as a second or third language in many Pakistani schools. But, because of its association with Shi'ite Iran, it too was

dropped and replaced by Arabic. The morphing of the traditional *'khuda hafiz'* [Persian for 'God be with you'] into *'allah hafiz'* [Arabic for 'God be with you'] took two decades to complete. The Arab import sounded odd and contrived, but ultimately the Arabic God won and the Persian God lost.[27]

None of the research participants I spoke to explicitly mentioned or referenced Shia Iran as a reason for using or not using the Persian-origin Bengali terms; however, several references were made to 'political changes' impacting the language use. Such references were made to the geopolitics of the Arabic-speaking Middle East and the exposure to the Arabic language that has been becoming a prominent feature during Friday sermons, not only in reciting passages of the Qur'an, but also in delivering the sermons themselves. A similar change has been noted in Bangladesh, where Arabic is favoured over the Bengali expressions. Ali Riaz contends that there is 'a growing tendency to accept and glorify practices akin to practices in Saudi Arabia',[28] while Taj Hashmi has framed this as a form of Arabisation of non-Arab Muslims, particularly those in South Asia.[29] Anders Härdig and Tazreena Sajjad describe the phenomenon as consisting of:

> a shift in everyday language relating to common religious practices such as the change from the use of the word 'Ramzan' to 'Ramadan'; saying 'Allah Hafiz' instead of the previously common 'Khuda Hafiz'; and there is a general vilification of local practices of Islam as being 'contaminated' by 'ignorant' cultural traditions. Informal conversations often reveal a desire among a younger generation, particularly urbanites, to learn about 'true Islam', as if the religious teachings they grew up with were tainted by Bengali cultural traditions and 'improper' Iranian influences. Arguably, by following an allegedly more 'pure' version of Islam, they are at once consumers and co-producers of an Arabized Islam, very different from the Sufi traditions that shaped Bengali culture for centuries.[30]

Although focused on Bangladesh, this reading can also be applied to the Bengali Muslim community in East London. Such a convergence raises the potent question: how do we explore the *impact* this is having? I am conscious of how the framings around Muslims and Arabic have been forged following the War on Terror and the consequent investment in producing terrorism 'logic'. Within this malignant framing of Muslims and the Arabic language, punitive measures have erupted to create the compliant and 'good' Muslim.[31] Instead, I am attempting to consider what being Muslim means for Muslims away from terrorism logic. How do Muslims contend with their diverse cultural expressions, which are not easily divorced from religious expressions? Yet, there is an attempt to create linearity that collapses diversity into a monolithic confession. In this vein, this pursuit examines how these oppositional responses locate and reimagine Muslimness in

East London, and what this particular expression contains. One participant who challenged the forging of a new(er) local discourse projecting a more Arabic-influenced Muslimness was Dr Imran (interviewed in March 2014). He pointed out that he continued to use *Khuda Hafiz*, which people around him had used when he was growing up. He then explained why others may have stopped using it:

> I use the word *Khuda Hafiz* because this is how it was when I was growing up. People I mixed with, [the] majority of people, used *Khuda Hafiz*. *Khuda Hafiz* is Persian, so I noticed many of my friends use the word *Allah Hafiz* because they sort of, like, saw the influence, or some influence came from somewhere, you know. Generally, what you see is the Persian influence. Strictly speaking, these are all cultural things, but in religious terms, right, yeah, it doesn't matter, yeah, you could even use *Bhagavan Hafiz* ... because we say, in this country, we say, ahh, 'God bless you' or whatever – we use the word 'God', so why can't we use the word *Bhagavan*? Some people might say *Bhagavan* refers to too many gods ... I use the word *Khuda Hafiz*, because this is how I work, but sometimes my friends say *Allah Hafiz*. I would still mostly use *Khuda Hafiz*.

Dr Imran did not go into any detail as to how this new trend emerged amongst his peers; however, it is evident that the formation of a language identity outlines the focus around which other culturally specific identities orbit. In this case, it may be due to the associations and meanings attributed to these terms, which provide purpose and significance for the individuals using them. Dr Imran points out that one could also use the phrase *Bhagavan hafiz*, which may appear controversial for Muslims. The word *Bhagavan* can serve as an epithet for God, precisely referencing the avatars of Krishna, Shiva and Vishnu. However, to Hindus the term also represents the concept of an abstract, genderless God. Dr Imran is aware of these distinctions; therefore, he emphasises how Muslims could technically use *Bhagavan hafiz*, though this is highly unlikely as the general understanding of *Bhagavan* is that it refers to multiple gods. He emphasises how such boundaries are blurred when one can easily find 'sameness' with other religious terms and that individuals negotiate complex socio-political landscapes in order to forge their identities. Individuals also seek to understand which aspects of competing cultural worlds they can and/or should accept and reject to delineate their identity, making it distinct from the 'other'.

The generational difference and approaches to languages are succinctly captured by Ismail's interview (interviewed in March 2014), who described how he used the Bengali terms with his parents. This was a theme throughout, where, as noted by the above interviews, exposure to Bengali terms through parents meant they were retained. However, Ismail noted how he did not use the Bengali terms with his children and instead switched to Arabic:

Me: Do you use terms such as *namaz*, *Khuda Hafiz*?
Ismail: No, I think with my mum and dad maybe [use] *namaz* sometimes. With my children, it's *salah*.
Me: So with your children it is *salah*?
Ismail: Yeah, because I think that's the way I grew up with my parents. My children would say *salah*, because that's what they … if I would say *namaz* they would be like 'huh?'.
Me: What about *Khuda Hafiz* or *jaynamaz*?
Ismail: We wouldn't say *jaynamaz*. We would in Bengali with my parents … *Khuda Hafiz*, not really …
Me: So how do you say goodbye?
Ismail: We just say *assalamu alaykum*. I'm trying to think have we ever used *Khuda Hafiz* in our family. I don't think we have. I know some people do, but I don't think in my family we've ever used that. I can't remember.

Ismail's insights signify a rupture to the continuity of these terms by displaying how younger Bengalis are less familiar with them because of a lack of exposure in the home that is further compounded by their context – for example, attending *madrasahs* after school emphasises the importance of Arabic. In this regard, his children cannot relate to the Bengali terms and use Arabic as their default religious language, which implies that his children's subjective certainty and understanding are ascertained through Arabic, thus providing meaning that they would not be able to confer to the Bengali language. His children's use of Arabic further suggests that religion is fostered through Arabic outside the home, creating a sense of collective belonging, loyalty and social cohesion among fellow young British Bangladeshi Muslims and other British Muslims. This turn to a resolute 'Muslim' identity, manifested through Arabic with the erasure of the Bengali words, represents shifts of emphasis within the community from the generation who uphold their 'Bengali consciousness' to a re-emerging 'Muslim consciousness', centring Arabic. The continuous existence of the Bengali terms, it appears, is due to the interaction some have with their parents, who continue to use these terms, keeping the language alive. Preoccupation with an Islam that is devoid of 'culture' is in line with Olivier Roy's argument that young European Muslims are pursuing a 'pure form of Islam', avoiding their cultural influences and defining it as a 'decultured Islam'. He elaborates:

> The construction of a 'deculturalised' Islam is a means of experiencing a religious identity that is not linked to a given culture and can therefore fit with every culture, or, more precisely, could be defined beyond the very notion of

culture ... The new generation of educated, Western born-again Muslims do not want to be Pakistanis or Turks; they want to be Muslims first.[32]

However, the concept of a 'deculturised Islam' is a redundant argument, as no expression of religion can exist in a vacuum. Yet, the expressions in Arabic derive from somewhere – from a 'culture' with its own confines and boundaries. British Bangladeshi Muslims, it seems, are ridding their religious identity of any 'cultural baggage' and employing a process whereby the experiences of being a Muslim in the UK are indicative of the processes and discourses that will continue to define and shape the religious identity of British Bangladeshi Muslims in the years or even decades to come. The parents' and grandparents' interaction with and use of the Bengali terms suggest the connectedness with their ethnic roots, which I argue is due to their ongoing attachment to Bangladesh. However, I contend that this attachment is imaginary and does not factor in the changes developing in Bangladesh, where there are rapidly shifting religious identifications. The British Bangladeshi Muslims who have grown up in the East End with parents, or at least one parent, already acculturated to the UK, are shifting the dynamics. They are shifting religious connotations and outward invocations to a more homogeneous outlook, and this is becoming a dominant feature. Yet, even if this religious identification appears to be homogeneous, I would still suggest that this perceived 'singular identity' is complex and nuanced *in itself*, and neither exists or gets produced *by itself*. The current recomposition involves a contained shared network and structure bearing on the unfolding domain. It is, of course, also likely to change, with other variables influencing this domain of negotiation.

Arabic: The lingua franca of Muslims?

For the majority of Muslims in the world, Arabic plays a crucial role in forging a religious identity, as all Muslims are required to learn Arabic for worship purposes or for the sake of pursuing theological knowledge. As Rosowsky notes, it is impossible for Muslims to pray without reading the opening chapter of the Qur'an, which is in Arabic.[33] Although most Muslims worldwide are of non-Arab origin, hearing Arabic words and utterances is a complete norm if there are conversations between Muslims. For example, many of the participants in my fieldwork used Arabic terms during their interview and in the conversation that followed it. Some of the most common terms included, but were not limited to, *in sha Allah, masha Allah, jazak Allah khairan, subhan Allah, assalamu alaikum, khair* and so on.[34] Until now, the focus has been on how Bengali words have slowly disappeared, incorporating the changes in Bangladesh. However, it thus becomes particularly urgent to pay attention to how Arabic is articulated, not necessarily as a spoken language but more in pursuit of religious authenticity. Out of the forty-three research participants interviewed, only two spoke Arabic. Interestingly, in their study on the role of Gurmukhi amongst South Asian Sikhs, Sanksrit amongst South Asian Hindus and Arabic amongst South Asian Muslims, Jaspal and Coyle note that 'religion also has its linguistic demands', and further argue that 'the role of language and religious identity is considered within the wider context of individuals' complex linguistic repertoires consisting of various languages'.[35] Thus, the aim is to explore the research participants' accounts of their upbringing with the Arabic language, as well as their daily management of the language and its implications for their religious identity constructions. I also aspire to observe how Arabic has shaped their religious observance, and whether it further consolidates their religious identity or merely acts as a religious language that allows them to observe their prayers.

Previous research on British Muslims has found that religion is becoming the more salient and precedent identity.[36] To complement this, a trend that emerged among the participants is their belief that knowing Arabic is far more critical in further entrenching their religious identity than it is their ethnic identity. In their study on second-generation South Asians, Jaspal and Coyle report having observed the relationship of South Asians with their religious languages, and the role of those languages in the formation of their religious identity.[37] Specifically, as one of Jaspal and Coyle's interviewees illustrated, 'Arabic is holy ... It's the language the Prophet Mohamed used to speak in so it's holy for Muslims.'[38] John Esposito attributes this view to Muslims' belief that Muhammad is the final and most influential Prophet and Allah's messenger, and to Muhammad's own use of Arabic, which has given it a level of sanctification not afforded other languages.[39] Lisa Bernasek and John Canning report that while most 'British Muslims are from a South Asian background, they are not "native speakers" of Arabic', and that the vast majority 'may have had formal or informal training in the language'.[40] Their training in the language discloses the existence of a network of relations that cultivates embeddedness into the British Muslim psyche, projected as a necessity to filter through the *ummah*. After sharing his thoughts on the Bengali terms, Shaju (interviewed in December 2014) elaborated on the function of Arabic in his daily interaction with other Muslims and what it symbolised for him:

> So, yeah, it's always been those small, minority changes, influences that have come into us, and actually, that kind of impacted the way Muslims view themselves. And I think those – coming back to your question, which I now remember, having introduced that cultural, kinda assimilating some of the words from Arabic, like *jazak Allahu khair* and things like *in sha Allah* or

alhamdulillah. People are quite proud of the fact that they can reference words like that in a normal conversation because it's a reinforcer. And sort of maintains that notion between people, of being brothers or sisters. So I think in that regard, it's becoming quite popular.

Centralising Arabic in the everyday signals the need to assert a religious identity in various settings, not just within the bounds of a religious institution. These everyday language parameters are drawn concerning the broader Muslim community, thus relying on producing the Muslim self to assert authoritative knowledge. As such, this assertion facilitates stability as one enters the space of collectivity. This particular framing of managing multiple identities while also claiming one of them is succinctly summed up by Stuart Hall, who argues that multiple identities emerge from the diaspora, declaring that people who belong to more than one culture:

> have succeeded in remaking themselves and fashioning new kinds of cultural identity by, consciously or unconsciously, drawing on more than one cultural repertoire. They are people who belong to more than one world, speak more than one language (literally and metaphorically), inhabit more than one identity, have more than one home, who have learned to negotiate and translate between cultures, and who, because they are irrevocably the product of several interlocking histories and cultures, have learned to live with, and indeed to speak from, difference.[41]

However, in Shaju's case, stripping away the difference is necessary to engage with, and entrench, the notion of one *ummah*, facilitated through Arabic. For Shaju, subjectivity and belonging are captured through language and allow him to inherit a form of 'rite of passage', i.e. 'a standardised pattern of social behaviour endorsed by the individual's parents, which allows initiation into the religious community and thus access to the religion',[42] although in Shaju's case this is taken not from his parents, but from his interaction and engagement with other young British Muslims. As Avtar Brah observes, 'identity ... is an enigma which, by its very nature, defies a precise definition'.[43] It is a transformative process for Shaju and others. The constant negotiation of their religious articulation and shaping their sense of self is an ever-continuous journey with different phases and moments, all of which define a form of grounded identity. This grounded identity then provides a basic framework, which I would argue has been approved and shaped by the relationship of other Muslims with spirituality and Arabic, and then used by individuals in order to mirror each other. For example, Shaju mentioned that people feel proud when they are able to use the terms in their daily conversations, as it allows and perpetuates a consensus viable for all Muslims. Therefore, the ability to use Arabic terms that others are using not only activates a religious-linguistic identity but also further cements it, as other Muslims reinforce and accept it.

Following further questioning on how this change occurred, he explained:

> Islam gave people a stronger identity than the one they probably grew up with, which is most likely to be more ethnic, and I think that Bengali identity where I grew up [was] certainly more stronger than the Muslim one that was initially during the nineties, but then people start to kind of 'wake up' and you had Islam coming into the scene, right? And there seems be more of an awakening attitude, a rise of Islam as something which could offer you a framework to live in. And not only that, but also when people started to empathise and, certainly in my case, sympathise, with what was happening across the globe to Muslims. They reacted, and that reaction didn't come from a bond which was based with some sort of other domain, like an ethnic. It came from the fact that these guys are Muslims like us. I mean I can only speak for myself but I think you have that general attitude, where Muslims start to actually become more conscious of the fact that they were Muslims. And also, with what was happening – the onslaught, the wars – it brought Muslims together regardless of where they were from. I think that process introduced that sort of lingo. Then, suddenly, you have a wave of people who start to become more practising and I'm certainly one of them.

The reference to the War on Terror is crucial in conceptualising how Arabic became more embedded every day, as this moment in history animated Muslims to command an affirmative Muslim identity in public. In addition, Nayanika Mookherjee notes that such influences can also occur by 'transnational, imagined and sub-continental discourses at a time of long-distance nationalism, deterritorialised nations and globalisation of domestic politics facilitated by satellite television and the internet'.[44] Further, Shaju's justification for the proliferation of Arabic as the central 'lingo' is the demand for an allegiance to faith forming part of a logic that defies upholding an identity strictly according to a bordered nation. Hoque states that it has become common for many young Bangladeshis to use Arabic 'lingo', uncommon among prior generations.[45] As Aminul Hoque contends, the use of Arabic 'provides a linguistic base for the development of British Islam'.[46] While this is a plausible argument, what it is vital to ascertain is that there is a proliferation of this 'lingo', but that this is developing in tandem with how other languages are deployed, in this case Bengali. In this regard, Jaspal and Coyle explain how 'individuals generally seek positive self-evaluation' that grounds the self with steadiness.[47] Furthermore, Kay Deaux notes that 'knowing which identities a person claims is not enough',[48] implying Jaspal's argument that 'the position of the identity within the broader identity structure and particularly in relation to other identities is likely to predict the individual's affective state and choice of behaviour'.[49] In that sense, the affective state and choice of behaviour arise for Shaju from his exposure to Muslims' suffering, invoking a 'reaction' and, consequently, making him pay less attention to his Bengali identity.

The research participants did not go into detail about how they were taught Arabic, but all of them knew how to recite the Qur'an. However, as mentioned earlier, apart from two, the participants were not able to write, speak or understand Arabic, typical of the lack of Arabic knowledge among British Bangladeshi Muslims, 'despite its religious significance in their lives'.[50] Most participants went to *fora*, which required them to travel to someone's house where other children would be taught *tajweed*, or they would stay at home with other children, and the *mesaab* came there.[51] This is an experience I am also familiar with, as I was sent to *fora* as a child, joined by ten other students. An elderly Bangladeshi woman taught me the pronunciation and recitation of the Qur'an. Interestingly, the vowel structure I was taught to memorise portions of the Qur'an and for recitation used Urdu, not Arabic. For example, to denote the vowel /a/, in Arabic one would use the word *fatha*; however, it is *zabar* in Urdu. Likewise, /u/ is *damma* in Arabic and *pesh* in Urdu, while /e/ *is kasra* in Arabic and *zer* in Urdu. Jahangir (interviewed in December 2014) studied Arabic for his undergraduate degree and, before that, had first become acquainted with Arabic as a child at *fora*. He remembered travelling to someone else's house every weekend for two hours daily. The *mesaab* would arrive to teach the basics of Arabic, then help the students recite the Qur'an and memorise some of the *surah*s.[52] When I asked Jahangir if he could speak Arabic, he responded:

> I mean, when someone asks me that question, I mean, I know the grammar and everything – that was second-year Arabic. I know the grammar, *alhamdulillah*, inside out – I would think so anyway. It's just speaking-wise, I don't get enough practice. If someone says *Hal takallum arabiyya?*, which means 'Do you speak Arabic?', I am like: 'No'. I don't get to practise whatsoever, and that's what the year abroad is all about.

Jahangir expressed frustration, and his few opportunities to practise the language orally meant he could not harness the skill further. He hoped that the year he was planning to spend abroad would allow him to access the language, use his grammar skills and actually speak it. Jahangir did not prioritise Arabic over Bengali or vice versa; however, he felt that speaking the language was crucial to maintaining a steady Bengali identity. His interest in learning to speak Arabic appears to have been triggered by his studies rather than by religion. Similarly, Sultana spoke of building and constructing a religious identity without speaking Arabic, but gave it utmost importance because of its role in the Qur'an. She mentioned that she would like to learn the language but acknowledged missing many of the 'real' meanings whilst reading the Qur'an because English cannot convey the 'proper' meaning. She asserted that one does not need to speak Arabic to have a sense of one's faith-based identity, but that it is necessary to understand what God is trying to convey:

> Speaking Arabic, erm, is not too important. I just want to be able to read the Qur'an. I think even I can't speak Bengali – I think it's more important for me to be able to speak Bengali than it is for me to speak Arabic because I don't deal with Arabic people too much and, in the mosque, we have a few people who come in and out, and we have the communication issue, but we can still communicate or get someone to translate, but there will always be people to help you. Living here, I think it's more important for me to speak Bengali, but more important for me is to understand Arabic, two different things.

She then went on to explain how religion can be accessed through other languages:

> They even have like German translation of the Qur'an and all that, but you always hear that it's not the same to read the translation [as] it is to read the actual Arabic, because one Arabic word is translated into a single word when in the Arabic it has so many meanings that can affect you in a different way, so in terms of the Islamic identity I think it's important that we all do learn Arabic. It's hard because the language, it's so complex, but it's a great thing if you can do it then.

The emphasis on losing out on the 'authenticity' of meanings and symbolism strengthens Sultana's argument that knowledge of Arabic is important but only insofar as one has the ability to understand it. Her conceptualisation of speaking Arabic is not related to actual communication with native Arabic speakers, nor does she relate it to that aspect of her religious identity. This suggests that 'the combination of vitality, contact, and competence variables is the language resource base whose ownership provides the power to influence linguistic behaviour and attitudes'.[53] The 'authenticity' argument also affords Arabic a hegemonic position as the language of Islam, reflecting 'the essence of the Koran' in a way that other langauges can't, as emphasised in Sultana's recognition that a German translation cannot accurately capture the sense of the original text.[54] The sanctification of Arabic is conceptualised as 'a process through which aspects of life are perceived as having divine character and significance'.[55] These respective and related themes confirm how Arabic is placed on a pedestal, as it is the 'most desirable linguistic code for Muslims solely because the Prophet used the language himself'.[56]

Husna, interviewed in October 2014 in her office at her law firm in East London, affirmed a similar position to Sultana's:

Me:	Do you speak Arabic?
Husna:	No. I was actually going to do Arabic courses here with my daughter, but then she had too much on. I don't speak Arabic. But I have also been back to Arabic classes when my children [not clear] Arabic. I realised actually my Arabic wasn't so good.
Me	When you say your Arabic wasn't so good, do you mean the recitation?
Husna:	Recitation, the pronunciation, the way I was reading – I had forgotten a lot of things.
Me:	Would you like to speak Arabic?
Husna:	I don't feel the need to speak Arabic, but it would be very useful to be able to read, to understand what I am reading when I do read the Qur'an, when I am reciting the *surah*, without having to go to translation – that would be perfect.
Me:	Why is language important, do you think – the Arabic language?
Husna:	The Arabic language is only important in my case because I would like to understand what am I reciting or reading. Other than that, I wouldn't be particularly interested in learning Arabic.

Husna, like Sultana, also emphasises the need to understand what she is reciting when reading the Qur'an, but feels it is unnecessary to learn to speak Arabic. The symbolism of the Arabic language as a crucial selected marker of one's religious identity; a steady and stable identity is externally imposed as a consequence of peer pressure and is then internally preserved. Jun Liu argues that language can become a form of 'cultural adaptive transformation', providing a way to navigate different spaces.[57] Arabic is not just a language that should be used to recite the Qur'an while adding little to one's development of a religious identity other than performing mimicry; Homi Bhabha argues that 'mimicry emerges as the representation of a difference that is itself a process of disavowal'.[58] I would argue that this disavowal has facilitated the need to learn Arabic to avoid mimicry; it also connotes the need to possess a sense of power over one's engagement with religious texts. This is an essential point: people's willingness to engage in the furtherance of their Arabic language skills has a unifying capacity, in that this opens up space to forge an ummatic experience of bringing Muslims together. It carries a recognition of difference while unifying through the use of Arabic.

On the one hand, Sultana emphasised that living 'here' – a reference to East London – she needed to maintain her Bengali language skills as opposed to Arabic, even though she mentioned in her comments that she struggled to communicate with women who came to her work place and needed a Bengali translator. Her emphasis on her ethnic identity, it appears, occurs because of her direct engagement with the local discourse, involving continuous engagement with the Bengali community. However, on the other hand, Khalid emphasised his religious identity over his ethnic one. He argued that he would invest money in learning Arabic, even if it meant travelling abroad to acquire the language skills. Like Sultana, Jahangir and Shaju, Khalid went to *tajweed* lessons after school every day for two hours. He regarded understanding what one is reading as very important because he was not interested in Bangladesh or retaining links with the country. In that regard, he prioritised fulfilling his religious needs:

> I think it is very important to understand. That's why, more and more, I think it's a good idea to learn what I'm reading because then you'd understand. Where I'm becoming more interested in religion itself, in Islam, I find myself, my Islam, my Muslim identity as a person, a Bangladeshi identity is: how to be a better Muslim? I think more and more of the fact that what am I reading, what's the purpose of this, what does this mean? I think more often of how can – I want to take more Arabic classes and learn what I'm reading better, pronunciation better. More than anything, I'd say, I need to go to a Bengali class and learn my Bengali. *Shuddho Bangaliye mattam kila? Hiktam kila?* [How will I speak Standard Bengali? How will I learn it?] That doesn't even come to my mind.

Herein, though this was a theme that emerged in the previous chapters regarding dress, the religious identity element is reified through language, thus confirming Gardner and Shukur's argument that more and more young Bengalis are now identifying themselves as 'first and foremost as Muslims rather than as Bengali or Bangladeshi'.[59] Khalid seems aware that he is disposing of his Bengali identity. In fact, he asserted that it does not even 'cross his mind' to take Bengali lessons. As Riaz contends, the 'diaspora community [are] not driven by nostalgia to recover and/maintain their "lost" identity but [by the need to] construct/discover/imagine who they are'.[60] In the process of discovering and constructing, there is an ostensible openness to how Muslimness is defined, albeit within the confines of religious sanctions. This means that although there may not be a fallback on nostalgia per se to develop a diasporic identity, a different form of nostalgia takes shape. For example, reminiscing about Islam's early history carries with it a desire to (re)imagine the self in relation to Muslimness. Brubaker and Cooper argue that 'if identity is something to be discovered, and something about which one can be mistaken, then one's momentary self-understanding may not correspond to one's abiding, underlying identity'.[61] Given this framing, it helps to understand that this conceptualisation of seeking 'authenticity' is in flux. The desire for 'authenticity' is further articulated by Ismail. Just as Sultana explained that understanding Arabic was far more important to her than actually speaking the language, Ismail similarly expressed that Arabic was essential to gaining an 'authentic' view and practice of Islam:

> It's very important, [be]cause if you want to understand your religion seriously, if you have proper Arabic understanding, language understanding, then

you get access to the proper material. But also to achieve the level of intimacy that's required in your religion, to understand when you're reciting what you're saying and everything else, it's more powerful.

In this respect, Kenneth Pargament and Annette Mahoney point out that the sanctification process is vital for the psychology of religion and that 'the sacred is not "out there", remote or disconnected from life; it is instead linked to people through feeling, thought, action, and motivation. We have relationships *with* the sacred.'[62] The salient feature of identifying with one's faith is predicted by the perceived benefits of establishing and forming a religious identity, including implementing the Arabic language. What transpires with other participants is that there were moments of rupture in the way they noted their children learning Arabic and how much it differed from their experience. For example, Nasima and Alom shared their memories of learning Arabic. They said that much had changed with time when they compared it to their adult children's experiences of learning the language. For example, Nasima (interviewed in June 2014) detailed her experience at *fora* and how her parents were disappointed at the Islamic teaching in London, where teachers were not qualified. This, in turn, made her parents decide to take her to Bangladesh for over a year so that she could access 'proper' Islamic teaching. She shared:

> So we would go every day five to seven to somebody's house, or somebody's place, and we didn't really learn anything but it was fun being out of the house. But then my parents thought 'okay, we need to go back to Bangladesh for a little while, so that they could actually learn the Islamic things'. We didn't go to school there, but my dad actually kept someone at home. Actually, I did go a few times to school, in the village, and it was nice, and we had a *mehsaab* who used to come, a young student who used to come, so we had to sit and learn Arabic and the Qur'an, so I learnt more when we stayed a little bit longer there than I did when I was here. But we didn't have mosque or anything like we do now, whereas everybody [now] has Islamic school, and every Sunday you go somewhere and you read *tajweed*. We never did have that. It was, again, my teaching in Arabic was how my mum was taught [and] you were just told how to recite the *kalimas*; you were never told what the meaning was, you never knew how to do the *tajweed* with the Qur'an and everything. So it's a different type of Islamic teaching now, to what myself and my peers went through, so we are having to readapt ourselves now. It's a learning process for me still – I'm learning much more about my Islamic background than I am my Bangladeshi background.

Her parents' perception of what is acceptable and 'actual' Islamic teaching highlights the significance of these spatial divisions. Nasima's parents felt they could, perhaps, identify a form of resonance with Bangladesh. They were familiar with the religious-teaching landscape there and felt assured that Arabic teaching would be of better quality, although this has evidently changed in the diaspora context. However, Nasima's reflections on her engagement with Arabic appear to be filled with a sense of disappointment. Although she was taught how to memorise verses from the Qur'an, she does not *understand* Arabic. Nasima also thought that she did not receive 'proper' *tajweed* lessons, contrasting her experience with that of her daughters. Nasima explained that her daughters received recitation lessons and continue to attend various East London institutions investing in qualified teachers. Consequently, Nasima feels that her children excel in their recitation, and that their Arabic pronunciation is 'much better' than hers.

Throughout the interview, Nasima emphasised the need to recite the holy text accurately by building a solid reading comprehension rather than learning to speak the language. Her reminiscence about how she was taught Arabic suggests that her exposure to different cultural settings where she learnt it have merged into her set identity. While there is this steadiness, she is now aware that she must 'readapt' to the newly emerging space through language. This new space's iteration articulates the desire to gain an 'authentic' access to one's religion. Therefore, she has to 'readapt' and endorse a new culture, dismantling the 'old system' of mere mimicry to perform religious rituals and forging a new(er) religious identity with much more meticulous precision in the Arabic recitation. In this respect, Anthony D. Smith argues that 'subjective perception and understanding of the communal past by each generation ... is a defining element in the concept of cultural identity'.[63] Furthermore, Hall argues that frustrations at creating identifications in a postcolonial world are inevitable, as identities for people from former colonial entities need to situate themselves within the 'historically specific developments and practices which have disturbed to the relatively "settled" character of many populations and cultures, above all in relation to the processes of globalization'.[64] Nasima's parents' reaction and their dismay at the lack of religious provision, thus disrupting her identity process, reiterat Hall's point that identities are actually 'about questions of using the resources of history, language and culture in the process of becoming rather than being: not "who we are" or "where we came from", so much as what we might become, how we have been represented and how that bears on how we might represent ourselves'.[65]

On the other hand, Alom (interviewed in January 2014) described a different experience of learning Arabic. He went to a local mosque in Bangladesh where he was taught to recite the Qur'an and, in common with other interviewees, Alom did not understand what he was reading or reciting. However, Alom has noticed the increased use of Arabic as part of one's religious expression in everyday interaction in the UK. Yet, before he shared his thoughts on the use of Arabic amongst younger Bangladeshis in East London, he explained that his family had the utmost respect for the Qur'an and made sure it was placed on the highest wardrobe or shelf in the house, representing its high status:

> [W]e paid the highest respect to the Qur'an. So after reading, it will be wrapped up and it will always be put in a higher place than your head. And I think any pages from the Qur'an, if [they were] seen lying around the floor then we'd pick [them] up and [they would be] kept in a safe place, but that's because it was from the Qur'an, not because it's Arabic language.

While the conversation continued, Alom discussed the use of Arabic in the UK and said he believed it to be part of a global project to promote Islamism:

Me: Do you hear the usage of Arabic language on a regular basis among Bengalis?

Alom: Nowadays, you hear a lot more *in sha Allah*, *masha Allah*, *jazak Allah* and a few others that I can't think of. In our days, the only two Arabic words that we used were *in sha Allah* and *masha Allah*. But nowadays, you hear more Islamic sayings and phrases.

Me: Do you think that's to do with religion becoming more important to Bengalis?

Alom: I think it's part of this revival of Islamism and, to me, *hijab* is an Islamists' agenda. So I think it's to do with this whole agenda to Islamise society. So those phrases are a part of that attempt, including the clothing and *hijab*. It's all part of the same project.

Here, Arabic is not addressed as a requirement for prayers or recitation; Alom notices its regular use and appearance among British Bengalis. This formulation of making Arabic appear in exchanges requires further examination. Multiple questions come to mind, including how the audience hearing the language is perceiving the use of that language while also considering the power dynamics at play.[66] This implies that, at times, Bengalis feel compelled to exhibit their faith through their constructed nostalgia for what it would have been like during the time of the Prophet Muhammad. Nevertheless, enjoining the language and making it appear in the everyday context, implicating it with Islamism and signifying it as rooted in an overall agenda, is a broad generalisation. This positioning delegitimises how younger Bengali Muslims are in a limboing process in configuring Arabic and its role in their life. This figuring-out process cannot be digestible in compartmentalised forms.

Notably, even an 'Islamist project' does not negate the adaptation or recreation of a religious identity. Some may argue that any religious/identity project relies on such a notion. For example, Catholicism does not look the same worldwide, even where the same orders moved around. As demonstrated through the narratives analysed, one of the primary functions of the close association with the language is that it serves as a device to appropriate the religious language for the performance of self-transformation. The continuous adapting, as well as adoption, of a religious identity in solace, and how it is also constitutive of the political in its expression, explains how Arabic is used to fulfil a perceived obligation to perform one's Muslim identity, mainly through language. The participants asserted that their journeys aided their discovery of the varying ways religion shapes them and informs the creation of their local identification. There is no doubt that there may be external powers outlining this emerging identity. Still, it would be erroneous to consider it the *sole* variable in determining a religious identity. In her study of young Bangladeshis in the UK and USA, Nazli Kibria argues that the 'weak' Bangladeshi public identity resisted by many younger-generation Bangladeshi Muslim young people stands as a point of contradistinction for their own modern 'new' Islamic identity.[67] In this regard, Alom is reifying the dominant political discourse's imagery of Muslims, which disregards the history of Islamism and invokes it as a way to scaremonger those unaware of its history. As a result, Alom is uncritically adopting this discourse, thereby dismissing how people in the everyday construct meanings around Islamism.

Fluency in Arabic and its role

Sohaib, one of the two participants who was fluent in Arabic, spoke very affectionately about the language, and when asked about how important it was to learn Arabic, he stated:

> I think it's very important. I think it's a religious obligation. If you ask me what it means to be Muslim, part of what it means to be Muslim is to learn the Arabic language, because it's the "lingua arabica", we say, as opposed to the lingua franca, of the Muslim world, and at one time it was of the whole world. And anybody who was anybody at one time needed to learn Arabic to study and go into higher education.

Not unrelatedly, others have already elaborated on how Arabic is the lingua franca. However, Sohaib (interviewed in January 2014) seeks to locate this in its entirety in his religious identity. For example, Shaju recognised it as a lingua franca concerning its daily use, contrasting vastly with how Sohaib conceptualises it as a religious obligation. Sohaib's preoccupation is with how the individual can become the centre of expression of religiosity solely by mastering the language through the core four skills of reading, listening, speaking and writing. After the interview, Sohaib shared that he had lived in Syria and had learned to speak, read and write Arabic there. When suggested that it might be sufficient just to be able to recite the Qur'an, he vehemently disagreed and pointed out that one ought to learn Arabic 'to be able to understand the Qur'an in its native tongue'. He expanded:

> And so, I don't believe that just understanding the Qur'an is the best way to learn the Arabic language; like any other language, you need to concentrate on all four skills, and if you do that, it transforms your life. Because if it's passive – if your knowledge of the Arabic language is passive, so you need the Qur'anic texts to be able to prompt you to comprehend it and then to understand it; and when it's not there, the Arabic isn't there, then it's not really part of your life, it hasn't transformed you. Whereas if it's inside you and it runs off your tongue, it's transforming you.

The hegemony of Arabic as the language of Islam is emphasised throughout Sohaib's other comments, in which he also asserts that English as a medium cannot accurately reflect the essence of the Qur'an. Hamid Dabashi, in *Being a Muslim in the World*, argues that Muslims, in order to conceptualise and craft 'a new language', must draw from their rich, cosmopolitan history, describing the Muslim as creative, imaginative and diverse.[68] This cosmopolitanism is a tool to decipher the multiplicity and heterogeneity of various Muslim societies, consisting in a Muslim's worldliness. However, Sohaib's response suggests that experiencing one's 'Muslimness' can only be achieved by learning Arabic. This position assumes that without Arabic one's Muslimness cannot be wholly experienced, or even fulfilled. For Sohaib, 'transformation' can occur in Arabic. While this is one reading of the role of language, other participants refuted such a position by invoking the need to acquaint themselves with the faith in ways that remain sincere in the pursuit and recognition of the struggle to learn an entirely new language.

Jahedur (interviewed in February 2014), another research participant who spoke Arabic and had lived in Jordan and Egypt to study the language, had a different stance. He prioritised Arabic over Bengali for his children and believed Bengali would provide no substance in the future. For now, it is a medium his children use to communicate with their grandparents. He shared:

> [I] don't really use Bengali anyway. I probably use more Arabic than Bengali because everyone speaks Arabic when I go to meetings, so I use that and practise it more, so there isn't necessarily a clash, no. I studied Bengali when I was young, so I have done whatever I could, but for my kids now actually there is a clash. Where is the priority? Is it Bengali? Is it Arabic? Or is it English? Of course English is first, [and] then I probably would say Arabic, then Bengali. This is my subjective worry as, obviously, that is what our people talk and the way I think because, to be honest, what would they need Bengali for in the long run?

Seen in these terms, the investment in Arabic thus goes beyond the confines of faith but is present in the arena of communicating with native speakers. This perspective presents the Arabic language as something beyond the hierarchy of prestige within Islam. Sohaib explains the changes across East London, which created a space for Arab culture to flourish at the expense of interest in Bangladesh:

> So what's happened with the Islam that's grown in East London in the last fifteen to twenty years is that it has been laced with a lot of Arabic culture, which is fine; it's not a problem, because Arabic is part of Islamic culture, you can't escape [it] – the Qur'an is in Arabic, there's a desire to learn Arabic language, to understand the Qur'an. I myself went abroad to study Arabic, and I teach Arabic, so there's no problem with that, but I think also [that] that's crowded out a concern for issues in Bangladesh.

The reference to the change in the landscape of East London is astute. This was very visible during the fieldwork process, where I noticed the presence of multiple institutions teaching Arabic. Arabic is ontologically tied to expressions of Muslimness, reasserted through what I would term the Arabic-learning economy. Through learning the language, there is a perceived perception that there is redemption in acquiring the idyllic Muslim position, and this helps to address what participants have intimated as an absence in their faith expression. This absence of the ability to understand Arabic is thus addressed by partaking and intervening in the knowledge production of how to be a 'proper' Muslim by embodying the language every day and incorporating it as a linguistic skill.

Conclusion

Over time, language has come to entail different meanings for each participant interviewed. Evidently, participants negotiate various discourses, but what was most evident is that more people are framing a Muslim subjectivity while relegating their heritage identity. On the one hand, some participants discussed how Arabic forges a religious identity. In the interviews, memorisation is not diminished or excluded, but there is an overall recognition that this particular form of learning is no longer sufficient in building a religious outlook. On the other hand, there was clear-cut boundedness when Arabic and Bengali terms were used, which was highly dependent on context. For instance, I discussed how these languages shape the boundaries that Bangladeshi Muslims create concerning home, other South Asian Muslims, non-South Asian Muslims and non-Muslims. The home and the family have become the leading sites where Bengali terms continue to be used. However, it is also noteworthy that while parents with adult children still used Bengali terms, the children were not necessarily doing the same. Instead, they were introducing more Arabic into the home than their parents.

The second part of the chapter concentrates on how Arabic operates within the British Bangladeshi Muslim community. The use of Arabic as the language that solidifies a strong Islamic religious identity was a consistent theme. This was conceptualised by connecting it to the past, particularly the time of the Prophet Muhammad. As Jaspal states, 'individuals subjectively perceive a unifying thread connecting past, present and future within identity, through the construction of a narrative explaining turning-points'.[69] The 'return' to Arabic suggests that the role of 'authenticity' forms a crucial marker for developing and constructing a religious identity with the need to 'deculturalise' from one's ethnic identity. Participants such as Husna and Sultana hoped to develop enough understanding to comprehend what they were reading, thus investing in the learning of Arabic without necessarily focusing on speaking the language. The participants who talked about feeling a sudden pressure to learn and know 'proper' Arabic are finding ways to balance relations and the demands of their parents or children. The dynamics around parents and children are essential because they challenge the binary idea that only younger Bangladeshi Muslims prioritise learning Arabic. As such, the complexities employed by participants whilst manoeuvring the demands of learning the language, and to what extent, are continuously in flux. The proliferation of institutions offering Arabic language courses has made accessing the language outside the bounds of the mosque easier. This particular development will have a compelling impact on future studies looking at how different Muslim communities (re)develop their relationship with Arabic and paying closer attention to how alternative modes of retrieving religion and religiosity are shape-shifting in the East End.

Notes

1 R. Soliman and S. Khalil, 'The teaching of Arabic as a community language in the UK', *International Journal of Bilingual Education and Bilingualism* (2022), 1–12, DOI: 10.1080/13670050.2022.2063686.
2 A. Rosowsky, 'The role of liturgical literacy in UK Muslim communities', in T. Omoniyi and J. A. Fishman (eds), *Explorations in the Sociology of Language and Religion* (Amsterdam: John Benjamins, 2006), pp. 309–324.
3 R. Jaspal and A. Coyle, '"My language, my people": Language and ethnic identity among British-born South Asians', *South Asian Diaspora* 2:2 (2010), 201–218. See also B. Norton, 'Language and identity', in N. Hornberger and

S. L. McKay (eds), *Sociolinguistics and Language Education* (Bristol: Short Run Press, 2010), pp. 349–368.
4. A. Ghosh, *Power in Print: Popular Publishing and the Politics of Language and Culture in a Colonial Society, 1778–1905* (New Delhi: Oxford University Press, 2006), p. 10.
5. Ibid., p. 42.
6. Ibid., p. 259.
7. Ibid., p. 266.
8. E. Goffman, *Stigma: Notes on the Management of Spoiled Identity* (New York: Prentice Hall, 1963).
9. M. Hasan, *Islam, Communities and the Nation: Muslim Identities in South Asia and Beyond* (New Delhi: Manohar, 1998), p. 13.
10. *Khuda Hafiz* means 'May God be with you', but Taj I. Hashmi contends that the Bangladeshi coalition government led by the Bangladesh Nationalist Party in 2001 introduced and replaced the Persian expression with the Arabic *Allah Hafiz*; T. I. Hashmi, 'Islamic resurgence in Bangladesh: Genesis, dynamics and implications', in S. P. Limaye, M. Malik and R. G. Wirsing (eds.), *Religious Radicalism and Security in South Asia* (Honolulu: Asia Pacific Centre for Security Studies, 2004), pp. 35–72. The word *Khuda* denotes Allah/Lord/God. *Namaz* is known as *salah* in Arabic, but is used by Central Asians as well as South Asians to refer to the five daily prayers, and *jaynamaz* refers to the prayer mat.
11. A. P. Ahmed, 'Islam's lesser Muslims: When "Khuda" became "Allah"', Lobelog (2 September 2016), https://lobelog.com/islams-lesser-muslims-when-khuda-became-allah/ (accessed 15 April 2024).
12. J. Eade, 'Nationalism and the quest for authenticity: The Bangladeshis in Tower Hamlets', *Journal of Ethnic and Migration Studies* 16.4 (1990), 493–503; K. Gardner and A. Shukur, ' "I'm Bengali, I'm Asian and I'm living here": The changing identity of British Bengalis', in R. Ballard (ed.), *Desh Pardesh: The South Asian Presence in Britain* (London: Hurst, 1994), pp. 142–165.
13. B. Parekh, 'The concept of national identity', *Journal of Ethnic and Migration Studies* 21:2 (1995), 255–268 (p. 264).
14. See P. G. Min and J. H. Kim, *Religions in Asian America: Building Faith Communities* (Walnut Creek, CA: AltaMira Press), cited in L. Peek, 'Becoming Muslim: The Development of a Religious Identity', *Sociology of Religion* 66:3 (2005), 215–242 (p. 240).
15. M. Bucholtz and K. Hall, 'Identity and interaction: A sociocultural linguistic approach', *Discourse Studies* 7:4–5 (2005), 585–614.
16. N. Meer, *Citizenship, Identity and the Politics of Multiculturalism: The Rise of Muslim Consciousness* (Basingstoke: Palgrave, 2010), p. 56 (emphasis in original).
17. A. Ramamurthy, *Black Star: Britain's Asian Youth Movements* (London: Pluto Press, 2013), p. 5.
18. E. H. Erikson, *The Life Cycle Completed* (New York: Norton, 1997), p. 74.
19. K. Woodward, 'Questions of identity', in K. Woodward (ed.), *Questioning Identity: Gender, Class and Ethnicity* (Bath: The Bath Press, 2004), pp. 5–42 (p. 39).

20 W. E. B. Du Bois, *The Souls of Black Folk* (New York: Modern Library, 2003).
21 *Assalamu alaykum* = 'May peace be upon you'; *wa alaykumu s-salaam* = 'and may peace be unto you too'; *masha Allah* is a term used to express joy or thankfulness; *in sha Allah* = 'God willing'.
22 P. Werbner, 'Introduction: The dialectics of cultural hybridity', in P. Werbner and T. Modood (eds), *Debating Cultural Hybridity* (London: Zed Books, 1997), pp. 1–26 (p. 5).
23 R. Jaspal and A. Coyle, '"Arabic is the language of the Muslims – that's how it was supposed to be": Exploring language and religious identity through reflective accounts from young British-born South Asians', *Mental Health, Religion and Culture* 13:1 (2009), 17–36 (p. 24).
24 Ibid.
25 B. Anderson, *Imagined Communities: Reflections on the Origin and Spread of Nationalism* (London: Verso, 1991).
26 T. Rahman, 'Language and ethnicity in Pakistan', *Asian Survey* 37:9 (1997), 833–839 (p. 835).
27 P. A. Hoodbhoy, 'Towards theocracy?', *India International Centre Quarterly* 35:3–4 (2008), 142–51 (p. 145).
28 A. Riaz, 'Religion and society in Bangladesh: Unpacking the multilayered relationships', in K. A. Jacobsen (ed.), *Routledge Handbook of South Asian Religions* (Abingdon: Routledge, 2020), pp. 300–315 (p. 312).
29 T. I. Hashmi, 'Arabisation of Bangladesh: An asset, liability or threat?', *Daily Star*, 14 July 2015.
30 A. C. Härdig and T. Sajjad, 'Between the secular and the sacred: The changing role of political Islam in Bangladesh', Woodrow Wilson International Center (9 December 2015), www.wilsoncenter.org/sites/default/files/media/documents/event/hardigsajjadpaperfinal.pdf (accessed 15 April 2024), p. 2.
31 K. El Shayyal, *Muslim Identity Politics: Islam, Activism and Equality in Britain* (London: Bloomsbury, 2019).
32 O. Roy, *Globalised Islam: The Search for a New Ummah* (New York: Columbia University Press, 2004), pp. 22–25.
33 Rosowsky, 'The role of liturgical literacy in UK Muslim communities'.
34 *Subhan Allah* = 'Glory be to God'; *jazak Allah khairan* = 'May Allah reward you with goodness'; *assalamu alaykum* = 'May peace be with you'; *khair* = 'good', 'goodness', 'better' or 'best', depending on context.
35 Jaspal and Coyle, 'Arabic is the language of the Muslims', pp. 18–19.
36 J. Gest, *Apart: Alienated and Engaged Muslims in the West* (London: Hurst, 2010).
37 Jaspal and Coyle, 'My language, my people'.
38 Jaspal and Coyle, 'Arabic is the language of the Muslims', p. 23.
39 J. Esposito, *What Everyone Needs to Know about Islam* (Oxford: Oxford University Press, 2002).
40 L. Bernasek and J. Canning, 'Influences on the teaching of Arabic and Islamic studies in UK higher education: Connections and disconnections', *Arts and Humanities in Higher Education* 8:3 (2009), 259–275.

41 S. Hall, 'From "routes" to roots', in I. Grewal and C. Kaplan (eds), *An Introduction to Women's Studies: Gender in a Transnational World* (New York: McGraw-Hill Higher Education, 2006), pp. 427–428 (p. 427).
42 Jaspal and Coyle, 'Arabic is the language of the Muslims', p. 19.
43 A. Brah, *Cartographies of Diaspora: Contesting Identities* (Abingdon: Routledge, 1996), p. 20.
44 N. Mookherjee, 'In pursuit of the "authentic" Bengali: Impressions and observations of a contested diaspora', in M. N. Chakraborty (ed.), *Being Bengali: At Home and in the World* (Abingdon: Routledge, 2014), pp. 140–158 (p. 145).
45 A. Hoque, *British-Islamic Identity: Third Generation Bangladeshis from East London* (London: Institute of Education Press, 2015), p. 70.
46 Ibid., p. 71.
47 Jaspal and Coyle, 'My language, my people', p. 207.
48 K. Deaux, 'Reconstructing social identity', *Personality and Social Psychology Bulletin* 19:1 (1993), 4–12 (p. 8).
49 R. Jaspal, 'Delineating ethnic and religious identities in research with British South Asians', *Psychological Studies* 56 (2011), 241–244 (p. 242).
50 S. Hamid, *Language Use and Identity: The Sylheti Bangladeshis in Leeds* (Bern: Peter Lang, 2011), p. 128.
51 *Tajweed* = the pronunciation and recitation of the Holy Qur'an; *mesaab* is a term used in Bengali to refer to the Qur'an teacher.
52 *Surah* is the Arabic word for chapter.
53 S. Lawson and I. Sachdev, 'Identity, language use, and attitudes: Some Sylheti-Bangladeshi data from London, UK', *Journal of Language and Social Psychology* 23:1 (2004), 49–69 (p. 57).
54 Jaspal and Coyle, 'Arabic is the language of the Muslims', p. 20.
55 K. I. Pargament and A. Mahoney, 'THEORY. "Sacred matters: Sanctification as a vital topic for the psychology of religion"', *The International Journal for the Psychology of Religion* 15:3 (2005), 178–198 (p. 183).
56 Jaspal and Coyle, 'Arabic is the language of the Muslims', p. 23.
57 J. Liu, 'Adaptive cultural transformation: Quest for dual social identities', in D. Nunan and J. Choi (eds), *Language and Culture: Reflective Narratives and the Emergence of Identity* (Abingdon: Routledge, 2010), pp. 125–130 (p. 129).
58 H. Bhabha, 'Of mimicry and man: The ambivalence of colonial discourse', *October* 28 (1984), 125–133 (p. 126).
59 Gardner and Shukur, 'I'm Bengali, I'm Asian and I'm living here', p. 163.
60 A. Riaz, 'Being Bengali abroad: Identity politics among the Bengali community in Britain', in M. N. Chakraborty (ed), *Being Bengali: At Home and in the World* (Abingdon: Routledge, 2014), pp. 159–180 (p. 165).
61 R. Brubaker and F. Cooper, 'Beyond "identity"', *Theory and Society* 29:1 (2000), 1–47 (p. 19).
62 Pargament and Mahoney, 'THEORY', p. 188.
63 A. D. Smith, 'National identity and the idea of European unity', *International Affairs* 68:1 (1992), 55–62 (p. 58).

64 S. Hall, 'Introduction: Who needs "identity"?', in S. Hall and P. Du Gay (eds), *Questions of Cultural Identity* (London: Sage Publications, 1996), pp. 1–17 (p. 4).
65 Ibid.
66 A. Lo, 'Whose hearing matters? Context and regimes of perception in sociolinguistics', *International Journal of the Sociology of Language* 267–268 (2021), 153–162.
67 N. Kibria, *Muslims in Motion: Islam and National Identity in the Bangladeshi Diaspora* (New Brunswick, NJ: Rutgers University Press, 2011).
68 H. Dabashi, *Being a Muslim in the World* (Basingstoke: Palgrave Macmillan, 2013).
69 R. Jaspal, 'The construction and management of national and ethnic identities among British South Asians: An identity process theory approach' (PhD thesis, Royal Holloway, University of London, 2011), p. 21.

Conclusion

Waking up in the morning and deciding what to wear is not as simple as one may think. The look of the day depends on your mood and how you feel but, more importantly, it is shaped by internal and external forces that can define your day and dictate how others will perceive you. In a similar vein, when one communicates with another person, they opt for the language that is best suited to or deemed most appropriate for the particular context they are in, or about to enter. These choices will, more than anything, also have a lasting impact on yourself and the wider world. Thinking back to the Modern Saree Centre on Brick Lane and how so many *sari* shops had left that iconic part of East London is an example of the inner debate British Bangladeshi Muslims in East London have when contesting the social meanings of their identities. This book aimed to demonstrate that, and presented the varying identification processes that emerge from the constant negotiation, reconciliation and exchanges among British Bangladeshi Muslims. This identity formation is also primarily influenced by the presence of other variables, most potently politics, which takes place on the local and global level. It involves the invention of multiple social identities through which the actors determine their affinities. On the one hand, religious affinities shape the construction and interactions of the Bangladeshi community, derived from exposure to the ever-changing discourses on British Muslims and their place in British society. On the other hand, ethnic affinities are shaped by engagements with family and the wider British Bangladeshi community in East London, and by the younger generation who are reshaping their understanding of their heritage identity. In the process of demonstrating this, I examined and denaturalised the ubiquitous and deeply problematic security lens through which knowledge of Muslims has been produced in the past two decades. While the national (dominant) discourse has mediated this lens, this work offers an alternative reading of the communities, and how their political subjectivities emerge via dress and language was a core focus.

I endeavoured to develop an approach to capture the multifaceted dimensions of forging an identity in the diaspora. To this end, the book considered the importance of a range of intersecting discursive traditions and practices, connecting them with the historical relations between the Bengalis and the British during the British Raj. However, the most important aspect I attempted to emphasise throughout this book was the significance of the Bangladeshi Muslims who experienced visceral forms of racist violence, their fight back, and their forms of reasoning and argumentation. The varying responses from the participants showcased how much local communitarian fights shaped the meaning-making of their heritage and religious identity, but how much of this was also informed by global political events' restructuring the local. I addressed this by investigating the role of dress and language, as these two variables are deemed key markers in forming an identity, particularly for diaspora communities. The various clothes identified as symbolising an ethnic and/or religious identity in the present study were *sari*, *shalwar kameez*, *funjabi*, *lungi*, *jilbab*, *hijab*, *niqab*, *thobe* and the wearing of the beard for men. For language, I focused on Arabic and Bengali while also paying attention to Persian-origin terms embedded within the Bengali language. These specificities and their relationship to social identity-making have rarely been unpacked, even though substantial literature exists on Muslim women's bodies and their sartorial practices.

Through the interviews, I illustrated the cultural, ethnic, and religious markers and boundaries created by the research participants, and how they continue to be significant in shaping and reshaping identities. However, I also sought to clarify and elaborate that these thoughts and expressions are representations of the forty-three individuals interviewed during my fieldwork, so they may not necessarily represent the experiences of other British Bangladeshis. This is an important point to make, as studies on ethnic minority groups can easily be used to represent the whole 'community', when in fact this is simply not feasible. As Sanjay Sharma, John Hutnyk and Ashwani Sharma argue, 'these cultural forms continue to be imbued with an exoticised, othered status in the West and our primary goal has been to break out of the Orientalist tradition of making knowable these cultural productions for an ever-eager academic audience and other agencies of control'.[1] Refusing the assumption of homogeneity allows the possibility of complicating the nebulous ways identity is presumed. Countering this point is crucial, as it is widely assumed that Muslims engender cultural or religious separatism, erasing the results of the inheritances of colonial conditions in the UK.

My point is not that the data used in this book reveal an unmediated 'reality' of the 'community'; instead, my claim is that the data I have discussed here represent a reality for the research participants themselves. I have presented the arguments through the British Bangladeshis' lived experiences and approached this by investigating the meanings and forms they attribute to themselves and their relations with others, such as friends, family and Muslim peers, as well as their relationship with God. Their experiences of dress and language were by no means idiosyncratic and, as Abner Cohen suggests, they can be 'subjectively' experienced by the actors and remain objective.[2] Among my main goals was to seek out how social and political circumstances shape 'how people make sense of the world and then act upon it.'[3] In that sense, the book considered *how* the research participants are able to make their decisions around dress and language and *in what way* those decisions, in turn, inform their experiences of dress and language. I examined how their identities intertwined with broader socio-political moments by exploring specific garments and languages. My analysis reveals how distinct articulations and identifications are emerging where the altered body via dress and language exposes volatile dimensions of such choices regarding which garment or language to utilise in tandem with racial formations.

In a similar vein, Claire Alexander argues that 'ethnography, at least at its theoretical margins, has developed a highly critical self-reflexive gaze that has undermined its claims to "truth" and to making known the "Other", and made explicit the relations of power that create and sustain it'.[4] In this book, I have attempted to show that the strategy I employed to present the data constitutes a dialogue with and between alternative forms of representation: my interviewees, my own positionality, as well as the hegemonic discourses surrounding ethnic minorities in Britain, particularly the hyperfocus and discourse on British Muslims. As Alexander continues to argue, 'rather than making the "Other" known, its aim has been to contest this possibility, to argue for a knowledge that is both highly located and shifting, structured through an unequal dialogue between researcher and subjects, and unavoidably compromised in the act of writing'.[5] Keeping this in mind, while certain theoretical tools and frameworks have provided insight, the importance of context has repeatedly made me consider the specificity of this book. I argue that the East End's symbolic heartland for the British Bangladeshi Muslim community has avenues to provide generalised assumptions and projections, but the terms in which Bengaliness emerges are not the same elsewhere because of the high density of Bangladeshis in the area.

Furthermore, my fieldwork has revealed the multiple themes that materialised and how these experiences outlined and informed the production of identities. The older research participants engaged with their identities vis-à-vis their strong links to 'back home', which seemed to help configure and transform their identity in Britain. However, the participants born and raised in the UK are reconfiguring their heritage and religious identities in relation to their home life in Britain with their experiences outside the home, including interaction with other British Bangladeshis. This group is restructuring their identities with little emphasis on Bangladesh, as many do not retain links with the country, apart from speaking to relatives over the phone or visiting the country with their family. In this context, the Bangladeshis who arrived as young children and spent their formative years in London are discursively positioned as the transient generation, with the majority retaining a much closer link to Bangladesh via their parents but also performing the customs that their seniors require of them. Such close links cannot be attributed to the third generation, who, unlike their parents, are not bound by those expectations and demands.[6] Consequently, I wanted to tell the story of people who encounter themselves through their own paradigmatic shifts while in conversation, specifically, with the local landscape, thus creating the possibility of coding these dress and language practices differently.

In this book, I wanted to familiarise the reader with the defining moments and conventions through a thorough insight into an abridged version of Bengali history, spanning over a few hundred years, including today's West Bengal and Bangladesh. I provided a detailed analysis of the period following the 1947 Partition, leading up to the independence of Bangladesh in 1971. Through this contextualisation, I linked the events occurring halfway across the world to various events unfolding in the UK. Focusing on international events and their impact on the British Bangladeshi community was significant in terms of explaining how the early migrants sought to establish themselves in the UK and, consequently, how the following generations, if at all, reflected upon their struggles to understand their positioning as British Bangladeshi Muslims. The first- and second-generation British Bangladeshi Muslims experienced widespread racial and cultural hostility, resulting in many deaths that led the community to seek protection and solace with other Bengalis in East London.[7] The book has contended that the historical and contemporary demarcations of Muslims are not simply about the difference but also relate to anxiety around the certainty that they pose in who they are and how they assert this by using religion as the core framework.

Dress and language, as demonstrated by the book, are no longer just an expression of a cultural possession or birthright but are part of a socially, historically and politically located struggle over meaning and identity. To reiterate Stuart Hall's idea, discussed in multiple chapters, cultural identity is a matter of 'becoming' as well as of 'being', which implies an ever-present negotiation, making it impossible for any researcher to 'capture' the identity of an individual or group.[8] The experiences and moments 'captured' in this book were from a specific location, space and time, so it cannot be argued that the same research participants would feel the same way now. Hall then states:

> [C]ultural identities come from somewhere, have histories. But like everything which is historical, they undergo constant transformation. Far from being eternally fixed in some essentialised past, they are subject to the continuous 'play' of history, culture and power.[9]

The area of Spitalfields provides a 'perfect laboratory for an exploration of the different stages of migration and settlement. It, and its inhabitants, demonstrate both the permanent and the transitory states.'[10] The location itself and the previous struggles of the French Huguenots and the Jewish communities suggest that young British Bangladeshi Muslims are able to use religion as a multi-purpose tool where 'it can aid to integration, a link between over here and over there'.[11] Though there can be similarities between the British Bangladeshis of today and the previous communities who settled in the area, it is not to say that my interviewees' thoughts can be perceived as belonging to a particular point of history or location. As Gayatri Spivak argues:

> [T]he space I occupy might be explained by my history. It is a position into which I have been written. I am not privileging it, but I do want to use it. I can't fully construct a position that is different from the one I am in … No one can quite articulate the space she herself inhabits. My attempt has been to describe this relatively ungraspable space in terms of what might be its history.[12]

Chapters 2 and 3, which looked at dress, revealed the various attitudes and perceptions and their multilocational manifestations. Many of the objections directed at the various forms of dress associated with their ethnic identity were related to the idea that the origins of such clothes are not Islamic but stem from Hinduism. The clothes' detachment from Islam caused much discussion, particularly around the *sari*. The insights of women, from both the first and second generations, were principally nuanced; these women appeared to be aware that, with a six-yard fabric, it is possible to cover one's whole body without revealing the midriff or back, as can be the case with the *sari*. However, the men appeared much more concerned, deeming the garment inappropriate and not Islamic enough because it reveals particular parts of the body. When discussing women's dress, the male participants argued that the *shalwar kameez* is a more appropriate form of clothing that better meets the Islamic requirements of modesty. Farhana even classified the garment as an 'Islamic' one, evident in Emma Tarlo's research on clothing in India and the fact that Hindus perceived the *shalwar kameez* as 'Muslim dress'.[13] However, in Bangladesh and India, the urban space defines the *shalwar kameez* as a garment for those working in the city, and it is still projected as a professional outfit.[14] The *funjabi* and *lungi*, on the other hand, are hardly visible, although the former makes appearances during special occasions, such as Eid, weddings and Friday prayers; beyond that, it is non-visible. Whilst my data attests to the negotiation of identities through space within evolving discussions around religion and its parameters for Muslim men, this negotiation remained closed for the *lungi*. The *lungi* challenged other elements, such as masculinity, and the sense of embarrassment associated with the *lungi* stems from the fact that it resembles the kilt-like style (worn with no undergarments), causing much caution among the participants who seek respectability from their Muslim peers, intensifying the possibility of facing mockery for wearing it.

On the other hand, the religious garments were defined and constructed vis-à-vis the understandings and boundaries of Islamic law and the modesty requirements set forth. The majority of the women I interviewed wore the *hijab*, with Sultana being an exception, preferring the *niqab*. Nasima, quite vocally, expressed her frustration at not being taught her religion properly and the fact that she was only now, slowly, understanding the wisdom behind wearing the *hijab*. Husna, also in her forties like Nasima, does not wear *hijab* but hopes to do so one day. The younger women interviewed conceptualised the *hijab* as a garment that a woman should have the right to choose whether or not to wear without force. This notion was conceptualised through a neo-liberal framing, centring the individual as the sole bearer of such a decision to emphasise self-expression and choice. Understanding men's relationship with and analysis of clothes was challenging, as I struggled to find academic literature on male Muslim dress. Nonetheless, in my data it emerged that Bangladeshi Muslim men who wore the *funjabi* to the mosque and as part of their daily religious expression assigned religiosity to the garment, while there was a recognition that the *thobe* had gained more prominence among younger Bangladeshis. Specifically, the *thobe* has become visible on the streets of East London, with young boys wearing it as part of their after-school *madrasah* uniform or, if they go to one permanently, as part of their school uniform. The wearing of the *thobe* is given more religious authenticity, as it originates from the same geographical region as the Prophet Muhammad (PBUH), asserting that following this dress code aligns with Islamic teachings.

Chapters 4 and 5 explored the role of language and its position in the lives of Bengali Muslims. Chapter 4 shows how standard Bengali and Sylheti were juxtaposed, even though the participants referenced what they spoke at home as Bengali. Showcasing this nuance of slipping between Bengali and Sylheti, or between Bangladeshi and Bengali, as synonyms, was common, reflecting the multilayered, structured ways that markers of identities evolve. The relationship with the Bengali language shifted so that it became more domesticated, bound to the home space. However, this home space was expansive, and included the vicinities of Tower Hamlets for many, as it facilitated interactions with other Bangladeshis. In Chapter 5, we see that, as some participants noted, *fora* for Bengali was no longer an option, as it had become dominated by Arabic classes only. The learning of Arabic was pursued no longer just for memorisation and prayer purposes but as a means to understand the same litanies and prayers they were reciting. The data also show that traditionally used Bengali terms such as *Khuda Hafiz*, *namaz* and *jaynamaz,* will soon no longer be in use, as more and more British Bangladeshi Muslims rely on Arabic to convey religious terms.

The salience of religious identity was complementary to the current canon. However, there was some divergence, in that the locality of Tower Hamlets provided access to a specific heritage-linked religious expression, albeit at a reduced level. As such, this strong identification with Islam demonstrates the external pressure that the Bangladeshi Muslim community faces from the media and elsewhere; however, it was also inseparable from the construction of 'the Bengali community'. In that regard, the book's findings will contribute to further study of British Bangladeshis and British Muslims. In writing this, I have provided as much detail as possible about the difficulties, intercessions and aspirations that my interviewees handle and deal with in order to understand their place in society. In this respect, the book will benefit those seeking to understand further the nuances of the British Muslim and the British Bangladeshi communities by considering the participants' observations above the mainstream theories, policies and political commentaries, paying attention to their unique insights into *their own* worlds.

Notes

1. S. Sharma, J. Hutnyk and A. Sharma, *Dis-Orienting Rhythms: The Politics of the New Asian Dance Music* (London: Zed Books, 1996), p. 2.
2. A. Cohen, *Custom and Politics in Urban Africa: A Study of Hausa Migrants in Yoruba Towns* (Berkeley: University of California Press, 1969).
3. A. Kundnani, *The Muslims are Coming: Islamophobia, Extremism, and the Domestic War on Terror* (London: Verso, 2014), p. 10.
4. C. Alexander, *The Asian Gang: Ethnicity, Identity, Masculinity* (Oxford: Berghahn Books, 2000), p. 225.
5. Ibid., p. 227.
6. A. Hoque, *British-Islamic Identity: Third Generation Bangladeshis from East London* (London: Institute of Education Press, 2015).
7. S. Begum, *From Sylhet to Spitalfields: Bengali Squatters in 1970s East London* (London: Lawrence Wishart, 2023).

8 S. Hall, 'Cultural identity and diaspora', in J. Rutherford (ed.), *Identity* (London: Lawrence Wishart, 1990).
9 Ibid., p. 225.
10 A. Kershen, *Strangers, Aliens and Asians: Huguenots, Jews and Bangladeshis in Spitalfields, 1666–2000* (Abingdon: Routledge, 2005), p. 230.
11 Ibid., p. 226.
12 G.C. Spivak, *The Post-Colonial Critic: Interview, Strategies, Dialogues* (Abingdon: Routledge, 1990), p. 68.
13 E. Tarlo, *Clothing Matters: Dress and Identity in India* (London: Hurst, 1996).
14 N. Hussein, 'Bangladeshi new women's "smart" dressing: Negotiating class, culture, and religion', in N. Hussein (ed.), *Rethinking New Womanhood* (Cham: Palgrave Macmillan, 2018), pp. 97–121.

Index

7/7 9, 20, 42–43
9/11 5, 9, 42–43, 103, 106, 152

Adams, Caroline 11, 22–24
Afghanistan 42–43
Ali, Altab 12, 31, 35–36, 38–39, 128
Ali, Monica 44
Ali, Quddus 41
Al-Qaeda 5
Altab Ali Park 31, 36, 128
anti-racism 34, 38–39
Awami League 32–33, 76, 129

Banglatown 40, 118
Bashani, Maulana 76–77, 122
Battle of Cable Street 41
Begum, Anwara 116–117
Begum, Shabina 66–68
Begum, Shabna 4, 11, 71
Brahmin 58
Brick Lane 1–3, 28, 35–37, 40, 42, 44, 77, 96, 178
British National Party 37, 41
British Nationality Act 35
burqa 67, 92–93, 100

Cameron, David 132
citizenship 35
Commonwealth Immigrants Act 29
community service language 126, 136

double surveillance 93–94, 109
Dwyer, Rachel 61, 64–65, 68–69, 95–96

Eade, John 12, 22, 40–41, 150
East India Company 14, 19–20

East London Mosque 20, 60, 71, 73, 87, 98, 105, 107, 109, 119, 127, 130–131
election 33, 40–44, 58, 126

fashion 78–80, 93, 94, 102, 104, 106, 110
fora 116, 118, 141, 147, 163, 167, 184

Galloway, George 43
Gandhi 3, 70, 77
Garbin, David 12, 22, 40–41
Gardner, Katy 11–12, 21–22, 33, 150, 166
Ghosh, Anindita 25–26, 148
Glynn, Sarah 12, 34, 110
Goffman, Erving 58, 71, 74, 93, 149

Hall, Stuart 16, 59, 61, 68, 109, 125, 129–130, 133, 136–138, 161, 168, 181–182
Hall, Tarquin 28
Hamida, Shahela 120, 128, 130, 139
Hoque, Aminul 11, 162
Hoque, Ashraf 64
Hoque, Nurul 116–117
Hussein, Nazia 58–59

Iraq War 43
Islamic Law 103, 183
Islamophobia 3, 43, 89, 106

Jagonari Centre 128
Johnson, Boris 2
Judaism 12, 28, 41, 85, 101, 138, 182
jumping ship 23

Kolkata (Calcutta) 19, 21–22, 25, 28–29, 76, 121

Labour Party 34, 39
language movement 19, 29, 31–32, 118, 136
lascars 11–12, 14, 20–24
Liberation War 26, 32, 34–35, 58
Luton 2, 32, 40, 64, 66

Madrasah 105, 135, 158, 183
Mahmood, Saba 7, 100–101
marriage 9, 21, 61, 89–90, 131, 138, 140–142
Middle East 10, 104, 108, 156
multiculturalism 7, 10–11, 39, 43
murobbi 74–75, 141
Musalmani Bengali 26, 148
Muslim consciousness 89, 95, 137, 151, 158
Muslimness 6, 15, 94, 96, 101, 103, 106, 109, 148, 153, 156–157, 166, 171–172
myth of return 20, 28–29

Newham 4, 13

Osmani Centre 37

'Paki bashing' 36–37, 43
para 4, 72, 74, 127, 138
Prevent Strategy 6

Rahman, Lutfur 8, 126, 133, 44
rivers 11, 19, 22, 40

Shaheed Minar 31
Shukur, Abdus 21, 150
Sivanandan, Ambalavaner 9, 41
Straw, Jack 2
synagogue 28, 101

Tarlo, Emma 55, 59, 62, 65, 67, 69, 76, 79, 86, 95, 97, 100, 106, 108
terrorism 6, 42–43, 99, 156
transnationalism 12–13, 27–28, 65, 129, 138–142, 162

ummah 20, 67, 105, 154, 160–161
ummatic identity 107, 149, 165
urban 12, 42, 59, 69–70, 100, 121, 182
Urdu 26, 29–32, 59, 120–121, 137, 148, 163
uthaan 4

war on terror 2, 42–43, 64, 106, 156, 162
Wemyss, Georgie 41
Whitechapel 2–3, 32, 36, 71, 85, 97, 126

Zeitlyn, Benjamin 13, 33, 118, 121, 126–127

EU authorised representative for GPSR:
Easy Access System Europe, Mustamäe tee 50,
10621 Tallinn, Estonia
gpsr.requests@easproject.com

www.ingramcontent.com/pod-product-compliance
Lightning Source LLC
Chambersburg PA
CBHW071204240426
43668CB00032B/2095